The POWER *of* STRANGERS

The POWER
of STRANGERS

The Benefits of Connecting in a Suspicious World

Joe KEOHANE

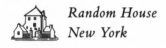

Random House
New York

Published in the United States by Random House, an imprint and division of
Penguin Random House LLC, New York.

RANDOM HOUSE and the HOUSE colophon are registered trademarks
of Penguin Random House LLC.

LIBRARY OF CONGRESS CATALOGING-IN-PUBLICATION DATA
Names: Keohane, Joe, author.
Title: The power of strangers : the benefits of connecting in a suspicious world / by Joe Keohane.
Description: First edition. | New York : Random House, [2020] | Includes bibliographical references
and index.
Identifiers: LCCN 2020048385 (print) | LCCN 2020048386 (ebook) | ISBN 9781984855770 (hard-
cover) | ISBN 9781984855787 (ebook)
Subjects: LCSH: Interpersonal relations. | Social interaction. | Strangers.
Classification: LCC HM1106 .K465 2020 (print) | LCC HM1106 (ebook) | DDC 302—dc23
LC record available at https://lccn.loc.gov/2020048385
LC ebook record available at https://lccn.loc.gov/2020048386

Printed in the United States of America on acid-free paper

randomhousebooks.com

9 8 7 6 5 4 3 2 1

First Edition

Book design by Diane Hobbing

For June

The only true voyage of discovery, the only fountain of Eternal Youth, would be not to visit strange lands but to possess other eyes, to behold the universe through the eyes of another, of a hundred others, to behold the hundred universes that each of them beholds, that each of them is.

—MARCEL PROUST

I know by my own experience how, from a stranger met by chance, there may come an irresistible appeal which overturns the habitual perspectives just as a gust of wind might tumble down the panels of a stage set—what had seemed near becomes infinitely remote and what had seemed distant seems to be close.

—GABRIEL MARCEL

People are strange when you're a stranger.

—JIM MORRISON

CONTENTS

PART II: WHY *DON'T* WE TALK TO STRANGERS?

PART III: HOW TO TALK TO STRANGERS

Strangers in a Cab

I have a story for you. It's about a stranger.

A couple of years ago, I had the obscene good fortune to spend two weeks on the island of Nantucket as part of a screenwriters' fellowship: three other writers and me living in a house, honing our craft, and meeting industry people, while going to parties and methodically divesting our host of liquor and food. Early one morning, after a party, the four of us are standing outside in the dark waiting for a cab. I'm telling them that while my business—print journalism—may indeed be hurtling toward oblivion, taking with it many of my prospects, hopes, dreams, etc., I wouldn't trade the experience for anything, because it gave me a chance to make a living by talking to strangers. And when you talk to people you don't know, I tell them, you learn that everyone has a bit of gold; everyone has at least one thing to say that will surprise you, amuse you, horrify you, edify you. They tell you things, usually with minimal prodding, and sometimes those things can deepen you, and awaken you to the richness and the grace and even the pain of the human experience. They show themselves to be freestanding worlds. When you're allowed in, you can internalize a little piece of that person, and by doing so, you grow a little. You gain a bit of empathy, wisdom, or understanding.

The cab finally shows up. It's driven by an older woman. We pile in, and I decide to show my friends what I was talking about. (As you'll see, I have a real fondness for cabdrivers.) I ask her about living on Nantucket. She answers. I ask something else. She answers. She gets comfortable, and, over the course of a twenty-minute drive, she tells us her life story. She was born into money on the Upper West Side of Manhattan. When she was small, there was some kind of deranged socialite fad her parents went in for that involved binding a child's calves. This, she explains, was meant to spare said socialites the humiliation of being seen with a child with inelegant calves.

Her parents crippled her with this treatment. She struggled to walk. What did they do when they realized what had happened? I ask her. Did they consult a surgeon, or a physical therapist? Did they try to redress the damage they had done and restore proper mobility to their daughter? Did they even apologize?

They did not, the cabdriver says.

"Then what did they do?"

"They made me take dancing lessons."

"Oh my god," I said. "Why did they make you take dancing lessons?"

"Because they wanted to teach me to fall down more gracefully," she says.

Reader, I'm the grandson, son, and brother of Irish Catholic funeral directors in Boston, Massachusetts. My background has shaped my worldview, my sense of humor, my whole sensibility. So believe me when I tell you that I have never in my life heard a more perfect summation of the human condition than what I heard from that random stranger, at that late hour, on that gilded little boomerang of an island in the Atlantic.

After that interaction, I started thinking a lot about strangers. *Why don't we talk to strangers?* I wondered. *When will we? And what happens when we do?* Because the fact was, outside of my job, I really hadn't been talking to strangers. Not in the wild, anyway. The dueling demands of a job and an infant daughter—the so-called work-life balance that so often feels like a war of attrition—left little time to hang around places where people do talk to strangers, and little energy with which to do it. Even when I did manage to carve out half an hour to stop into a bar or café, I didn't talk to people. When I did, it went badly. This, I expect, was because, as any parent of a very young child can attest, my brain didn't really work anymore. I found myself withdrawing—either reading or, more shamefully, staring at my phone, numbly consuming "content" that just minutes later I would have absolutely no recollection of, but that still left me feeling vaguely unwell. In time, I stopped talking to anyone. I barely made eye contact. Even that felt like a chore.

What struck me was just how easy it was to withdraw, to absent myself from most human interaction. Throughout his career studying cities, the sociologist Richard Sennett has praised the idea of *friction* in life: those little inefficiencies that force you to interact with strangers—like asking a butcher for grilling tips, or asking for directions, or just ordering a pizza over the phone. With the march of technological progress, those interactions have become increasingly unnecessary. And that, I suspected, was eroding our social skills. I was evidence of this. Why did I always pick the self-checkout lane at CVS even when there was no line? Why did I get annoyed with a store clerk when he asked what my plans were for the day? Why did I stop chatting with strangers and disappear into my phone when I knew from experience that what they would tell me would usually be far more interesting than whatever toxic slurry was coursing through Twitter at that moment? I don't know. But I did. And I did not feel great about it.

Still, though, there were times, like on Nantucket, when I did wind up talking to a stranger, and it went well, and a little world opened. I gained something: an insight, a joke, a different way of thinking about things, a good story. But more than that, I felt, as strange as it is to say, *relieved*. And I wanted to understand why.

Those questions crept into my day job. When I was interviewing the actor Alan Alda about his work teaching communication skills to scientists, I mentioned the curious sense of relief I feel after talking to a stranger. He lit up. "That sense of relief is such a palpable thing to me," he said. "So much so that I wonder why relating to others isn't self-reinforcing. Why we don't just tend toward it naturally?"

Why don't we?

Well, for starters, strangers have gotten a pretty bad rap. The great country singer Merle Haggard didn't name his band the Strangers because he wanted us to believe they were good citizens. He did it because he wanted us to believe they were dangerous. The Hitchcock film *Strangers on a Train* wasn't about meeting a romantic partner or client or new friend on a train, nor was it about having your mind expanded by one of those intense random conversations people can fall into while traveling. It's about how, if you're not careful, a charming psychopath will trap you into a murder plot concerning your wife and his father. William Golding's *Lord of the Flies* wasn't originally titled *Strangers from Within* because the ordeal of being marooned on an island brought out the very best in English schoolboys.

And of course, there's the most famous stranger of all. Albert Camus's novel *The Stranger* wasn't a story about a guy from Algiers making a good life for himself in France and introducing the locals to the rich traditions of Algerian food and culture. It's about a man who is so alienated from the world that he becomes a stranger to himself—feeling nothing when his own mother dies, killing a man, and contemplating, as he faces the gallows, that the only thing that will make him feel less alone is if there is "a large crowd of spectators the day of my execution and that they greet me with cries of hate"—in effect, making him the first internet troll.

The fear that strangers—even ones that appear friendly—are agents of chaos, treachery, and moral and even physical pollution has been with us for as long as there have been strangers. It has persisted from hunter-gatherer times, to the rise of villages, cities, and nations, to the stranger-danger hysteria of the 1980s, to Elon Musk describing the subway as "a bunch of random strangers, one of who might be a serial killer," to the sheriff of Harris County, Georgia—an affluent area—installing a sign in 2018 reading "Welcome to Harris County,

Georgia. Our citizens have concealed weapons. If you kill someone, we might kill you back. We have ONE jail and 356 cemeteries. Enjoy your stay!"

Today, our difficulties with strangers continue. The West is experiencing widespread political upheaval, caused in part by the migration of cultural strangers—people fleeing war, privation, and tyranny—seeking safety and opportunity. For many who live in the host countries, this has delivered a shock to our sense of belonging, to our sense of who we are.

These new faces have supercharged our already rather robust tendency to fear strangers, and the backlash has been ferocious—abetted, in part, by a deficit of understanding. According to several polls, Westerners display a wild overestimation of the scale of immigration and a wild underestimation of the degree to which the newcomers fit into their new countries.

At the same time, political polarization, segregation, discrimination, and inequality have conspired to turn fellow citizens into strangers. The fact is, in America anyway, we simply cannot stand the sight of one another. In 2016, Pew found that "Partisans' views of the opposing party are now more negative than at any point in nearly a quarter of a century." Three years later, Pew reported, "the level of division and animosity . . . has only deepened," with a growing percentage of each side believing the other is more immoral, and more close-minded, than they are. Each side is at a loss to understand the other, because neither is trying. Friendships across the aisle are increasingly rare. Polarization is keeping them separate, rendering them not only unwilling to speak to one another, but unwilling to even momentarily entertain the thought that their opponent is anything more than a mindless organism devoid of will, empathy, or complex motivation; a malignant simpleton; a garbage person. If they're a person at all.

And yet, ironically, in a political climate marked by ceaseless demands for solidarity with those on our side, we've also become deeply and dangerously alone. Studies have found epidemic levels of loneliness in the United States and United Kingdom—affecting everyone, but especially the young, who, in a remarkable development, report levels of loneliness that surpass even those of the elderly. And loneliness, medical researchers have found, is as bad for you as smoking, making it a bona fide public health threat.

The causes of loneliness are complex. When technology eliminates the need to talk to strangers, our social skills erode, weakening our ability to meet new people. As more and more of us move to cities, we trade familiar friends and family members for a rotating cast of strangers that can make it difficult to feel connected to our own neighborhoods. As globalization continues and millions migrate, we become as likely to talk to a stranger in India as the one who lives next door to us. This has created a phenomenon political scientist Chris Rumford called strangeness.

"Familiar places, close to us in our daily existence, may no longer feel entirely 'ours,'" he wrote. "In our local communities and neighborhoods we get the sense that we are living side-by-side but also living apart from people who we might otherwise be tempted to believe comprise our local community. . . . We are no longer sure who 'we' are, and we find it difficult to say who belongs to 'our' group and who comes from outside. . . . Strangeness means that we must recognize that 'we' are probably also strangers (to somebody)."

This is not limited to cities, of course. Something similar is happening in small towns, where population shifts and social and economic forces can combine to wreak profound changes that can render even our hometowns virtually unrecognizable, so we become strangers in our own lands. And as we'll see, when areas become more diverse, we can become anxious about the prospect of even talking to the newcomers, regardless of our political orientation. Sometimes this anxiety leads us to avoid contact not just with different people, but with our own kind as well.

As a result of all these factors, we feel rootless, disengaged from our world. "We have radically changed our environment," wrote the late neuroscientist John Cacioppo, who spent his career studying loneliness. "As career patterns, housing patterns, mortality patterns, and social policies follow the lead of global capitalism, much of the world seems determined to adopt a lifestyle that will compound and reinforce the chronic sense of isolation that millions of individuals already feel."

Given the sheer tonnage of bad PR strangers have gotten over the last, say, two million years, it's a wonder anyone ever talks to them. And yet we do. And we must. Because we would be nowhere without them. My own history stands as evidence. I am no Pollyanna. I am aware of and despairing of the damage humans do to one another, and four decades into life in this world I am shocked anew by how needless and pointless and gratuitous that damage is. *Homo sapiens,* to me, is all too often a creature of monstrous confusion and contradiction and destruction. And yet, some of the most formative experiences of my life have come from talking to strangers.

In college, I was playing bass guitar in a music store outside of Philadelphia when a middle-aged Black man in a cowboy hat appeared, looked at me, looked at the bass, looked back at me, and drawled, "Motherfucker, you look like *Conan O'Brien.*" He hired me on the spot to play with a twelve-piece funk band he had formed. That led to club gigs around Philly and, later, gospel gigs in Baptist churches where I was often the lone white person. For a twenty-year-old kid from a largely white neighborhood, that experience—from the mentorship of the older musicians to the kind hospitality the churchgoers extended to this pasty heathen interloper—was absolutely formative to who I am and how I view the world.

After graduation, I found a strange flyer in the pages of a book at a bookstore seeking writers for a new publication. Something about it struck me, so I emailed the author. The publication never materialized, but he happened to be the distribution manager for a small weekly newspaper. We became friends, then roommates. He introduced me to the editor of the paper. I started writing for them, and in a few years I was running it. That was my start in journalism. Talking to strangers is good for business, good for your career. If it weren't for that flyer, I simply would not have the life I have now.

And I'd be criminally remiss if I didn't mention the Irish coworker who a year or so later dragged me to a party, where I met a stranger who became a friend and who happened to work with another stranger who became my wife and the mother of our four-year-old daughter—who, apropos of the topic of stranger danger, told me the other day, "Dada, some people might be afraid of you. But I'm not, because I've known you a long time."

What's more, my parents, Ed and Joan, are world champions at talking to strangers. Everywhere they go, they make friends: at home, on vacation, in restaurants, on the street. It's a never-ending accumulation of friends and acquaintances. While many older people sit passively while their social circles contract, my parents are relentless in the acquisition of new friends. Talking to strangers for them—and for many of their friends—is simply indistinguishable from being alive.

Without question, I am who I am, and I do what I do, and I think what I think, and I live where I live, because of strangers. And yet here I am, sitting in a bar, inches from another person, head down, eyes down, and mute, my face bathed in the cold blue glow of my phone. And I don't feel great about it.

Why don't we talk to strangers? When will we? What happens when we do?

This book is the result of my quest to answer these questions. And what happens is this: We become better, smarter, and happier people, and strangers—and by extension, the world—become less scary to us. A raft of new research is finding that talking to strangers can help expand us personally, opening us to new opportunities, relationships, and perspectives. It can alleviate our loneliness, and enhance our sense of belonging to the places where we live, even when those places are changing. Talking to strangers, whether they be refugees or political opponents, can even reduce prejudice, cool off partisanship, and help mend fractured societies. As philosopher Kwame Anthony Appiah wrote of these exchanges, "When a stranger is no longer imaginary, but real and present, sharing a human social life, you may like or dislike him, you may agree or disagree; but if it is what you both want, you can make sense of each other in the end."

While we travel together through these pages, we're going to go from the small to the large. We'll start with the new insights psychologists are discovering about what happens when we have even a passing interaction with a stranger. Then we're going to go deeper. Why does it feel good to have a passing interaction with a stranger? We'll look at the dawn of humanity, and our ape ancestors for the answer. We'll see how we became what scientists call *the ultra-cooperative ape,* a creature that both fears and needs strangers. We'll see how hunter-gatherers created ways to safely talk to strangers as a means of survival. We'll look at how hospitality toward strangers became a cornerstone of civilization. We'll see how mass religion's true, transformative genius was in making strangers familiar without ever having to meet them. We'll see how cities rose because people wanted to be around *more* strangers, not fewer. We'll see how human civilization happened in large part because humans found a way to reconcile the fear strangers inspire with the opportunities they offer. And we'll investigate all the factors that keep us from talking to strangers—from technology to politics to citizenship in the fine if very quiet nation of Finland.

And of course, we'll meet a lot of strangers: people off the street, and the activists and researchers who are trying to forge a culture of talking to strangers to help address the ravages of some of our most pressing social problems. While we do, we'll get some useful lessons on how we can go about doing it in our own lives—techniques I'll try out myself, as I try to rebuild myself as a more social person.

In the end, by going back some two million years and ending at the present day, what I hope to do is make the case for talking to strangers. To show, contrary to the stranger-danger line we have been fed for many years by the media, politicians, schools, police, and so forth, that talking to strangers is, in fact, considerably less dangerous than not talking to them.

Talking to strangers isn't just a way to live. It is a way to survive.

Part I

What Happens When We Talk
to Strangers?

Chapter 1

Strangers in a Classroom

In which I travel all the way to London to relearn what should be a laughably rudimentary human skill, and am made to feel uncomfortable—a sign of things to come.

Our journey begins on a bright day in a small classroom at Regent's University in London. I'm sitting on a chair, palsied with jet lag, clutching my third cup of coffee. There are four other people there, too. They appear to be functioning at a higher level than I am, thankfully. We have come here to learn how to talk to strangers. Our teacher in this endeavor is an energetic twenty-nine-year-old named Georgie Nightingall. Georgie is the founder of Trigger Conversations, a London-based "human connection organization" that hosts social events aimed at facilitating meaningful conversations among strangers. Georgie had been recommended to me by a renowned psychologist whom we will meet soon. I got in touch with her, and when she told me that she was planning an immersive three-day seminar on talking to strangers, I bought a plane ticket. Not long after, I landed in London, slept a couple of hours, and then arrived bright and early to a classroom, more coffee than man, but ready to learn.

Georgie started Trigger Conversations in 2016. Up until then, her background had been eclectic. She had graduated from college in

2014, where she was pursuing both an undergraduate degree in philosophy and a master's in "emotions, credibility, and deception, from a psychology and linguistics angle," as she says. That got her interested in language and conversation. After school, she tried her hand at a few different jobs. She interned at a start-up, worked a series of jobs as a project manager, and was for a time at the Francis Crick Institute, a world-renowned biomedical research facility. "That was my last real job," Georgie says. After that she struck out on her own.

She was always a talker, though the prospect of talking to strangers made her a little hesitant, "partly because of some social anxiety about the fact that it wasn't normal to speak to strangers," she says. However, she had also grown bored with the conversations she *was* having with new people—the usual "What do you do?" and "How was your day?" interactions that never go anywhere. She wanted to help introduce people to the idea that these conversations don't have to be dull or formulaic. They can be scintillating, informative, and exploratory. After she founded Trigger Conversations, she drafted a short manifesto along those lines: "We are adventurers in conversation," she wrote. "We are travelers without a destination. Exploring the unknown, without expectation. Each one of us a teacher and every person an opportunity."

Georgie, as it turns out, was exploring the unknown in particularly treacherous territory, conversation-wise. London in particular, and the United Kingdom in general, is something of a global center of a nascent talking-to-strangers movement—in large part because of a concerted national effort to combat the nation's loneliness epidemic. A recent study by the British Red Cross found that a fifth of the British population often or always feels lonely. In 2018, the United Kingdom appointed its first "loneliness minister," a high-ranking government official who steers policy geared toward repairing frayed social ties and reinforcing social cohesion.

In the past few years, numerous grassroots groups have cropped up to try to get Britons to talk to strangers in cafés, pubs, or on mass transit. A "Chatty Café" initiative, in which pubs and cafés set up specially marked tables where strangers can chat, has spread to more than nine hundred locations throughout the United Kingdom and beyond. In 2019, the BBC launched a series called *Crossing Divides* that sought to inspire people to connect over social, cultural, or ideological differences. This included a "chatty bus" day, during which riders were encouraged to talk to one another, because that "may be the only time we are exposed to others outside the cocoons of our family, friends and colleagues," wrote Emily Kasriel, the BBC's head of special projects.

This was, shall we say, a departure from how the English, and particularly Londoners, usually behave on mass transit.* And yet, despite the egregious violation of a time-honored social norm,† chatty bus day was a success. "It's the best bus I've been on," one woman told the BBC, confessing that she usually suffers from acute social anxiety. Some members of the general public have expressed skepticism, if not hostility, toward these initiatives, believing it to be at best an open question as to how compatible the Londoner temperament is with such shenanigans. When I met an English friend for a beer in London and told him I was in town to learn how to talk to strangers, he replied, "You do know that we're like the worst in the world at it, yeah?"

Georgie was understandably nervous about her new venture early on—and not just because of the local horror at the prospect of chatting on the Tube. She worried that there wouldn't be an audience for an organization that tries to facilitate conversations with strangers, or

---

* Coldness is such a part of the local character that when a Hungarian immigrant to Britain named George Mikes wrote a series of guides from the 1940s to the 1970s instructing others on how to be British, his advice on talking to strangers on mass transit included this macabre tale:

> In the late nineteen-fifties, a man committed a murder in the Midlands. Afterwards, near the scene of the crime a man covered with blood was seen to board a bus with about fifty people on it. Yet when he got off, leaving a pool of blood on the floor, not one single passenger bothered to ask him what he had been doing lately. They were true Britons, minding their own business. . . . If another man had been carrying some victim's decapitated head under his arm, that would not make the slightest difference. The parcel you carry is your own business.

† Here I feel compelled to add that according to a 2020 poll commissioned during the COVID-19 crisis by that august polling body Absolut Vodka, 23 percent of young Brits say they miss chatting with strangers.

if there was, people may try it, but they wouldn't like it. When she started running her first conversation events, she was forced to grapple with the norms and anxieties that kept people from talking. What would they say? Where would they start? How should they engage? There was a problem of "people not knowing how to be," she says. "Because if you say to someone 'Come to an event with meaningful conversations with strangers—we won't talk about work; we won't talk about, like, where you live,' they're like, 'So what *can* I talk about?' Suddenly they don't know what's okay and what's not okay."

Georgie eventually realized that the way to get past that initial awkwardness wasn't to offer more freedom, but less. She would gather people in groups of two or three, give them cards with specific questions on them, and set a time limit. That way, all the groundwork that must be done in order to start a conversation—meeting someone, initiating a conversation, and finding something to talk about—would be taken care of. The possibility of rejection would be nil, and there'd be no fear about not knowing how to end the conversation. People could just jump right in, and then when the buzzer sounded, walk away without guilt. "That's incredibly liberating," she says.

Since she founded Trigger Conversations in 2016, Georgie has done more than one hundred events and many training sessions—with strangers, companies, communities, universities, and conferences, both in London and around the world. In 2020, for instance, she developed a program with the University College London to help college students get better at connecting with one another—something, as we'll see, they struggle with. She's seen people come away from these engagements transformed—more confident, more curious, more optimistic about the potential of incorporating these conversations into their lives more regularly. "So many people were coming to these events and being like, 'How do I do this in real life? I want to talk to strangers, but I can't just go up to them with a question card and say, *Do you want to answer a question?*'" she says.

This apparent pent-up demand gave Georgie an idea. She wanted to create a class that could teach people the skills to strike up these conversations in their everyday lives. She started attending self-development seminars and reading everything she could find that could help her understand all the moving parts that made up something as seemingly simple as a chat with a stranger. "How do you start a conversation that's cold and make it warm very fast?" she wondered. "And how do you ask the right questions in order to establish rapport, or go deep or be creative and playful? How can you be authentic? What are the limiting beliefs you are having about yourself, or the beliefs about the other person that are affecting your ability to take risks?"

Georgie learned that for a lot of people, the hardest thing about talking to strangers is initiating the conversation: approaching someone, making them feel safe, and quickly conveying the idea that you don't have an agenda, that you're just being friendly or curious. She found that older people are much more likely to initiate a conversation, for instance, whereas younger people require a little more assurance. She noticed if you answered the question "How are you?" honestly, it created a little bond among strangers and cleared the way for a conversation because it showed vulnerability and curiosity, and encouraged people to respond in kind. She found that in all her attempts, the vast majority of people did in fact engage with her, most of those interactions were substantial, and many were, she says, "meaningful."

As she went about gathering ideas and experimenting with techniques, she gained a clearer insight into the potential value of talking to strangers. Georgie recalls an attendee at one of her early events coming up to her and thanking her. "It was remarkable," the man told her. "I never would have chosen to speak to that person. And yet when I did, I discovered that actually we had so much in common, and it was remarkable how connected I felt to someone who is completely not like me."

Georgie says she now feels that way every day. "I find that as soon as I'm able to see how I relate to somebody, in any particular way, it means I like them more, I trust them more, and I feel like we're actually part of a bigger world, rather than just in our own silos," she says. "And it just makes life so much more fruitful, more fulfilling. I feel less irritated and angry because I know that everyone is just being in the world, like I am, and everyone has a backstory, like I do, and our experiences probably aren't that different."

She came to believe, too—and this is important—that making a practice of talking to strangers could offer more than a jolt of good feeling for an individual. There was real joy in it, profundity, real communion. If practiced widely enough, she believed it could help repair a fracturing society. "We're not just talking about a few individualized things," she says. "We're talking about a systemic issue. A different way to live."

Georgie stands before our class, bright, engaging, and articulate, and walks us through what to expect over the coming days. She wants to take us "from unconscious incompetence, to conscious incompetence, to conscious competence, to unconscious competence," she says. In other words, we are currently bad at this and we don't know why. We will learn what we are lacking. We will improve on it. And we will hopefully become so proficient that it will become second nature to us.

We go around the room and introduce ourselves. I say I'm here mostly because I'm writing a book, but I'm writing the book because I've seen what talking to strangers does for my parents, how naturally it comes to them, and I want to get better at it. Justine,* who is in her early forties, says she came to London from Australia. At home, the culture encouraged talking to strangers, and she liked that. But when she got to London, anytime she'd be friendly, people would regard her warily. She'd say hello to a guy in a pub—not flirting, just friendly—and he'd immediately tell her he has a girlfriend. Those reactions eroded her confidence and caused her to withdraw. She wonders if the reason people don't want to talk to her is "because I'm fat." She says she notices that the seats next to her on the Tube are always the last ones filled. She works from home and thus doesn't get much human contact. And she wants to talk to strangers, but she isn't sure what to say.

---

* Names have been changed to protect the privacy of the other students.

The next student, Paula, late twenties, bright and personable, says she works a lot, and her job requires her to spend a great deal of time being efficient and polite, which might come across as a little chilly. When she does talk, "the things I'm saying aren't meaningful, and because I'm on autopilot I'm not sharing the true me," she says. "I think that blocks people from connecting with me." Paula says she has old friends who told her they don't really know who she is. "That's really hurtful," she says. Still, she's afraid if she does open up, people will not be interested in what she has to say.

Another student, Nicky, twenties, diminutive and quiet, was raised on a farm and recently moved to the outskirts of London. He gets nervous in conversations, he tells us, and struggles to say what he means. He wants to be more creative, to ask better questions. Later he tells me at lunch that he wants to get better at talking to strangers "so I can be free." He has aspirations to travel, and he believes that with improved social skills, he will be able to fit in anywhere—that learning to talk to strangers will be the key that opens the world to him. He will be a stranger nowhere in the world.

A fifth student, Margot, is the youngest. Early twenties. She tells us that she's simply not interested in other people, but she also wants to get out of her own head. She's suspicious, resistant, and quiet, but also absolutely without mercy or tact when it comes to speaking her mind. This, she explains, has not made things easy for her socially. When we're asked to imagine a scenario in which we want to connect with someone, and then devise an opener, I propose "a waiter."

"Why would you want to talk to a waiter?" she says.

I say because it always strikes me as awkward that you treat the person bringing you your food like they're a robot. She says, "That's because you're an American." Later, during a particularly intense conversational exercise in which one partner expresses personal feelings uninterrupted for several minutes, and the other tells them how they seem based on what they said, Margot tells me I seem to be very stable, but I also remind her of her father, and that's both comforting and freaking her out. I don't quite know how to respond to this.

That will not be the only uncomfortable moment I have in the class. In the days ahead, we will be made to have very personal conversations with one another. To stare each other in the eyes for long periods. To intensely monitor what we feel and how we think when we talk to people we don't know. To touch each other's arms to signal friendliness. My discomfort was not limited to the class, or the campus, or the city of London. I was in for a fair amount of it. I had set out on a mission to become good at talking to strangers, to build myself up as a much more social creature, and as it turned out, I had a lot to learn.

Chapter 2

A Readily Available Source of Happiness That We Almost Never Take Advantage Of

In which we learn that talking to strangers can make us happier, healthier, and less lonely—and also that we seldom do it, because we're not completely sure that strangers are entirely human.

Now, I can't really sell you on the value of a *class* on talking to strangers without first taking you for a brief tour through the growing body of recent psychology research that shows what happens when we talk to strangers. Over the past decade and a half, researchers have found that talking to strangers can make us happier, more connected to the places in which we live, mentally sharper, healthier, and more trustful and optimistic. We're going to meet some of those researchers in this chapter, and we're going to take a look at what they've learned. This is the foundation for everything you and I are going to encounter over the course of our time together. But first, I want to introduce you to someone who has lived what these scientists have found. Her name is Nic, she's a nurse in Las Vegas, and talking to strangers has changed her life.

Nic grew up in a small beach town in Santa Cruz County, California, the child of a volatile father and a mother who had experienced a great deal of trauma and transferred much of it onto her daughter. She was raised to be a fearful child. "My primitive brain was programmed to be afraid of everybody, because *everybody's evil and they're gonna hurt you,*" Nic tells me. "I thought I was supposed to be afraid of everything."

And she was. Nic spent most of her childhood avoiding people. "I was safe that way," she says. "I had my billions of books. I had my dog, I had my cats and my random rodents, as pets. I didn't really need anything else," she says. "I had the safety of those that knew me best, which were animals, and they would never hurt me."

Nic's teenage years were rough. She is a mix of Egyptian Jewish and Scottish stock, and her thick hair and cystic acne made her stick out in her mostly lily-white schools. "I was harassed a *lot,*" she says. But there was an upside to being the outcast. Nic invariably ended up making friends with other kids who looked different or came from different backgrounds. If there was a new Black or Latina student, say, they'd naturally fall in together. "I remember meeting a girl from France who got transferred into our elementary school, and of course she and I became best friends, because I was alone and she was alone," Nic tells me. Friendship bloomed from their mutual estrangement.

Nic had been raised to fear strangers—by her mother, of course, but also by a country in which the phrase "stranger danger" is practically tattooed onto the foreheads of children at birth. But as Nic connected with these particular strangers, she found that they weren't dangerous or scary. They were actually a source of comfort to her, and belonging. They expanded her world. By seeking them out, her life became better. "I met a lot of incredible people that way, as a kid," she says. "That probably started the whole thing: *I'm okay with strangers, but I'm not supposed to be okay with strangers.*"

That "whole thing" she's referring to is something Nic calls Greyhound Therapy, a practice she developed as she got older that helped her manage her fear of strangers and secure for herself a place in the world.* Its roots were in her childhood. Her family never traveled

---

* Not to be confused with the pejorative term that is used to describe the practice—all too common in America, unfortunately—of healthcare providers shipping troubled patients

because they were afraid to. And as it so often happens, this immobility sparked in young Nic a burning, Springsteen-grade desire *to get the hell out of town*. "Something in me decided along the way that I wanted out," she says. Her early experiences meeting new and unusual people had given her a taste for a world beyond the stultifying and paranoid confines of her childhood, and she wanted at it. *God made a huge Earth with a shit-ton of people in it,* she remembers thinking, *and I have to meet 'em.*

And so she did. At seventeen, Nic was offered a chance to travel to Europe for ten days with her high school, and what she experienced shocked her. "That's when random people started talking to *me*," she says. "In Europe, they find out you're American—oh my goodness, I met so many great people that way." That gave her some confidence. "If people in Europe randomly talked to me, then maybe I'm not so bad," she figured. "Maybe I'm not gonna die if I randomly talk to *them*."

At eighteen, she took her first solo road trip. She drove to Eureka, California, just because she liked the name. She stayed one night in a hotel by herself and drove home. It was a short trip, but it was another nickel in the confidence bank. She took more trips, and started talking to more people. She was anxious about these encounters, wired for fear and expecting the worst, but they always went well. "That's when I started *really* trying to expand my horizons and talk to people randomly," she says. That was the start of Greyhound Therapy. In the literal sense, it refers to talking to your seatmate on a long-haul bus. But Nic came to apply it to talking to strangers anywhere—at a restaurant, at a bus stop, in a grocery store—wherever there were strangers.

Life did not get easier, however. She graduated from nursing school at twenty-one, and a few years later fell into a serious relationship with a man. They connected over a shared love for driving and cars—which Nic got from her father, a trucker. It was the only thing she could reliably talk with her dad about. She married the man, but he ended up being volatile and abusive. They didn't make it to their

---

elsewhere instead of offering them the treatment they need.

first anniversary. She wound up in the hospital with stitches and a broken tooth.

She met another man, a larger-than-life New Yorker, and moved to the city to be with him. "He was a New Yorker by birth, and he was absolutely obnoxious and the complete and total opposite of me," she says. He was a chef at a university, which gave him plenty of time off, and he had wanderlust, too. They drove to Alaska, down to Mexico, and back to New York, talking to people the whole way. She and the man stayed together for four years, but the kitchen life takes a toll. He got into coke and started drinking heavily, and turned into a different person. Having been down this road before, she left. He eventually succumbed to his addictions, but the good influence he had on her remained.

Nic was on her own for a while after that, living in an apartment in a strange place. And she was lonely, "which is shocking because I never thought I would be lonely—as an introvert," she says. "So, there was a whole period of time where I would seek out Greyhound Therapy. I would seek out that human interaction just to stave off the loneliness."

"And it worked?" I ask.

"Oh god, yes," she says. "And I would go home with some amazing stories—granted, nobody to share them with, but I still had the stories—they were mine." It was also a way to "test my mettle, if you will," she says. "The more I interacted with people, the more confident as an adult I became."

It changed her life. These days, Nic is a successful nurse with an uncanny gift for connecting with her patients, happily married to a kind and sociable man, and living in Las Vegas, which, she says, "is awesome." She travels as much as ever, and when she's alone on the road, she still seeks out Greyhound Therapy. She'll size up her seatmate, or someone sitting alone at a table or the bar. If they have headphones on, or they're giving off a disinterested vibe, she'll leave them alone. But if they seem receptive, she'll say, "Hi, I'm Nic," and see where it goes. She's not reckless, or naïve. She isn't striking up a conversation with a stranger in a dark alley in an unfamiliar town. Like many children of chaotic parents, her radar is keen; she has a gift for reading people and situations and detecting trouble. But the conversations tend to go well, and each one, in turn, "reinforces that not everybody's going to hurt me."

"I've had a few crucibles in my life," Nic says. But those crucibles, and the strangers she turned to in order to help get through them, to reassure her that there is a goodness in the world, and the possibility of belonging, taught her something invaluable, she says: "Never underestimate the power of even the most minute positive connection."

So—what is that power? In psychology, the sorts of exchanges Nic is talking about are known as "minimal social interactions." And the Canadian psychologist Gillian Sandstrom had a similar epiphany about them about a decade ago. Only hers concerned a hot dog cart, and it led to a series of discoveries about talking to strangers that have established Sandstrom, now based at the University of Essex, northeast of London, as a rising academic star in the social sciences.

Sandstrom, forty-eight, was raised in Canada by extroverts, both teachers. "My father is the king of talking to strangers," she says. "He can't help himself, he has to talk to everyone." Her mother talks to strangers, too, though she tends to seek out people—adults and kids—who seem alone, or left out, in an effort to include them. One day, Sandstrom, who had always considered herself an introvert, realized something. She noticed that she always looked down when she walked along the street. She would make eye contact with someone and then immediately look back down at the sidewalk.

"I thought, *Well, that's dumb,*" she says. So she started looking up and holding eye contact with people. "That was my first step to talking to strangers," she says. "I was just trying to fix this weird habit." As she did, Sandstrom found that not only was making eye contact *not* weird, but it actually felt pretty good, and her fellow pedestrians didn't seem to object to it either, even if it was unusual. She had two separate instances in which people on the subway in Toronto told her unprompted that she must not be from around here. When she asked why, they told her it was because she was actually looking at people. "I thought, *Oh my gosh—how sad!* I didn't really notice that people were just looking at the ceiling or the floor, but not looking at each other," she says.

Before long, Sandstrom wasn't just looking at strangers, but talking to them. She was surprised at how easy it was, and how fun it was. "I thought, *Oh, that's why my dad does this!*" She recalls one conversation on the subway. A woman was holding a box of elaborately decorated cupcakes, and Sandstrom asked about them. They started talking. "I don't know how the conversation got there, but she taught me that humans can ride ostriches," she says. That was it. "I was *sold*. That was just a delightful conversation. I wanted to do it again, and I started doing it more often." With that epiphany, her future direction as a researcher started to come into view.

The next epiphany came in in 2007, when Sandstrom was studying for her master's degree at Ryerson University in Toronto. Grad school was hard, and Sandstrom often felt like an imposter—not an uncommon affliction in grad school or, if we're being honest here, in life—and she had plenty of time to ponder her perceived inadequacy in transit. Her lab was in one building, and her supervisor was in another, and the walk between the two was long. Every day, while making this trek, Sandstrom passed a woman selling hot dogs from a cart. One day, she smiled and waved at the woman, and the woman waved and smiled back. Sandstrom felt a little spark. After that, it became part of her routine. "Every time I passed, I looked for her, to try to make that little connection," she says. "And I realized that when I saw her, and when she acknowledged me, it made me feel good. I felt like, *Yeah, I belong here.*" She laughs at the absurdity of it. "I felt like I belonged because the hot dog lady knew who I was."

Sandstrom began looking at what was happening: why these connections felt so good. She and her PhD supervisor at the University of British Columbia, Elizabeth Dunn, a widely respected psychologist who studies happiness, conducted an experiment. They asked a group of adults to try to chat with the barista at their local Starbucks when they got their morning coffee. This is an unusual request. People—especially, but not exclusively, in cities—tend to favor efficiency in transactions like these. They rarely talk. Sometimes they don't even make eye contact. But Sandstrom and Dunn had the idea that by *not* engaging with counter workers—by essentially treating them as insensate service modules and not, say, actual humans—we may be denying ourselves something that could potentially be beneficial. "Might we be missing out on a hidden source of belonging and happiness?" they wondered.

The idea was, and still is, pretty novel in the field of psychology. A hefty body of research over the years has found that the single best predictor of happiness and well-being is the quality of a person's social relationships. People who have good relationships are healthier in mind and in body; people who don't are more susceptible to everything from mental disorders to cardiovascular disease. Simple. But those studies generally looked at only *close* relationships: family, friends, coworkers. Sandstrom and Dunn wanted to see if interacting with *strangers* could be good for us, too: not as a replacement for close relationships, but as a complement—a way to help create a more balanced social diet, as it were.

Sandstrom and Dunn recruited sixty adults—thirty men and thirty women, across a range of ages—from in front of a Starbucks in a busy shopping district. Half of these participants were instructed to interact with their baristas—to "smile, make eye contact to establish a connection, and have a brief conversation." The other half were told to make their transaction as efficient as possible. Both groups were asked to report back afterward. As it turns out, Sandstrom and Dunn's hypothesis was correct. The participants who talked to their baristas reported feeling a stronger sense of belonging and an improved mood, as well as greater satisfaction with their overall experience. Thus, the authors concluded in a 2013 paper, "The next time you need a little pick-me-up, you might consider interacting with the Starbucks barista as if they were [an acquaintance] instead of a stranger, thereby mining this readily available source of happiness."

Around the same time, Sandstrom and Dunn launched another study that spoke to why waving to the hot dog lady every day somehow made Sandstrom feel like she belonged. Researchers have long found that people are happier on days where they socialize more, but no one had studied interactions with "weak ties"—which could be passing acquaintances, or people we know by sight who aren't necessarily friends. To see if interactions with these people could affect levels of happiness and belonging, Sandstrom and Dunn gave red and black clickers to fifty-eight students—fifteen men, forty-three women—and instructed them to click red when they encountered a "strong tie"—a friend or family member, say—and click black when they encountered a "weak tie"—like the hot dog lady. At the end of every day, they tallied the number of interactions and asked participants a series of questions about whether they felt socially connected or lonely, and whether they felt they had social support and experienced a sense of community. The researchers found that those who had more interactions with strong ties felt happiest and more connected to their communities. That wasn't surprising. What was surprising is that people who had more interactions with *weak ties*—like the hot dog lady—were happier and felt a greater sense of belonging than those who had fewer. What's more, people were happier on days they had more weak-tie interactions than days when they had fewer.

These were college students, though—which means they may not be all that representative of humanity. So Sandstrom and Dunn recreated the experiment using forty-one members of the community—thirty female, eleven male, all over twenty-five years of age—and they got the same result. Across both studies they found that interactions with weak ties were even more potent on days when the participants had fewer overall interactions—a valuable insight in an age of loneliness. Like food for the hungry, or water for the parched, an interaction with a weak tie on a solitary day felt nourishing.

Sandstrom wasn't the only one mining this newly discovered vein. In 2013, the University of Chicago psychologist Nicholas Epley and his then-student Juliana Schroeder were wondering why an ultrasocial species like *Homo sapiens* is so often hesitant about talking to strangers, inspired by the silence they observed on the crowded subway at rush hour. "From trains to cabs to airplanes to waiting rooms, strangers may sit millimeters apart while completely ignoring each other, treating one another as objects rather than as sources of well-being," they noted. "For a species that seems to benefit so much from connecting to others, why would people in close proximity so routinely seem to prefer isolation instead? Why are such highly social animals, at times, so distinctly unsocial?" Epley and Schroeder hypothesized that the reason people didn't talk to strangers is because they think it would be less pleasant than just keeping to themselves.

They created a series of experiments in which they instructed participants to—heaven forfend—talk to strangers on mass transit, in taxis, and in waiting rooms. Their first experiment involved ninety-seven commuters with a median age of forty-nine—61 percent of them women—in suburban Illinois. The participants were divided up into three groups. One was instructed: "Please have a conversation with a new person on the train today. Try to make a connection. Find out something interesting about him or her and tell them something about you. The longer the conversation, the better." A second group was told, "Please keep to yourself and enjoy your solitude on the train today. Take this time to sit alone with your thoughts. Your goal is to focus on yourself and the day ahead of you." And a third group was told to commute the way they always do. Afterward, the participants were instructed to fill out a questionnaire about their personalities and their experiences during their commute.

True to the researchers' prediction, the people who talked to strangers reported a significantly more positive, enjoyable commute than those who didn't. Conversations lasted an average of 14.2 minutes, and the talker came away with a positive impression of the strangers they'd talked to. Not one of them reported having a negative experience. Positive effects were reported regardless of the talker's personality type. Extroverts and introverts both had a good experience.

Now, if talking to a stranger during your commute is so pleasant, why don't people do it? To answer that question, Epley and Schroeder recruited sixty-six commuters—66 percent of them women, with a median age of forty-four—and asked them to imagine how they would *feel* if they participated in the three conditions of the previous study: if they talked to a stranger, remained solitary and focused on themselves, or just did what they always did. While in the previous study, those who talked to strangers reported having a significantly more positive commute than those who did not, here, those who *imagined* talking to a stranger predicted their commutes would be significantly worse.

Epley and Schroeder repeated these experiments on buses in downtown Chicago with a new sample, this one with a median age of twenty-seven—49 percent of them women—and got similar results. Riders predicted they would have a negative experience talking to strangers, when in reality those who actually did ended up having an overwhelmingly positive one. Another study based in taxis got a similar result. People who talked to their drivers enjoyed their ride more, and liked the driver more, than people who did not.

They then reproduced the previous experiments, only this time they wanted to see if a fear of rejection was a major barrier to interaction. And it was.

Participants believed they were significantly more interested in talking to strangers than strangers were in talking to them. They predicted, on average, that fewer than 47 percent of the people they approached would talk to them. They expected it would be hard to start the conversation. And they were wrong. It was easier than they'd predicted. People *were* interested in talking to them, and not a single one was rejected. "Commuters appeared to think that talking to a stranger posed a meaningful risk of social rejection," Epley and Schroeder wrote. "As far as we can tell, it posed no risk at all."

By now, skeptics among us are thinking the same thing I was thinking when I first read these studies: Sure, talking to strangers might be enjoyable if you're the one doing the talking. But what about the stranger? Are they enjoying it? After all, every one of us has at one time or another been trapped in an enclosed space by a talker who proved agonizingly impervious to social cues indicating that you're not in the mood.

So, to test whether the enjoyment went both ways, Epley and Schroeder created yet another experiment—this time in a laboratory meant to resemble a waiting room. They assigned participants some tasks unrelated to the research at hand—to throw them off the scent of the real aims of the experiment. But between those tasks, the researchers had them take a ten-minute break in the waiting room. Some of these subjects were told to talk to the other person in the room, some were told not to talk, and some were told to do whatever they wanted. The ones who talked—both the people who started the conversation *and* the people they talked to—reported having a much more positive experience than those who did not. That happened regardless of whether the initiator of the conversation was told to talk or just decided to on their own, and it happened regardless of personality type.

Finally, lest anyone think that these results were skewed due to the general friendliness of Midwesterners, Epley and Schroeder recreated the experiment in London, in 2019 at the behest of the BBC. Londoners' expectations for these interactions were even lower than their American counterparts, but Epley and Schroeder got the same results. "Our commuters estimated that only about 40% of their fellow train passengers would be willing to talk to them," they reported. "Yet every participant in our experiment who actually tried to talk to a stranger found the person sitting next to them was happy to chat."

Juliana Schroeder let me take a look at the survey responses she and Epley solicited from participants. "Quite a surprising outcome," one reported. "Being a Londoner, it is not in my nature to start conversations with strangers on public transport. But a couple sat next to me when changing trains. I asked them a question about the next train, and struck up a conversation until their train came ten minutes later." Another added, "It was nice! I enjoyed my conversation and it made me think I should talk to strangers more."

The results of all these studies were heartening—it's easier and more enjoyable to talk to strangers than we think—but there was also an undertone of alarm to the researchers' conclusions. "It is possible," they write, "even in situations where social interaction is neither required nor the norm . . . that engaging a stranger in conversation may actually be *more* pleasant than remaining isolated. This suggests a . . . profound misunderstanding of social interactions: Members of a highly social species may ignore other people because they expect that connecting with a stranger will be more negative than remaining isolated. . . . Humans may indeed be social animals but may not always be social enough for their own well-being. On an increasingly crowded planet, misunderstanding the benefits of social engagement could be increasingly problematic."

The participants in all these studies predicted that their interactions with strangers would go badly—they would be hard, and people would reject them—and they were delighted to find that they did not. And when they did strike up these conversations, they were happier, and felt a stronger sense of belonging. So why don't people talk to one another on the subway? Epley and Schroeder argued that it's not that everyone really prefers silence, but that they all assume no one else wants to talk, and they believe it will go poorly if they try. This is known in the field as *pluralistic ignorance*. Basically, it means everyone having the wrong idea about everyone else.

But there is a deeper force at play here, too. Participants in these studies expect to be rejected, yes. But judging from their responses, they also expected little from the conversations themselves. That's why they were so pleasantly surprised. Why? Why did it come as such a shock that a random stranger could be approachable, cordial, and interesting? Because, simply put, *we don't expect them to be fully human*.

Part of the inspiration behind the subway experiments, Schroeder tells me, is the idea that "being surrounded by people and not engaging with them is fundamentally dehumanizing." Put it this way: It's dehumanizing to me, because I lose an opportunity to be a social being, which is my nature as a human. And it's dehumanizing to them, because when I don't talk to them, I never really experience more than a superficial glimpse of their full humanity. "In big cities, you get this phenomenon where you're treating people like obstacles," Schroeder says. And this creates a sort of loop: City dwellers think of strangers as objects, so we don't talk to them; and because we don't talk to them, it never fully occurs to us that they are, in fact, really people. We know intellectually that they are, of course, but we often act like we don't.*

This is *the lesser minds problem,* so-dubbed by Epley and psychologist Adam Waytz, in 2010. This is important. Lesser minds, they explain, works like this: Because we can't see what's happening in other people's heads, we have "what appears to be a universal tendency to assume that others' minds are less sophisticated and more superficial than one's own." That means we chronically underestimate strangers' intelligence, their willpower, and their ability to feel human emotions like pride, embarrassment, and shame. Perhaps this is why we expect interactions with strangers to go poorly: because we subconsciously believe they just don't have much to offer.† There is a passage about Theodore Roosevelt in historian Doris Kearns Goodwin's *Leadership: In Turbulent Times* that perfectly captures this dynamic:

> Week after week, Theodore visited Morton Hall, relaxing with working-class Irish and German immigrants, with butchers, carpenters, and grooms as they drank beer and smoked cigars, listening to their stories, joining them in

---

* And let me just say, I am judging no one here. I live in New York City. When I went out to get lunch just now and people kept walking in front of me on the sidewalk and weaving and stopping short, did I pause and reflect on their capacity for thought and agency? Did I consider their dreams and feelings? The richness and individuality of their experiences? I did not. I lumped them all together and dismissed them as witless bovine obstructions, and, reader, I seethed at them.

† I recall when I was starting this book, I used to tell people that I believed if you talked to a stranger—really engaged—that you will discover that everyone has at least *one* meaningful thing to share. At least one! I realize now that that is a monstrously condescending thought and offer my apologies to the world.

games of cards, thoroughly enjoying the convivial, masculine atmosphere.

> "I went around often enough to have the men get accustomed to me and to have me get accustomed to them," he later said, "so that we began to speak the same language and so that each could begin to live down in the other's mind what [nineteenth-century American author] Bret Harte has called 'the defective quality of being a stranger.'"

The lesser minds problem turns up in everyone, but it can be especially potent if these strangers belong to different groups than we do: if they are a member of an *out-group,* meaning a different race, nationality, or party.* Studies have found that we don't believe out-group members think as well as we do, feel as deeply, or have the same degree of self-control. One study, conducted by Carleton University psychologist Michael Wohl, found that apologies from a fictitious group of Afghani soldiers for a friendly fire incident fell flat because the Canadian study participants didn't quite believe the Afghanis had the capacity to feel genuine guilt.† Lesser minds often manifests in subtle ways, but history furnishes us with many examples of the monstrous dimensions it can take on if provoked. (We will return to those later.)

Obviously, going through life thinking other people aren't *really* human is not ideal—not if we want to make progress on the great experiment that is human civilization. So what can we do about the lesser minds problem? Schroeder explains: Since it is "a function of being stuck inside of our own perspectives all the time, the way to counteract it is to actually sit down and engage with the person in a more meaningful way—which involves language," she says. "That's

---

* A well-meaning socialite once asked the anthropologist Hortense Powdermaker about her time among native tribes in New Guinea: "Don't you think that the natives are *just like human beings?*" she asked. "And have you noticed that they *really* appreciate kindness?"

† And these were *Canadians!*

kind of why language developed, for these social purposes of finding out what's going on in the minds of others."

In other words: We can address it by talking to strangers.

Okay. Now let's return to Gillian Sandstrom. After her initial breakthroughs, which attracted international media attention, she began examining what was keeping people from taking advantage of this "readily available source of happiness." While Epley and Schroeder believed that lesser minds and pessimism were keeping us apart, Sandstrom had a simpler explanation: She believed people just didn't know how to do it.

This insight arose in part from a collaboration she had with a London group called Talk to Me, cofounded in 2012 by two young women named Polly Akhurst and Ann Don Bosco. The group distributed "Talk to Me" buttons to signal a willingness to talk in public, and set up "talk bars" in public spaces, pubs, and bus stops, offering people sets of questions to get the conversations started. There was predictable pushback from some Londoners aghast at the violation of this sacred social norm, but Akhurst says she saw results immediately. "Some people said that they feel differently about London," she says, "and even feel safer living in the city after realizing who the actual strangers *are*."

In 2014, as Talk to Me garnered attention in the international press, Don Bosco reached out to Sandstrom to ask if she was interested in working together. She was, and they set about thinking of what she could contribute. "Then one day I just had this revelation," Sandstrom says. "I was playing the piano, and all of a sudden this idea popped in my head: *Maybe people just don't know how to talk to strangers.*" She whipped out her phone and started making notes for a workshop in which she could help them learn.

Sandstrom ended up running six of these events, and in addition to showing attendees how fruitful and enjoyable talking to strangers can be, the workshops also gave Sandstrom an opportunity to compile data for what she came to call her "fears inventory"—a list of the factors that keep people from talking. Echoing Epley and Schroeder's findings, workshop attendees worried that the other person wouldn't be interested in talking to *them*. They worried they didn't have permission to do it; they worried they wouldn't know how to end such a conversation once it began. They worried they wouldn't enjoy it. And—in what is perhaps the most English thing I have ever encountered—they worried that once they started talking, they'd wind up revealing too much about themselves. (Later, in an analysis of seven studies on talking to strangers, Sandstrom and a colleague found no notable difference between men and women when it comes to these fears—though they did find that people who are shy or more socially anxious experience them more acutely.)

Sandstrom has since developed some techniques to help allay these fears. For instance, she tells people to follow their curiosity—notice something, compliment a person, or ask them a question. Generally, though, she just told people who attended these workshops to talk to one another, and watched as they figured it out themselves. They'd shuffle in beforehand, and it would be quiet and awkward. She'd tell them to pick someone they'd never spoken to and just talk to them. When they had gotten over the initial hump, they'd find it came to them quite naturally. "It doesn't take any time at all before they're into the conversation, and by the end they don't want to stop talking," she says. "It's fascinating. You can't shut them up. I love it."

In 2018, Sandstrom worked as part of a team of researchers on a series of experiments led by psychologist Erica Boothby that took place in a lab, a freshman college dorm, and a personal development workshop in the community, in which participants interacted with strangers. Afterward, the participants reported back on how much they liked the stranger, and how much they believed the stranger liked them.

The researchers found again and again that there was a gap between perception and reality—participants believed that they liked the stranger more than the stranger liked them. This effect was particularly strong among people who rated high for shyness. The researchers called this *the liking gap,* and it's not hard to see how this could be a deterrent to seeking out connections with strangers. Even if a conversation goes well, if you believe the other person doesn't like you that much, you probably won't keep seeking out these interactions, and that could deprive you of the benefits of talking to strangers—from short-term boosts of happiness and belonging to more lasting benefits, like meeting new friends, romantic partners, or business contacts. "Conversations have the power to turn strangers into friends, coffee dates into marriages, and interviews into jobs," concluded the authors. "But part of what makes conversations difficult is that people . . . systemically underestimate how much their conversation partners like them and enjoy their company."

Where does this gap come from? The answer is a Gordian knot of norms, neuroses, and misunderstandings. Conversations with new people are "conspiracies of politeness" in which people can mask their true feelings, making it hard to read one another. They are more cognitively demanding than conversations with people we know; because you have no frame of reference for the person you're speaking to, you have to listen more closely, remember what they said, and think about what you're saying and how it's being perceived.* Because you're putting so much effort into simply maintaining the conversation, you tend to miss the signs of positive feedback from your partner. At the same time, you tend to assume that your own inner thoughts and feelings—such as awkwardness or insecurity—are far more visible to your partner than they actually are. And, cherry on top, we have a tendency to compare all of our conversational performances with our all-time greatest conversational performances, and we assume that others hold us to the same pitiless standard. And ironically, while we expect a great performance from ourselves, we expect very little from others. Call it the upside of the lesser minds problem: low expectations. So while we're frequently disappointed by how we do, we're usually delighted to discover that what we had previously believed to be a more or less witless husk standing before us *actually contains a thinking, feeling human being.* Good job, everybody.

---

* The psychologist Oscar Ybarra has actually found across two separate studies that talking to strangers can lead to gains in cognitive functioning—in part because it's hard to do: like exercising.

As Gillian Sandstrom continued her research, she found that in addition to the fear of incompetence, which can be addressed easily enough, there was a much more insidious obstacle against talking to strangers: a social norm against it—a belief that this is simply not done where we live. We're going to get more deeply into how cultures evolve to be for or against talking to strangers a little later in this book.* But it's worth dipping a toe in now, just to help us get a good foundation in place for what's coming our way.

Sandstrom had encountered the social norm against talking to strangers in an experiment she did in conjunction with the Tate Modern museum in London in 2013, the results of which have not yet been published. She asked volunteers at the museum to strike up conversations with museumgoers at an exhibit in the facility's cavernous Turbine Hall. These volunteers weren't given any special training on the exhibit itself, or any instructions on what to talk about. They were just told to ask people what they thought, or how the art made them feel.

Afterward, researchers interviewed volunteers and visitors alike and found that, across the board, visitors who spoke to volunteers felt more connected to the exhibit, to the other people at the exhibit, and to humanity in general, and volunteers who sought out these interactions also felt happier and more connected than those who did not. Sandstrom recalls one participant telling her, "It's gone better than I expected; I didn't realize that people would enjoy talking so much." Yet, when Sandstrom asked her whether she'd keep striking up conversations with strangers in the future, she got a hard no. The reason, Sandstrom believed, was the social norm against talking to strangers. "By participating in this study, she had permission to go up and talk to people," she says. "But without that permission, she was just like: *Nope. Not doing it.*"

Sandstrom started to think about ways to push back against the norm. Her previous experiments, though successful, were one-offs. Participants would unfailingly have positive experiences, but those

* The explanations include diversity, fear of disease, wealth, living in a big city, bad public architecture, and/or residence in the country of Finland.

experiences never became a habit. "When you ask people about the next conversation, they're really worried again," she says. She wanted to try to address this by engineering a situation in which talking to strangers, through sheer repetition, would become natural enough to people that they would simply begin to do it out of habit, free of all the usual fears and social encumbrances. The trick, she believed, was "to get people to have a *lot* of conversations." She hoped that by doing enough of them, people would eventually overcome their anxiety and change their behavior in a more lasting way.

In 2019, using an app called GooseChase, Sandstrom created a scavenger hunt that gave ninety-two members of the general public a list of types of people with whom to strike up conversations: people who were smiley, people who looked "artsy," people trying to carry a lot of things, people who looked sad, people who seemed nice or fashionable or sporty or who were tattooed or wearing a "striking tie." Before dispatching the participants, Sandstrom asked them to predict how interested strangers would be in talking to them, how many people they'd need to approach before one talked to them, how hard it would be to start and maintain the conversation, and how long they thought the conversations would last. As usual, their expectations were low. "People are remarkably pessimistic about talking to strangers," Sandstrom writes.

They were then asked to have at least one conversation, after which they were to report back on their experience. You can probably guess what the preliminary findings indicate. While only 24 percent of participants predicted the first person they approached would talk to them, in reality, the first person talked to them 90 percent of the time. Plus, the conversations lasted twice as long as they predicted.

Sandstrom was curious if having more conversations could correct that pessimism. She recruited 286 students—209 women, 75 men, and two who declined to say, with a median age of twenty—from a university in the United States and one in the United Kingdom. They were divided into two groups. One group was instructed to talk to strangers every day for five days, using the scavenger hunt app, and another was simply asked to find the people on the list, but not to talk to them.

The results, again, were striking. Participants found it was much easier to start and maintain a conversation with a stranger, and the conversations lasted three times longer than they predicted. Eighty-two percent of participants said they learned something they didn't know. But it was more than a pleasant way to pass some time. Relationships formed. Forty-two percent said they exchanged contact information with someone. Participants made friends, went on dates, got coffee. Many of them said it was just great to meet new people. And true to Sandstrom's prediction, their pessimism about the prospect of talking to strangers was eased, and their expectations were brought closer to reality. A week after completing the scavenger hunt, participants were more confident of their conversational abilities and less afraid of rejection.

Sandstrom let me look over the students' responses from the scavenger hunt survey, and I found many of them to be poignant, coming from such young people.

> I liked most of the people that I talked with. . . . I realised that it was easier talking to strangers than my friends because they did not know about my problems. Most of the conversations were small talk but they made me happy because sometimes you realise that others are also having a bad day or agree that the weather was terrible.

> I felt that the missions helped me be friendlier to people I otherwise would not talk to day to day. I was also able to create conversations out of interactions that might have only been a couple of words, and this made me feel happier and more fulfilled.

> Strangers are generally friendly and helpful.

> I enjoy my own company and being alone, but have found recently that I have been missing social contact a little. I felt like I had forgotten how to make friends, but this study reminded me that most people are friendly and you just need to put yourself out there.

I feel more connection to the world and also I feel people around me are more friendly. The conversation is pretty good. Although sometimes I have nothing to say, the strangers would try to save the conversation, which warms my heart.

The experience was marvelous. . . . I am an exchange student for the autumn term and I hardly know any locals or other students (apart from some other exchange students). It was really helpful to connect an "outsider" with the community and reduce my homesickness (haha!). . . . I talked to classmates I never talked to before, and I made actual friends that I would be able to meet again during my study. Thank you very much for giving the opportunity for an exchange student!

I met a really nice girl. Super friendly. It's always nice making new friends.

With a little effort you can find friends easily.

I met people who I believe will become my good friends.

I met a friend in the girls toilets.

New friend!

Some of these experiences, of course, have to do with the college setting. Everyone has some things in common—shared age, shared student life, shared toilets. Still, the results were heartening. "It feels pretty great to enable that many people to meet new friends," Sandstrom says. "It baffles me how many students have trouble getting to know each other."

After COVID-19 hit, Sandstrom tried another experiment. This time she wanted to see if talking to strangers could serve as a treatment for loneliness—an already serious social problem that was exacerbated by the pandemic. She had students talk to strangers online, via Zoom, Google Hangouts, or other platforms. She asked them the usual questions—how hard they thought it would be to have the conversation and how long it would last, and so on—but this time, she asked them how benevolent they believed people are in general, and how lonely, socially isolated, and socially connected they felt. Again, the participants found that talking to strangers was easy, and the conversations lasted longer than they expected—even online. But they also reported feeling less lonely and isolated afterward, and had a stronger belief in the benevolence of other people.

As I read through the survey responses from Sandstrom's study, I kept coming upon what seemed like a subtle undertone of relief—which I recognized, having wondered myself, *Why do I feel a sense of relief after a pleasant exchange with a stranger?* I asked Sandstrom about this, and she paused for a moment, and then said something that took me back to the story of Nic, her fearful childhood, and her experience with Greyhound Therapy. "I think that relief might just be the feeling that we're sold this message that the world is a scary place," Sandstrom says, "and then you have a chat with someone, some random person, and it goes well, and it's sorta like, *Maybe the world isn't so bad after all.*"

This takes us to a big question: *Why?* Why would such fleeting, seemingly commonplace interactions make us feel so good? Why does the prospect of talking to strangers feel so unnatural, but when we do it, once we get past our initial anxiety, it feels like we'd been designed to act this way? The answer is, *because we have been designed to act this way.* A long process brought us here. We not only evolved to do this: We evolved *because* we did it. And we have been doing it for a very long time.

Sometime, deep in human history, we started meeting strangers. Those we didn't kill or avoid, we learned from and traded with. We gained access to their resources and companionship, and we parlayed those relationships into introductions with their more distant neighbors, and *their* resources, skills, and ideas. Out of this came civilization—but also a new kind of species. We became the sort of creature that can get a charge out of talking to a stranger, even waving to a stranger, even looking at a stranger. A creature that, at its best, naturally seeks out new people. We became something scientists have called "a spectacular evolutionary anomaly": the ultra-cooperative ape—that rare beast that can work and live with strangers.

And if we want to understand how that happened, how we became a species that is capable of experiencing what we've seen so far, you and I are going to take a trip to Georgia. We need to see a lady about some chimps.

Chapter 3

Hello Through the Howdy Door

In which we take a brief detour to meet our two closest genetic relatives—one who loves strangers, and one who goes berserk around them—learn how they got that way, and begin to understand why we are the way we are.

Every once in a while, Dr. Joyce Cohen has to introduce a chimp to a stranger. Dr. Cohen is the associate director of the Division of Animal Resources at the Yerkes National Primate Research Center, a facility affiliated with Emory University in Atlanta, Georgia, and the reasons why she may have to introduce a chimp to a stranger can vary. Perhaps there has been a death in a group of chimps and the remaining animals need to be introduced to other groups. Maybe the center is planning geriatric housing and wants to form a new group with older chimps, or they have a renovation in the works and need to combine groups to make room. But whatever the reason, they have to be careful, because chimps have a tendency to go berserk in the presence of strangers.

"The process starts with a tremendous amount of conversation," says Dr. Cohen—pausing to issue what sounds to me like a weary chuckle—"among all the people who help take care of all the chimps." This includes animal care staff who work with the animals every day, veterinarians who provide their healthcare, and behavioral management staffers who know their personalities. The team gathers everything they know about the chimps in question and makes a list of potential matches, looking for instances in which the animals might have encountered one another in the past. Then they think about relationships: If they put Chimp A in with Group B, what will it do to the existing hierarchy? What alliances might be affected, broken, or formed with the addition of a new member? "Chimp society is very much based on who your buddies are, who will support you if you get in a tiff or something," says Dr. Cohen. "So we have to try to stack things equally."

Having an existing relationship between a member of the group and the stranger can make the process easier. One chimp essentially vouches for the other, same as humans. But there are instances in which the staff has no choice but to introduce a total stranger to a group, and this, as Dr. Cohen puts it dryly, is "challenging."

To minimize the potential for bedlam, the team might first pull a single chimp out of a group to meet the newcomer—the thinking being that if they get along, then that's a potential alliance that could ease the stranger's entry into the larger group. They never just throw the two strange chimps into the same room together, though. Instead, Dr. Cohen's team places them in adjacent enclosures separated by what she calls a "howdy door"—a clear panel or a panel with holes through which the animals can see each other.

Then the scientists just watch. "If there is really aggressive behavior being displayed, we may reconsider the whole strategy," Dr. Cohen says. But if the apes find the sight of each other tolerable, the staff might, after a reasonable amount of time, open the howdy door a crack so the chimps can touch fingers. If that goes well—and it may not, but if it does—the staff will slowly work their way up toward letting the chimps be together. When this happens, some animals may begin to bond. They may pant-hoot happily or hug. If that's the case, the team might consider leaving them together for a few days or a week to let them bond further. If they do, the team might add a third chimp to the group to grow a fledgling alliance, or they might separate the first two and reintroduce the stranger to another single member of the group through the same drawn-out process. If it doesn't work out, the researchers might separate the pair completely and start over. Or they might just let the animals resolve their differences on their own. Maybe the chimps scream it out, or there's mounting behavior or biting or slapping to establish the nature of their relationship. After that, hopefully there are gestures of reconciliation, like handshakes, pats, or hugs. "Sometimes they work out their differences and it's fine," says Dr. Cohen. But sometimes it isn't.

"It can go horribly wrong," she says. "It can result in death."*

Now, let's look at what happens when another ape meets a stranger. Bonobos are almost genetically identical to chimpanzees—which means they're almost genetically identical to humans. But unlike chimps, bonobos have been observed mixing with other groups in the wild, and even sharing food with strangers. Where chimpanzees are xenophobic, bonobos are regarded as *xenophilic*—meaning that they can actually prefer the company of strangers over members of their own groups.

A few years back, Duke University researchers Brian Hare and Jingzhi Tan, working at the Lola ya Bonobo Sanctuary in the Democratic Republic of the Congo, launched a series of experiments to see how far this tendency could go. They placed a bonobo in a room full of food. On either side were two other rooms. One held a stranger, and one held a member of the bonobo's own group. The subject could choose to eat all the food themselves, or they could share it with the friend or the stranger by opening the respective door.

What happened? The subjects not only preferred to share—*they preferred to share with the stranger*. This was repeated across several experiments of varying design. Each time, the subject preferred to share, and they preferred to share with strangers over friends. Only when they didn't have the opportunity to meet the stranger did the bonobos keep the food to themselves. In contrast with chimps, there

---

* To the credit of her team, it hasn't resulted in death during Dr. Cohen's decade and a half at Yerkes.

was no aggressive behavior. Bonobo strangers entering the room even allowed themselves to be outnumbered by members of another group, which, the researchers wrote in 2013, "contrasts sharply with the xenophobic response of wild chimpanzees [who] rapidly retreat if they do not outnumber strangers by a factor of three."

Why do bonobos act like this? It's simple: For them, the upside of being generous with strangers—a potential relationship—outweighs the downside. It's pragmatic. It's the same for bonobos as it is for humans at a networking event: They want to make a connection, add someone to their network. As Tan put it later, "You meet a stranger, and this individual could become your future friend or ally. . . . You want to be nice to someone who's going to be important for you."

Now, if chimpanzees and bonobos are genetically almost identical, why is one so welcoming to strangers and the other so hostile? The answer to that question lies between the serpentine banks of the Congo River. Chimpanzees and bonobos—who are descended from our last shared ancestor, ancestral *Pan*—diverged between 875,000 and 2.1 million years ago. According to Harvard University primatologist Richard Wrangham, the initial split likely occurred during the Pleistocene ice age, during which Earth became cooler and drier. As rainfall slowed, the Congo River dried up—at least enough for chimpanzees to cross it, which they hadn't been able to do before. Some did. There were gorillas in the region, too, but since their food supply was in the mountains on one side of the river, they didn't migrate.

After a few thousand generations, the rains returned and the river swelled, severing the ape populations from one another. The land on both sides of the river became lush with vegetation. The big difference now, however, was that one group of chimpanzees had to share land with the gorillas, while the other had the land pretty much to themselves. That meant life was easier for what would become the bonobos, and harder for the chimpanzees. The bonobos never had to go far for a meal; the chimps, locked in perpetual competition with gorillas for food, always did, searching, often in solitude, across great distances.

Because chimps were often out foraging alone, Wrangham argues, it was easier for the males to target solitary females and coerce them into sex. Therefore, the most aggressive ones mated the most frequently, which meant that, over time, the species selected for aggression and dominance. The bonobos, on the other hand, didn't have to travel far. Females could stay closer to home, together, forming tighter social bonds with one another and mustering the strength of numbers needed to fend off male aggression. Female bonobos, thus endowed with more power than their chimp counterparts, began selecting less aggressive males to mate with, and the species evolved to be both matriarchal and docile. As a result, male bonobos form close bonds with their mothers; they show little sexual aggression toward females; and they don't try to stop other males from mating. No male bonobo has ever been seen killing an infant, unlike chimps, and no bonobo in captivity has ever been seen killing another bonobo. If there is tension, it is normally resolved through play or sex. While chimps conduct border patrols and will attempt to seize territory from other groups, confronting and sometimes killing others, bonobos' relations with other groups can be positive, playful, and, again, sexual. Bonobos share readily; chimps are loath to share even with their own children. Bonobo males sire more children than chimp males, presumably because they're not spending so much time fighting and jockeying. And while introducing a chimpanzee to a new group is fraught, with bonobos it's much easier. "A new bonobo, even as an infant, can be introduced without incident," writes Brian Hare. "And two groups, including multiple adult males separated for weeks, months or years, can be reintegrated with little more than play and sexual contact as a result."

Chimpanzees are still very social creatures. They are capable of affection, they can help one another, and they are intelligent and can be collaborative—at least within their own groups—but their relationships are often more tenuous and transactional. Alliances are critical, but they can also shift without warning. In 1978, the legendary primatologist Jane Goodall watched aghast as one group of chimps at the Gombe reserve in Tanzania set about systematically exterminating another group for no clear reason, and a marauding mother-daughter pair killed and ate ten newborns. "I always thought that chimps were rather nice, more gentle [than humans]," Goodall told *Science News* at the time. "Now we know there is a strong similarity to humans."*

The differences between chimps and bonobos go beyond their behavioral traits. The animals actually look a little different. "Chimps are brawny bodybuilders, whereas [bonobos] look almost intellectual," writes primatologist Frans de Waal, who has studied both. "With their thin necks and piano player hands, they seemed to belong in the library rather than the gym." Despite their "intellectual" appearance, however, bonobos have smaller brains. Male bonobo faces are more feminine than those of male chimps. Their skulls are shorter and wider, and their eyes are bigger. They have smaller canine teeth, and their lips and tails are paler than those of chimps. Bonobos also show lower levels of serotonin, which has been linked to decreased aggressiveness, and they have more gray matter in areas of the brain connected to perceiving the distress of others and controlling aggressive impulses. While male chimps exhibit heightened testosterone levels as they pass through puberty—making sharing a dicey proposition—male bonobos' testosterone levels stay mostly stable, which is to say, pretty low.

These are all symptoms of what scientists call "domestication syndrome" and they appear in other domesticated animals, such as silver foxes bred in captivity and dogs and guinea pigs, all of which also show lower levels of aggression and higher levels of prosocial behavior and playfulness than their undomesticated counterparts. But unlike silver foxes, guinea pigs, and to some extent dogs, bonobos self-domesticated. They weren't made docile by breeders. They made *themselves* friendly because that was what worked best in their environment. It was adaptive for them. And it was adaptive for another ape: *us*.

---

* Say what you will about us, but, in our defense, we do generally manage to refrain from eating one another's infants.

Chapter 4

Human Makes Friend

In which we learn how another ape became the sort of creature that could sit down at a table full of strangers and enjoy it a great deal, thanks to three factors: weather, meat, and murder.

A few years ago, I was standing on the Second Avenue Subway platform in Manhattan when a scene played out above me. A mother, white, maybe in her thirties, was approaching the lip of the stairs with a baby carriage. A Black teenager and his girlfriend were coming from another direction. In a sequence that plays out countless times every day in New York City, the young man registered what was happening, trotted over, and offered to help carry the stroller. The mother accepted his offer. He hefted the front of the stroller, she grabbed the back, and together they started down a set of stairs begrimed—as are all stairs in the New York City subway system—with a troubling mix of brake dust and human moisture.

As the mother, child, and young man descended, the F train rumbled in—a fact that the teen's girlfriend noted with mounting exasperation. By the time they reached the bottom of the stairs, the car doors were closing and the girl's impatience had turned into anger. The young man gently set the stroller on the platform. The woman politely thanked him and moved on. The girlfriend unloaded on him for missing the train. Seeing this, an older man in a suit walked over and told the kid, "Good work, young man." I did the same. I told him that my wife and I had recently had a baby, too, and things like this really mean a lot. I did it partly because it was indeed good work, as the older man had said, but also because the kid was getting lit up like a Christmas tree and I felt bad. We chatted for a minute. Another train came, the doors opened, and off they went.

As I said: This was not an unusual sight in New York City—a place where a baby is born every 4.4 minutes, and only a quarter of the city's nearly five hundred subway stations are equipped with elevators. And yet let's pause for a moment and consider what happened. A young male helped a strange woman—a person of a different gender, race, and age whom he had never met and will probably never see again, in a city of 8.4 million strangers, in a pathologically individualistic country of 328 million strangers whose history is marred by racism. Yes, there were some outward indications of similarity between these two to patch over some of the differences: They were both wearing Western-style clothing, they were both no doubt acquainted with the serial degradations and unpleasantries of the MTA, and no one was barking like a seal or wielding a clawhammer, which no doubt helped.

But still, these were total strangers. And in helping this stranger, the young man incurred two costs. One was time. He made himself late. And two—and not to put too fine a point on this—but, biologically speaking, he may have squandered an opportunity to pass along his genes. This is extraordinary in the context of the natural world, where the whole point of the game is to multiply. Had a trio of chimpanzees found themselves in the same situation, things would have gone very differently. The mother could have been attacked, the baby possibly eaten, and the stairs would have gotten even grosser than they already were.

So why did this young man do it? The eighteenth-century thinker Adam Smith wrote about our seemingly innate desire to be "praiseworthy," and indeed, the young man did win a measure of praise.

But attaboys from two random strangers and one dead economist are cold comfort when you're getting yelled at by your girlfriend. So let's look beyond this scene.

Why does anyone ever help a stranger? Evolutionary scientists and philosophers have been grappling with this phenomenon for many years. They call it *the altruism paradox*. It is a universal feature of the human experience, and it is key to understanding our species' curious relationship to strangers. If people are supposed to have evolved on the basis of individual fitness, selfishly favoring themselves and their close relatives in a ruthless bid to ensure passage of genetic material to future generations, how is it that we so frequently expend time, effort, and money—and sometimes even risk our lives—to help people who we've never met before, and will never see again, and who will almost certainly never pay back the favor? For many years, economists argued that scenes like this one were either the result of a glitch—normal familial altruism spilling out toward friends and strangers like a bowl of soup served by a clumsy waiter—or the product of calculation: something we do because we are selfish and we are rational, and we ran the odds and figured that altruism would pay out in our favor.

The idea that humans have that much control over their rational faculties is immediately hilarious to anyone who has spent more than a few weeks on this rock, but still, such pessimistic appraisals of human nature have always found a receptive audience. We are, so we have been told, irretrievably fallen. From Adam and Eve, Pandora's box, Thomas Hobbes's natural state of "war of all against all," and eighteenth-century preacher Jonathan Edwards's contention that we make God sick to his stomach, to shows like *Breaking Bad* and *Veep,* there is a persistent belief that people, in their heart of hearts, are irredeemably selfish and awful, and that civilization, for all its achievements, its refinements and laws, is just a brittle crust of rock trembling atop a cauldron of swinishness, greed, and violence. And there is plenty of evidence to back that up.

As a resident of Earth who's not a complete idiot (generally), I am well aware of the astonishing feats of cruelty humans are capable of visiting upon one another. As a Bostonian of Irish extraction, I am a member of an ethnicity that famously worships at the altar of Our Lady of Perpetual Antagonism. And as a resident of New York City, I spend a solid 20 percent of my time raging against people who stand in the doorways of subway cars, who carry golf umbrellas on crowded city sidewalks, or who don't merge properly in traffic, perceiving their deeds as irrefutable evidence that Jonathan Edwards was right.

All of which is to say that the idea that humans are docile—that we are self-domesticated and xenophilic like bonobos—is not one that would have occurred to me on my own.* The idea, in fact, initially struck me as saccharine at best, dangerously naïve at worst. But if it seems implausible that humans are domesticated, it may be because we've got the wrong baseline. Yes, a man was rude to me on the subway the other day, and tense words were exchanged. But put fifty strange chimps on that same subway car and you would be able to see the carnage from Jupiter's moons.

The idea of self-domestication is key to helping us understand how we came to be a species that is able to live among total strangers, and it helps explain why it can feel so good to talk to them. It suggests that connecting with strangers is an innate skill that humans possess. Which itself suggests that this ability is somehow adaptive—that there is an evolutionary advantage to being able to talk to strangers. That's why we're rewarded when we do it. And to understand how we got to be that way, we have to leave our friend on the subway platform, wishing him the best, and return to deep history.

This story starts about 2.5 million years ago, during the same Pleistocene ice age that gave the world our randy little pal, the bonobo.

---

* The Enlightenment thinker Johann Friedrich Blumenbach had a similar idea, which is worth citing both as a testament to his insight and intelligence, but also because it's hilarious:

> Man is a domestic animal. But in order that other animals might be made domestic about him, individuals of their species were first of all torn from their wild condition, and made to live under cover, and become tame; whereas he on the contrary was born and appointed by nature the most completely domesticated animal. Other domesticated animals were first brought to that state of perfection through *him*. He is the only one who brought *himself* to perfection.

The air cooled and the rain dried up, and our distant ancestors were forced from the woods and out into arid, open grasslands. Like Adam and Eve expelled from the garden, these early humans found themselves in strange country, prowled by predators and haunted by the ever-present specters of starvation and drought. Surviving in this environment was hard, and it required some social innovations that put us on a path to becoming the creatures we are today.

The first pertained to food. At some point, perhaps two million years ago, perhaps more, humans began scavenging large carcasses, and later they began hunting.* The payoff for eating meat was considerable—a bounty of nutritious, fatty food—but the work was hard. The open savanna made people vulnerable to predators, and it put them into competition with big cats and hyenas for the best kills and carcasses. To survive, people had to band together. Of *Homo habilis*—the first in the line of *Homo,* emerging some two and a half million years ago—British archaeologist Steven Mithen wrote, "At just 1.5 m and 50 kg in weight at most, and no more than a few lumps of stone to throw, they were not particularly well equipped for hand-to-hyena combat. So group living seems a necessity." Those groups eventually evolved into what we know today as hunter-gatherers or nomadic foragers—the oldest continuous form of human social organization on Earth, and the way we lived for 99 percent of our time on this planet.

Eating meat drove the expansion of body and brain, and by 1.5 million years ago, the bigger, smarter, longer-legged *Homo erectus* began to travel. "These were the first humans to have done so in sizable numbers," writes Rick Potts, a paleoanthropologist who directs the Smithsonian's Human Origins Program. With long legs and meat in

---

* It's not clear exactly when. For years it was believed that *Homo habilis*—the first in the genus *Homo*—started supplementing their diets with bits of meat scavenged from carcasses, and then humans began to hunt a million years later. But a recent find in Kenya suggests that some people were already hunting with stone tools by then, evidenced by cut marks on the bones of small gazelles. Another recent find—a set of tools discovered in 2011 on the shores of Lake Turkana in Kenya, dates back 3.3 million years, predating early humans by hundreds of thousands of years.

their diet, the nomadic *Homo erectus* had an advantage over more stubby-legged and finicky creatures. This is because meat, wherever it is, is always pretty much edible—unlike, say, randomly encountered grasses and mushrooms, which can offer a fast track to a fantastically unpleasant end.

Now, even if these humans did manage to avoid being mangled by predators while looking for food, they still had to grapple with the logistical challenges of hunting big game. Tracking and killing the animals, hauling them back to camp, butchering them, preparing them, and distributing them—all these tasks presented logistical and social difficulties beyond the ken of other animals. So early humans learned to cooperate. And this was novel. Whereas most apes gather their food alone, early humans learned to do it together. This was because they had to. "They had no or few satisfactory fallback options if the collaboration failed," writes Duke University developmental psychologist Michael Tomasello, who has done a great deal of research on apes and human evolution. "They had to collaborate with others on a daily basis or else starve."

We don't know much about these people. As scientists put it, behavior doesn't fossilize, which is another way of saying that hunter-gatherers were bad about archiving their emails. But we can draw some inferences about how food sourcing may have worked from more recent field studies of hunter-gatherer societies. The anthropologist Kim Hill, who has done extensive fieldwork on the Aché people in the forests of eastern Paraguay since the 1970s, recounts how food was shared in that society:

> When the meat is cooked an older male (not the hunter) usually divides it up into pieces, or piles of pieces, and hands them out, often with the help of another male who calls out the names of each family that should receive a share. Other band members are quick to remind the distributors which family has yet to receive a share (they never mention themselves, only others that they know have not eaten yet). All meat is pooled and shared equally

among adult band members; however, the hunter of the game usually does not eat from his own kill. Wives and children of hunters receive no greater portion of meat than any other individual in the band.

Variations on this type of system in hunter-gatherer cultures around the world have been observed by anthropologists. These variations set us apart from apes. While chimpanzees tend to be strict tit-for-tat kinds of cooperators—the you-scratch-my-back-I'll-scratch-yours variety also known as *direct reciprocity*—early humans developed a capacity for something far more flexible, fruitful, and, as time would show, powerful: *indirect reciprocity.* Indirect reciprocity worked like an insurance policy, a pooling of risk with others. And as with insurance, it required people to develop a few capabilities: trust, good faith, and a tolerance for delayed gratification. If you were a hunter who'd had a bad day, you could rely on other band members to cover your shortfall. And they'd do it, not because they expected you to compensate them for the exact amount of meat they had given you, but because they had faith that the system would make them whole when they themselves came up short.

In order to live cooperatively like this, humans had to evolve a few novel psychological capabilities that are relevant to our project here: *joint intentionality* and *collective intentionality,* which is the ability to articulate goals to others and approach them as a pair or a group; *theory of mind,* which is the ability to understand that other people have different thoughts than we do, and to infer what those thoughts might be; and *self-other equivalence,* which is a recognition that our partner or partners are just as human and deserving of sympathy as we are.

Membership in these early bands was not irrevocable—granted by simply being there or being kin. Cooperation was the god of the group, the karma, and like those supernatural forces, it dispensed benefits to those who honored it, and punishments for those who did not. Depending on the seriousness of the transgression, these sanctions could arrive in the form of criticism, gossip, ridicule, shaming, ostracism, even execution, all dished out by one's peers. Selfish behavior imperiled the group. Done egregiously enough, it voided your membership and rendered you a stranger, a subhuman, an animal, summarily vomited up out of the *we* and into a likely oblivion— a measure the Mbuti people of what is now modern-day Congo memorably referred to as "leaving matters to the forest."*

It's important to note that cooperation didn't happen because people were trying to be nice, or to aspire to some higher moral plane, or to signal virtue. They were doing it to survive.† For Michael Tomasello, a developmental psychologist who has studied human evolution extensively, this cooperative effort was the beginning of human morality, a new way of balancing the needs of the individual and the needs of the group. It was a new means of relating to other people. As humans hunted together, ate together, raised children together, and intuited one another's thoughts and needs, the line between individual and group began to blur. Yes, people have always had distinct personalities, but because there was no *me* without *us,* and maybe no *us* without *me,* humans became somewhat permeable, fuzzy around the edges, susceptible to influence, and capable of empathy toward members of our groups. The *I* merged with *you,* and out of it came *us.* I'm going to talk about a few social renaissances in this book. This

---

* The British anthropologist Colin Turnbull published an account in 1961 that sheds light on how powerful even the threat of estrangement might have played out in hunter-gatherer bands, based on his time among the Mbuti in Congo. A hunter named Cephu was caught stealing meat from the hunt, a transgression Turnbull called "one of the most heinous crimes in Pygmy eyes, and one that rarely occurs." When Cephu returned to camp, the atmosphere was tense, and he was denied a chair by a youth, which was humiliating for a skilled hunter. When Cephu demanded a chair from another member of the band, he was told, "Animals lie on the ground." According to Turnbull, things escalated, and another band member told Cephu "he hoped Cephu would fall on his spear and kill himself like the animal he was. Who but an animal would steal meat from others?" Cephu told them he shouldn't be treated this way, that he was the best hunter. The argument flopped. After great gales of derision and threats of expulsion for Cephu and his family, Cephu broke down in tears, apologized, and returned the meat. With that, he was permitted to rejoin the group, and by extension, the human race.

† It's little wonder, then, that we still have such a visceral response to greed or freeloading— why we often dehumanize those we believe to be taking more than their fair share, or not doing their part. For 99 percent of our time as a species, greed and freeloading could cost us our lives.

is the first: the first time that humans became social as a response to an existential threat.

Okay, big deal, you say. You just described tribalism. We know very well that humans can be sweet and kind to members of their own groups while being absolute bastards to strangers. We see it frequently. It's real, it's profound, and it is part of us—even on a biochemical level. Humans produce a hormone known as oxytocin. Oxytocin is most closely associated with mothers and their babies—it's what triggers milk production, for instance, and it's released in the brains of the mother and the baby during nursing to help them bond. But oxytocin also plays a larger role in holding groups together. When we produce oxytocin, it enables us to like and empathize with others in our groups, to follow shared norms, and to trust our fellow group members and cooperate with them. The flip side is, when we are threatened by other groups, oxytocin helps us defend our own tribes against them by dehumanizing the others and blinding us to their pain. It's all the sweetness and horror of human existence in one terrifying little molecule.

So, yes: We are programmed to favor our own kind. This is probably the most well-established fact in the field of psychology. But the thing with tribalism is that the common understanding of it is actually off base. The belief that humans have for two million years stayed with their own little family bands, on their own little pieces of turf, and barred the door against strangers until they suddenly, through some fluke of history or grievous miscalculation, ended up surrounded by them in cities and towns, is a false one. The reality is, we've been moving and mixing for a very long time. The Harvard geneticist David Reich, who studies human migration in deep history by analyzing ancient DNA, has found that the conventional wisdom about humans—that there was a single people that in time branched out into all these different groups—is false, at least in terms of what science has been able to establish. "It has been mixtures all the way down," he writes. "Mixture is fundamental to who we are, and we need to embrace it, not deny that it occurred."

Indeed, as human populations grew and migrated, hunter-gatherer bands had more contact with strangers: neighboring bands who might try to steal their territory through violent incursions. This is how male chimpanzees expand their holdings, using a tactic primatologists call *lethal coalitionary aggression*. But according to the cultural anthropologist Raymond Kelly, a technological innovation may have set us on a less warlike path.

Kelly* argued that the spread of human beings was accelerated by the invention of the throwing spear, about four hundred thousand years ago. The weapon, which allowed people to kill from a distance, imposed lethal consequences on any attempts to seize territory by force. Prior to that, aggression may have just been a question of numbers. Ten men with hand axes could overwhelm two men with hand axes and seize a piece of land. With the spear, however, those raids became riskier. Ten men could enter another band's territory, and one assailant in a tree could pick off three of them sight unseen. This made dominance over another group unattainable, and ushered in what Kelly calls a "period of Paleolithic warlessness."†

And apart from suppressing violent conflict, the advent of the spear may have also led to something more lasting: the potential for positive social relationships among different bands. In a 2005 paper, Kelly wrote:

> These developments marked a major turning point in the evolution of lethal intergroup violence and in the character of interrelations between neighboring groups. . . . Selective circumstances no longer favored aggression as a means of achieving territorial gain. Conflict avoidance

---

* It's worth noting that Kelly was in no way insulated from the darker side of human nature. When he was in the field, studying the Etoro tribe in Papua New Guinea, someone in the tribe kept burning his hut down.

† "War" is a slippery term. Some scientists, like Richard Wrangham, define war as any time a group of men gang up on an enemy—which is the chimp way of conflict. For humanity, however, the archaeological record has produced no evidence of any large-scale slaughter. The earliest evidence of mass killing dates only to about ten thousand years ago, around the dawn of the agricultural revolution.

and the development of intergroup relations of friendship, mutuality, sharing, and cooperation were favored instead.

With that, we moved toward becoming a species that helped strangers
on the subway.

Then, around three hundred thousand years ago, came *Homo sapiens*: "Man the wise." (Which is pretty rich, but we still call lightbulbs
"lightbulbs" even though they're off most of the time.) Because people couldn't steal land without risk of getting a spear whistled
through a lung, as populations grew, groups had two choices if they
needed space: either fight or find new land. This desire to avoid conflict drove them to travel farther and farther out, Kelly argues, and
that paved the way for early humans to wander beyond Africa: another critical development that now defines the nature of our ambu-
latory species. We are wanderers and wayfarers, strangers and
sojourners. "We now realize that migration across great distances is
one of the fundamental processes of human history," write archaeologist Clive Gamble and anthropologist Timothy Earle. "We seem
to be made for travel; we evolved in transit."

As we traveled and mingled and populations grew, we commenced
the process of self-domestication. We started to look different. We
shed our heavy brows; our faces became shorter and more feminized;
our canine teeth got shorter; and our cranial capacity shrunk slightly,
which is associated with an increase in serotonin in domesticated
animals—which, as you'll recall, controls aggression. Our eyes got
bigger, and their sclera lost their pigment, giving us the whites of our
eyes, which telegraphed to others what we were looking at. For a
chimp or a wolf, this would be a significant disadvantage—think of a
quarterback who telegraphs every throw. But for humans, the value
in being able to quickly and nonverbally communicate our intentions
outweighed the downside of potential enemies being able to predict
our next move, because it made cooperation with others easier and
more efficient.

At some point along the way, *Homo sapiens* began to speak. It's unknown exactly when language came to be, but many scientists believe it likely evolved as a partial result of expanding group size. The British anthropologist Robin Dunbar found that as primate group size increases, so does the amount of time apes spend grooming one another. Grooming, of course, is about more than simply cleaning; it's about bonding and communication. So, as groups got bigger, it became impossible to attend to all of the other members in the manner to which they had been accustomed. A more efficient form of conveying social information was needed. Dunbar believed that for humans, that was language.

Now, what did self-domestication offer a hunter-gatherer? For one thing: greater ease of movement. When you're open to cooperating with strangers and they are open to cooperating with you, it gives you more options than just fight or flight. Based on what we know from contemporary studies of these groups over the last century and a half or so, the prevailing model of hunter-gatherer life is called *fission-fusion*. In fission-fusion societies, you moved among bands. Sometimes you left your band to join another one; sometimes you married into a new band, or a woman from another band married into yours; or a cousin left and then came back with a friend you'd never met—whom you could mate with instead of, well, your cousin. Sometimes bands grew too big to be sustained and splintered off into smaller bands.

As a result of the traffic of people among groups, the groups themselves became more diverse than you might expect. A statistical analysis of thirty-two contemporary hunter-gatherer societies conducted in 2011 found that on average, only about a quarter of members of each band were genetically related, a quarter were related by marriage, a quarter were distantly related by marriage (the spouse of your husband's brother, say), and a quarter were not related at all. They were genetic strangers, in the scientific parlance, and yet, they were treated like family. Today, anthropologists have a name for this social category: *honorary kin*.

This isn't to say there was no conflict or territoriality in hunter-gatherer life. There was. If there was crowding, or competition over resources, that might bestir our inner chimps. But according to American anthropologist Douglas Fry, the foremost expert on violence in hunter-gatherer societies—which he calls *nomadic forager* societies—the web of relationships in fission-fusion societies served as a "powerful obstacle" against the sort of us-them hostility that has marked humanity's most egregious misadventures. This is because, as Fry puts it, "group loyalties cannot exist in the absence of clearly defined groups." If there's not a stable *us,* in other words, there's no stable *them.*

In 2013, Fry and his colleague Patrik Söderberg investigated instances of deadly violence in a representative sample of twenty-one true hunter-gatherer societies, drawing upon data from past field studies. They had grown tired of non-anthropologists confidently theorizing that early man lived in a state of perpetual warfare, based on studies of societies that weren't true hunter-gatherers. (Some of the ones most frequently cited were actually more complex societies, with status, or they had negative contacts with more complex societies, or they had access to things like alcohol.) In their analysis, Fry and Söderberg found that most deadly incidents "were perpetrated by lone individuals, and almost two-thirds resulted from accidents, interfamilial disputes, within-group executions [for violating the rules], or interpersonal motives such as competition over a particular woman." Three societies had no killings at all. Open conflict among groups was rare.

The fact is, for much of human history, killing strangers usually didn't make sense.* For many of the hunter-gather societies that anthropologists have studied, xenophobia and violence were costly. They restricted movement and limited options. Think about it. The terrain was often unpredictable. Sometimes food would be abundant, sometimes not. Sometimes water would be easy to come by,

---

* Polly Wiessner told me a story about her time with the Ju/Wasi in the Kalahari Desert that speaks to this. She once told them that, in America, sometimes people murder strangers. "Everybody was just laughing," she said. "Like: 'Why would you murder someone you didn't know? You'd murder your brother if he had something you didn't have, but you're not going to murder someone you *don't know*!'" We will return to the odds of murdering, and being murdered by, a stranger later in this book.

sometimes not. So bands had to develop relationships with other bands. When times were hard, they could rely on help from the neighbors; when times were good, the neighbors relied on help from them. "We know little about the evolution of [these] egalitarian societies," the anthropologist Polly Wiessner has written. "What is clear, however, is that once established, egalitarian relations between individuals and social groups greatly facilitate sharing, reciprocity, and mobility."

Anthropologist Robert Tonkinson observed this firsthand while studying the Mardu people in Australia's vast Western Desert. "To permit intergroup conflict or feuding to harden social and territorial boundaries would be literally suicidal, since no group can expect the existing water and food resources of its territory to tide it over until the next rains," he wrote in 2004. "It is not surprising, then, that the Mardu have no word for either 'feud' or 'warfare' and there is no evidence for the kinds of long-standing intergroup animosity one associates with feuding."

As I said earlier, we often think the worst about our species, and persistent beliefs about the supposed hatred and ultraviolence our ancient forebears directed toward strangers has left us with the impression that our nature is inherently xenophobic, and that dealing peaceably with strangers is the exception, not the rule. Our chronic misunderstanding of hunter-gatherer societies has reinforced that belief. "The term 'tribe' continues in use and fosters the misconception that [these] peoples were organized in closed territorially defined units, uniformly obeying the mandates of custom and controlled by the authority," lamented the anthropologist Eleanor Leacock in 1976. "People were far more cosmopolitan than the term 'tribesmen' suggests. They moved about, traded, and negotiated, and constantly chose among the various alternatives for action."*

---

* These bands also accorded equal status to men and women, Leacock noted. There wasn't the same subjugation and estrangement more complex societies experienced. "Nothing in the structure of egalitarian band societies necessitated special deference to men," she wrote. "There were no economic and social liabilities that bound women to be more sensitive to men's needs and feelings than vice versa." They had different jobs, but there was no disparity between the prestige of what a woman did—foraging and childrearing—and what a man

Douglas Fry told me something similar. "The idea of the fission-fusion cultural organization is really interesting because it mirrors what we have today—where at least chunks of the West are steering toward a certain cosmopolitanism, in which it's not immediately clear what group you even belong to anymore," Fry says. "People treat that as though it's unprecedented, but the work on a lot of the nomadic foragers suggests that a liquid approach to group identities has been the way for the bulk of human existence." Simply put, according to Fry and Söderberg, hunter-gatherer society "is not conducive to making war. The nomadic forager default is getting along with neighbors, not warring with them. Of any lessons we derive from nomadic forager studies about war, peace, and human nature, this one is the centerpiece."

It's certainly another way we differ from our chimpanzee cousins. "The mere sight of an unknown chimpanzee sparks fear, hostility, and aggression" in chimps, note biologist Peter Richerson and anthropologist Joe Henrich. "Humans treat other humans not known to be a threat, or not obviously a member of a group assumed to be hostile, as potentially cooperative." That's self-domestication at work.

As bands met, and social networks grew, the relationships formed among them represented indirect reciprocity writ larger—an expansion of the *us* well beyond the level of our bands. Brian Hare, the leading proponent of the self-domestication hypothesis, calls this "a unique type of friendliness," and believes that "human cultural innovation was supercharged because hundreds and then millions of innovators were uniquely able to accept and cooperate with strangers." With a greater density of people came more ideas and more refined practices, in addition to a greater number of potential mates and companions. In his book *The Secret of Our Success: How Culture Is Driving Human Evolution, Domesticating Our Species, and Making Us Smarter,* the anthropologist Joe Henrich offers a good metaphor of the value of larger populations of cooperative humans:

---

did—hunting and defense. Both were equally critical to the survival of the band and thus respected.

Consider two very large prehuman populations, the *Geniuses* and the *Butterflies*. Suppose the Geniuses will devise an invention once in 10 lifetimes. The Butterflies are much dumber, only devising the same invention once in 1000 lifetimes. So, this means that the Geniuses are 100 times smarter than the Butterflies. However, the Geniuses are not very social and have only 1 friend they can learn from. The Butterflies have 10 friends, making them 10 times more social. Now, everyone in both populations tries to obtain an invention, both by figuring it out for themselves and by learning from friends. Suppose learning from friends is difficult: if a friend has it, a learner only learns it in half the time. After everyone has done their own individual learning and tried to learn from friends, do you think the innovation will be more common among the Geniuses or the Butterflies?

Well, among the Geniuses a bit fewer than 1 out of 5 individuals (18%) will end up with the invention. Half of those Geniuses will have figured it out all by themselves. Meanwhile, 99.9% of Butterflies will have the innovation, but only 0.1% will have figured it out by themselves.

These early humans still favored their groups. But their groups were getting bigger. As they did, they needed a way to signal membership quickly, so they could establish on sight that they were part of the group. This led to the rise of what we now know as cultures. People developed shared dialects and shared customs, and they used material culture to demonstrate belonging. Archaeologists have discovered decorative shells and carved objects in Africa and southwestern Asia that date back seventy thousand to ninety thousand years, which were likely traded or given as gifts, and worn to show to whomever the wearer encountered that while they were strangers, they weren't really *strangers*. This, again, was our own unique chemistry doing its work. "With oxytocin, even at a distance, we could feel kindness toward an approaching stranger we could see was like us," writes Brian Hare. This is our next social renaissance.

There is a concept in psychology that helps shed some light on how culture works, and how little it can actually take to alleviate the fear of a stranger. It's called *mere belonging*. Let me give you an example: I sometimes wear a Red Sox hat. As I mentioned, I live in New York, so wearing a Red Sox cap makes me an outlier. Not a hated Other, like Yankees fans are in Boston, but a tolerated minority. And when I wear this hat in New York, strangers just start talking to me in the street—almost every single time I wear it. That is the power of the hat. Even though they know nothing about me, the hat signals that I am safe for them to talk to, and convinces them that we will have something to discuss.

The problem is, I haven't actively followed the Sox in a long time. I became disenchanted years ago. I wear it because Boston is my hometown, and because it's the best-looking hat in the major leagues. So when some random stranger walks up to me on the street and starts talking about the game last night, I have to attempt to explain to him my long and tortured personal history with the Boston Red Sox, which is a story that could fill a book—ideally a psychology textbook. Invariably the person's face clouds with incomprehension. It's as if I was walking around in a burka, and a Muslim man walked over and said, *"As-Salaam-Alaikum!"* and I said, "Oh, this? No, I just like it. I'm actually an Episcopalian."*

According to the social psychologists who advanced the idea of mere belonging, Gregory Walton and Geoffrey Cohen, humans "are highly sensitive to even minor cues of social connection." When

---

* I had the pleasure of speaking to a rabbi by the name of Ethan Tucker while researching this book, after he had just completed a forty-mile bike tour through New York City. "I was on this thing with thirty thousand total strangers," he said, and it was striking to me the number of times that little conversations cropped up between me and another person." What struck him was the ease with which these conversations occurred. "We were strangers, but with a sort of shared minority uniform," he says. "I'm on this shut-down street wearing a weird purple helmet cover, and on this weird contraption, and we're all grappling with the same elements," he says. "It's almost like the strangeness was completely lifted. It's like there's this instinct." He was right. There is.

we find some small similarity, it serves as "an entryway to a social relationship—a small cue of social connection to another person or group." Humans have a powerful need to belong, so we look for what are called *incidental similarities* when we encounter strangers. These reassure us by signaling that we have something in common, that we belong together. If we have something in common with a stranger, however insignificant, we will be far more likely to like them, trust them, and talk to them because we consider them one of us. This could be a Red Sox hat, even though historically that's certainly been no guarantee of levelheadedness or civility, or it could be a pet dog, even though Hitler had a dog, her name was Blondi,* and he grieved her when she died.

There's a robust body of research into the power of these similarities, showing that having even meaningless things in common makes strangers like one another more, and help one another more. One study, led by psychologist Yarrow Dunham, involved a group of five-year-old children. The experimenters split the kids into a red group and a blue group based on the flip of a coin, gave them red or blue T-shirts to match their groups, and then showed them pictures of strange kids wearing red or blue shirts. The participants were asked to rate each picture in terms of how much he or she liked the kid. They were given five coins to distribute to the kids in the photos as they saw fit, and asked questions like "Who made cookies for all their friends?" and "Who took some money without asking?," and directed to select potential playmates from the pictures. The kids showed the strongest preference for their own gender, but after that, they overwhelmingly liked members of their own red or blue groups more, gave them more coins, wanted to play with them, and made more positive judgments about their character.

Other studies have shown that people can look more favorably upon others even if the similarities are completely inane. One found that when undergraduates were told that they shared a birthday or a first name with a stranger, or had a similar fingerprint, they were more likely to comply with that person's request to donate money or

* Of *course* she was named Blondi.

offer feedback on a paper. Another found that people were far more inclined to like a salesperson—and showed a stronger intention to buy from them—if they were told they shared a birthday.

Another still, run by psychologist James Jones, presented participants with partners bearing meaningless similarities—like last names with some of the same letters, and seemingly randomly assigned participant code numbers that resembled their own birth dates—and asked, "How much do you look forward to getting to know this person during the upcoming conversation?" and "How much do you think you would like this person if you got to know her?" Participants were more attracted to the people who had the meaningless similarities. In a later study, Jones and company created a sense of threat by asking participants to write about their biggest drawbacks as potential dating partners, and found that the people who felt threatened were even *more* attracted to hypothetical partners with a similar last name to theirs. In times of threat, we band together with our own, even when the definition of "our own" is patently ludicrous.

Another study, done by psychologists John Finch and Robert Cialdini in 1989, took this tendency to even more absurd heights. They had participants read a biographical article on Rasputin, "the Mad Monk of Russia." Half of the participants were led to believe they shared a birthday with Rasputin, and the other half were given no birth date for him. The ones that shared a birthday with Rasputin expressed far more favorable views of this sadistic megalomaniac's character. That's how powerful mere belonging can be. It speaks to both our well-documented affinity for our groups, but also how flexible our definitions of our groups can be, and how easily they can be—and have been—expanded throughout human history. Under the right circumstances, it just doesn't take that much.

Now, I want to make something clear. None of this is to say people are inherently *good,* because the thing that drove the spread of humanity wasn't about goodness; it was about expansion, multiplication, and empowerment. Hyper-cooperation is a double-edged

sword, after all. It can bind a group together to raise a stranger's or-
phaned child or wage a campaign of ethnic cleansing against that
child's clan. But the instinct to cooperate and expand our groups, and
our success at doing so, is evidence that we are in possession of an
unusually potent ability to connect with strangers, work with strangers, and, yes, talk to strangers. It is innate. As the Roman emperor
Marcus Aurelius wrote of his fellow man nearly two thousand years
ago: "He and I were born to work together, like a man's two hands,
feet, or eyelids, or like the upper and lower rows of his teeth. To ob-
struct each other is against Nature's law."

After all, if our distant ancestors killed every stranger they met,
we wouldn't have made it very far as a species. We certainly wouldn't
have traveled the way we did, developed complex cultures and technologies, learned to thrive in all climates, and built cities in which
millions of people somehow manage to live without a rolling slaughter, if we'd spent our formative millennia crouched in a state of constant hypervigilance, never straying far from our camps, never
mingling with anyone new, forever at war. This is heartening to me.
It's also, I'm willing to bet, why I'm having such a hard time finding
children's books promoting lethal male coalitionary violence.

So no, we're not inherently good or bad. What we are is *variable*.
The primatologist Frans de Waal has called humans "bipolar apes," a
phrase I like. But Allen Buchanan and Russell Powell, professors at
Duke and Boston University, respectively, who between them specialize in an intimidating array of disciplines, came up with a better
metaphor. They argue that humans have a moral "dial," which, depending on the circumstances, can be adjusted to become more inclu-
sive or more exclusionary. Inclusion, for our purposes, means we
accord strangers full moral consideration and treat them as equals;
exclusion means we believe the stranger is not a person at all and can
be tortured or killed without care.

Based on the archaeological record, we do know this: War as we
know it, the large-scale slaughter occurring when group fights group,
is a relatively modern phenomenon. The earliest archaeological evidence of mass murder, for instance, dates back just ten thousand
years, shortly after the advent of agriculture, and was found by Lake

Turkana in Kenya. A similar discovery in Germany, believed to be a mass execution, dates back some seven thousand years. All the victims' shinbones had been shattered. Analysis of isotopes taken from the remains shows them to have been outsiders.

It was around twelve thousand years ago, around the dawn of agriculture, that the hunter-gatherer mode of social organization gave way to more complex societies such as chiefdoms and nations, which had features like wealth, status, and possessions—things that could be hoarded and coveted and fought over. Agriculture led to an explosion of human populations, but it also rooted humans to fixed parcels of land for the first time. No longer could our ancestors disappear into the forest or move away in times of conflict. They now had something to defend, which means the neighbors did, too, which meant the neighbors had something worth stealing. War as we know it began. So did social stratification—classes and political hierarchies rose, with their attendant jockeying and jealousy. The new societies oriented themselves around dominance and not cooperation. The position of women was degraded as societies focused more on trading and fighting. Religions formed and, along with them, their own male hierarchies, which merged with political power and the will to conquer.

The hunter-gatherer tradition lived on in spots, but its decline was hastened after contact with European explorers and colonists, who at best fatally disrupted the delicate balance of these egalitarian societies, and at worst exterminated them. In many cases, the traditional societies that came to be known by early anthropologists as the most violent and xenophobic toward strangers were the ones that had tragic contact with strangers hailing from more complex societies.

In 1835, Alexis de Tocqueville wrote of the condition of indigenous people in the United States: "By dispersing their families, by obscuring their traditions, by disrupting their chain of memories . . . European tyranny has made them more unruly and less civilized than they were before." A decade and a half before that, the American geographer Jedidiah Morse made the same observation, writing to the U.S. secretary of war after a tour of Native American communities in 1820: "I have always experienced the greatest hospitality and kindness among those Indians who have had the least intercourse with white people," he wrote.

This has happened around the globe. The Andaman islanders, who live on an archipelago in the Bay of Bengal between India and Myanmar are known to be ferociously xenophobic. Believed to have migrated from Africa fifty thousand years ago and remained largely untouched since, the fiercely private Andamanese have been called "arguably the most enigmatic people on our planet." It's tempting to believe, then, that their posture toward strangers is our nature. But they also have a history of trauma. Upon initial contact with European outsiders beginning in the eighteenth century, the population was decimated by violence and pathogens brought by the newcomers. After that, fear of strangers took on a supernatural dimension for the Andamanese. "The body of a stranger who dies or is killed is not buried, but is thrown into the sea or cut up and burnt," anthropologist A. R. Radcliffe-Brown observed in 1906. "The explanation that the natives give of this custom . . . is that it serves to dispel danger that might accrue from the presence of a dead body of a stranger. The blood and fat of the dead man, from which they appear to fear evil influences, are, they say, driven up to the sky in the smoke of the fire and are thus rendered harmless."

From what we know about hunter-gatherers, however, murdering strangers remained a capacity—a thing that *could* be done—while cooperation was a tendency, a thing that was regularly done. As the human population grew in number, and in sophistication, our moral dial twisted and turned. Sometimes it was cranked to maximum exclusion, and all hell broke loose. But more often it was turned, slightly perhaps, in the opposite direction, and our unique social genius led to a more elastic and expansive definition of *us*. Yes, we favored our kind, but it turned out that "our kind" could be an amorphous concept indeed. The cultural and psychological lines dividing *us* and *them,* so often misunderstood by cynics and ideologues and extremists today as ironclad and inviolable, could be, under the right conditions, as porous as a picket fence. We just had to meet.

Chapter 5

How to Talk to Half a Dozen Strangers at Once

In which, armed with evidence of how talking to strangers is good for us, I commence rebuilding my social muscles by talking to seven strangers and a man in a yellow hat, and come away feeling slightly better about our ability to discuss sensitive topics without visiting violence and vituperation on one another.

All right. So, what do we know? We know that talking to strangers makes us happier, healthier, and a little smarter, and helps us feel like we belong in a world that can be chaotic and alienating. We know that talking to strangers is far easier than we think, that other people are far more receptive to it than we might expect, and that when we talk to them, we are often pleasantly surprised. Admittedly, this is partially because we suspect these other people are maybe not *entirely* human, so the bar is quite low. But I'll take it. We can build on it. We have.

As I started out on my quest to master talking to strangers, I wanted to find something suitable for beginners. Something structured, that would circumvent the norm against talking to strangers and minimize my fear of rejection and disaster. I need something easy. And that's how I find myself sitting at a diner in Midtown Manhattan across from a man in a yellow hat.

Ron Gross, eighty-four, is an author and celebrated educator at Columbia University. He's also the cofounder of an organization called Conversations New York (CNY), which he's helped run for some twenty-five years. CNY holds regular, free group conversations, largely among strangers. Before we meet, Gross tells me in an email that he'll "wear a yellow cap, as recommended by Immanuel Kant." I don't have the foggiest idea what this means. When I show up, there he is, wearing a bright yellow hat. "I wear this when I'm traveling," he explains. "So if I'm being picked up at my destination, for a speaking engagement or something, the guy can find me."

"What's it have to do with Kant?" I ask.

"I'm sure you're well acquainted with Kant's categorical imperative," Gross tells me, "that we should all act such that our action could be made a rule for mankind. So a couple years ago, this driver says to me, 'You know, Mr. Gross: That's a great idea, that hat—I just wish everybody arriving at the airport would wear a hat like that!' And I thought, *Ah! The man has refuted Kant!* I, of course, agreed with him heartily on his insight." Yellow hats have since become the de facto uniform for all volunteers of CNY.

Gross is an unlikely figure to run an organization like this. He's animated and talkative one-on-one, but he's not the type to talk to strangers out in the wild. He's an introvert. He tells me he once spent an entire summer avoiding the community pool by his house in Long Island because all people did there was talk. When his wife finally managed to drag him out, "I found a place, a table and a chair, and I brought some work," he says. "It's pretty much the same now. Basically, this is the last thing I would have thought that I would've done."

So why is he doing it? "I kind of realized that I was making myself inaccessible to a lot," he says. "I really needed to do something to countervail this propensity to hunker down." He knew from his own work—including an acclaimed book on Socrates—the vital importance of conversation as a tool for learning. But he also wanted to explore, as he says, "what happens when you are open to other people."

CNY events are held at colleges, or in the park, and each gathering attracts forty to eighty people. Attendees are divided into groups and talk for ninety minutes, working from a list of topical or philosophical questions. These gatherings attract a surprisingly wide variety of people—cutting across ages, genders, races, ethnicities, and personalities—all talking, with Gross overseeing, eavesdropping, steering, and occasionally ejecting people who get too aggressive or won't let others talk.

On its face, the content of the conversations at CNY seems to be the point. People are exchanging ideas and stories. But Gross has another agenda, too, which is relevant for us. He wants to teach people *how* to have good conversations. "What I want is for people to begin to learn that to be in a conversation, they need to maintain a kind of double consciousness, even a triple consciousness," he says. "The consciousness of what the conversation is, the consciousness of what they want to say, and then the kind of meta-consciousness of *Am I contributing to the process of this conversation in a good way? Or Am I being overbearing? Am I being irrelevant? Am I not trying to build?* That's the undercurrent."

That triple consciousness, as he calls it, is why having conversations with strangers can be so cognitively demanding, as we saw in chapter 2. As a journalist, this sort of thing is a fact of life for me: You're having a conversation, and you're listening intently, but you're also noting things that you want to follow up on and asking yourself how best to follow up on them, and trying to get the person to like you, *and* quite often quietly panicking that you won't get what you need for the story and therefore will never be paid. This has always been challenging enough for me one-on-one—to say I have the attention span of a squirrel is to do a disservice to squirrels. But I was drawn to CNY because I felt that doing it with a table of seven total strangers from all walks of life at a contentious moment in American history would be especially good practice.

I take part in two conversation events with CNY, and while the exchanges are lively and interesting, the most fascinating aspect is watching a group conversation organize itself—in effect, watching the group orient itself to itself and eventually find a sort of equilibrium. You can see many of the elements we discussed in chapter 4 at work. We had the collective intention to have a conversation. We took it for granted that people had different thoughts than we did and we tried to understand them—that was basically the point—and we treated one another as equals, with no one dictating to the others when they were allowed to speak. Those capacities, formed many years ago and coupled with language—are why the conversation worked.

A group conversation is in essence a cooperative venture, after all, and like all cooperative ventures, it takes a little time to figure out the best way to go about it and establish who's going to do what, and how everyone will fit together. In a discussion about racism with, for example, a group that includes an Indian American, two young Asian Americans, a Trump voter, a retired white male corporate executive, and a younger Black woman, people at first are gun-shy, or defensive. Things move haltingly. A couple people snap at each other. This is perfectly understandable. You don't know who these people are, and, frankly, you're not expecting much. Maybe you expect people to live up to their respective stereotypes, and that keeps you from really listening to what they're saying. Maybe you've dismissed them before they even speak.

But as you sit there across from these people, you start to care what they think or say. You can't help it. They are right there, after all. You see their eyes, hear their voices, observe their body language, and quickly discover that these are not lesser minds. Their humanity is undeniable. And as they speak, and stubbornly refuse to conform to type, their complexity reveals itself. It's a world apart from a lot of debate on Facebook or Twitter, where you can say whatever you want without ever having to register the look of pain or anger on the face of the person you've insulted, and they can do the same to you, and where likes and clicks and approval from your allies serve as incentives to reduce the complexity of others. Here, however, these are no avatars. And being in the physical company of these individuals both makes for a better conversation and keeps the conversation on the rails.

After fifteen awkward minutes of sorting things out, the group begins to cohere. It's like magic. It happens so smoothly and quickly.

People get comfortable, and a spirit of good faith breaks across the proceedings; it permits people to be curious about things that they may have been touchy about before, and it lets them push back on each other without fear of it being seen as a personal attack or having their noses bitten off. They allow themselves to be surprised by these strangers, and I come to realize how long it has been since I was genuinely surprised by something someone said to me—thanks, I suppose, to the filter bubble I spend much of my life inside. Some talk, and others listen. *I* listen, which, ordinarily, is not a great skill of mine. As my wife is fond of saying, I'm an "alpha talker," unpracticed in the rare and neglected discipline of conversational restraint. But here I am, engrossed.

Minutes tick past and the conversation deepens. People begin sharing personal stories to flesh out their arguments. That gives permission to others to do the same, and naturally, almost effortlessly, the group falls into a great conversation that reveals unexpected sides of everyone there. The former executive turns out to have been a conscientious objector during the Vietnam War, for instance. As we discuss the idea that curiosity is a hedge against prejudice, he says, "To remain curious about other people, and why they feel the way they do, is to be curious about why *I* feel the way I do." The young Asian American woman recounts bitter experiences she's had with discrimination: "The *one* thing I cannot change is the color of my skin," she says, exasperated. The Trump supporter tells her, "If someone throws an epithet at you, just say, 'Thank you. Do you feel better now?'" One participant in the midst of a personal tragedy remarks, with a hint of anguish, "I am who I am, but I'm not the same person I used to be." In very little time, personal disclosure begets personal disclosure, and we're onto something much more interesting than the questions we've been given.

Research bears this out. Studies have shown that when one person expresses something personal, the other person will match them. They will, in fact, follow one another in terms of the depths of their own disclosures. This is known as *the disclosure-reciprocity effect*. That keeps the conversation developing. Moreover, the simple act of making such disclosures is pleasurable, so much so that it registers physically. The psychologist Diana Tamir led a study that found that when people disclose something personal, it stimulates brain regions that form the mesolimbic dopaminergic system, which are associated with reward. "The human tendency to convey information about personal experience may arise from the intrinsic value associated with self-disclosure," writes Tamir. That value is that personal disclosures can foster deeper conversations, and, by extension, deeper connections, which can then lead to new relationships, or strengthen existing ones.

This seems like the sort of thing a chronic oversharer would use as a license to unburden their innermost thoughts and fears on everyone within earshot, but an analysis of existing studies by psychologists Nancy Collins and Lynn Carol Miller found that people who disclose—as long as it's appropriate and you're not immediately emptying your weirdest, darkest stuff on a person riding the bus—are perceived as more likable. While the effect was stronger among people who already knew each other, "it is important not to overlook the impact of self-disclosure among strangers in first encounters," the researchers write. The effect, they found, goes both ways. We also tend to like people to whom we disclose something. This is also adaptive, because it leads to intimacy, helping us to develop new relationships and deepen existing ones.

According to the psychologist Zick Rubin, part of what happens in these exchanges is modeling. One person sets the terms of the interaction, and the other follows and refines those terms. It's a kind of improvisation. "People look to one another for cues as to what sort of response is called for. If a person sitting next to you on a train talks about the fuel shortage, you are likely to respond in kind. If he proceeds to become more personal and tells you about his recent divorce, and if at the same time he seems to be in command of the situation, you may well infer that disclosing personal matters is the expected and proper thing to do," writes Rubin.

There's also the matter of trust. "When another person reveals himself to you, you are likely to conclude that he likes and trusts you," Rubin writes. "A common response in such a situation is to demonstrate to the other person that his affection and trust are well-placed." To not respond in kind is to imply judgment. For instance, if one of my partners at Conversations New York said, "Someone called me a vicious racial slur on the train yesterday and I broke down and wept," and I replied by asking, "You see the game last night?" she will assume her trust has been misplaced, and the conversation will cease.

Back at CNY, our group conversation continues, and the time, which moved slowly at first, speeds up, then flies, and then it's over. Afterward, all of our different bands gather in a circle to debrief, with Ron Gross overseeing it. Some marvel at how well their groups worked. More questions are raised. One man asks, "Is it possible to respect someone you dislike?" He sheepishly admits there are two people in his life he dislikes. "Only two?" Ron Gross cackles. "I can think of dozens, you piker." A Latino man named Angel dryly points out the irony that he was paired with an older, rough-looking character named, yes, Satan. "Only here can that happen," says Angel. Another, a middle-aged Black participant, described his group thusly: "We grew together. We grew wise together."

Ron Gross says he hears from participants all the time who tell him how profound an experience these events have been—even those who hardly seemed to talk. "I am constantly amazed when I get something from somebody who says, 'I just want to tell you what this year in the CNY has meant to me,'" he says. One person emailed to say they started attending at a low point in their lives, and the experience has really helped them pick themselves back up. "I had no idea that this was having this kind of an influence," Gross says. "To my utter astonishment, it does seem to have quite a profound effect on a few people."

I'm not immune myself, as it turns out. After my first CNY conversation—I eventually did several—I step out into a cool spring evening and take the subway home. I feel tired—these conversations are demanding, as we know—but pleasantly so, and a bit exhilarated.

I'm not going to say I became wiser, but having a deep discussion with strangers whose lives are different from my own stood as a good reminder to me that the path to wisdom has always been lined with new people. People we haven't met yet. It's not the only way to get there, of course. But it's a pretty good way.

Chapter 6

Talking to Strangers: Paleolithic Edition

*In which we meet a man at the library, and then learn how
greeting rituals helped turn strangers—aka "dead nonhuman
monsters"—into friends, mates, and collaborators.*

Let me tell you another story. A while back, I was sitting in a branch
of the public library near my apartment, working, when nature
called. I leaned over to the man across from me. I'd never seen him
before. He was thin, maybe early fifties. "Excuse me," I said, quietly.
He looked up. "Would you mind watching my computer? I gotta
run to the men's room," I said. "Sure," he said, in heavily accented
English. "Go." I went, and I came back and thanked him. "No problem," he said. A few minutes later, his phone buzzed. "Sorry," he
said, pointing at his laptop. "Do you mind?"

"Of course, yeah, go ahead," I said.

Now, my laptop cost about a grand. It's small and easily hidden
and weighs almost nothing. I would be in serious trouble without it.
I assume his laptop was also valuable to him. When each of us was off
conducting our business, the other could have easily grabbed the
stranger's computer, hustled out the door, and disappeared into the
city. Sure, there are laws, but the cops aren't exactly going to get
the chopper out to locate a stolen laptop. And yes, there's always the

possibility that the aggrieved party might manage to sprint and catch the thief out in the street and administer a good thrashing, but you don't see many brawlers in the library, and I haven't thrown a punch in years. Plus, I hate running.

What I'm saying is, in the grand scheme of larceny, this was a pretty easy score.

And yet, we didn't do it. Nor did we even balk at the prospect of defending the other person's property from a third party—which is always a distant possibility, as my beloved local branch plays host to a small but visible population of troubled people. No: I asked the man for his assistance in protecting my property, and he granted it. Then he asked, and I returned the favor. That was it. We are domesticated, after all. We are ultra-cooperative apes.

Later, as I sat at a table outside eating lunch, he came over and struck up a conversation. He was from Haiti, he said. He'd been here for a year. When he wasn't juggling jobs to stay afloat and studying in the library, he liked to sit out here and talk to people to practice his English. He was quiet, friendly, and earnest, and he was happy to be here, he said, and his company stood as one of those vaguely embarrassing reminders of just how hard some people have to work to attain the thing that fell so gently upon me at birth like a blessing, like a feather.

What happened between that man and me is a common scenario. We all do things like this, all the time. But the fact that we do so readily, and with so little thought, is itself remarkable. As it turns out, simple but structured interactions like these have been with us in one form or another for a very long time. Examples of humans' social genius, they've evolved as a mechanism to help us interact peacefully and fruitfully with strangers. Anthropologists call them greeting rituals. And like me, once you understand how they work, and why they came to be, you will see them absolutely everywhere.*

---

* An important note: The ideas and observations below are drawn from anthropological field studies of hunter-gatherer societies, most conducted in the twentieth century, some

For hunter-gatherer bands, it would have been pretty rare to meet a total stranger—someone with no social connection to anyone you knew. But as social networks grew, there came the first budding examples of a whole new social category: *in-group strangers,* which emerged maybe one hundred thousand years ago. Harvard anthropologist Joe Henrich explains it this way: "They're not a stranger in the sense that you're socially disconnected from them. They're a stranger in the sense that it's possible you might not have met them, or it might take a couple of decades until you've met everybody in the overall group." Anthropologists have estimated that those overall groups—known as *band nexuses*—could consist of seven hundred to one thousand people. They were held together by culture, as we discussed in chapter 4.

How might these in-group strangers have met? All societies are different, and as I said, the ones studied by anthropologists could have been different from our ancient forebears', so it's impossible to say for sure. But many societies around the world developed greeting rituals. These are "very stylized ways of interacting, which allowed strangers to approach," Henrich says. They were a way of processing new people, of remaining open to the possibility of a fruitful exchange, while also being cautious about the chaos a stranger could bring to your group.

A little more psychological background is helpful here. We know about the lesser minds problem—the tendency to believe that strangers in general, and out-group strangers in particular, have lesser minds than we do. And we know that we tend to think more highly of our own groups. In psychology, this is known as *in-group favoritism*. It doesn't necessarily mean we hate other groups. But under threat—real or merely perceived—our moral dial can turn and we can rather

---

predating it. Because humans were hunter-gatherers for 95 percent of their time on Earth, researchers often turn to the anthropological record to speculate about how human societies might have functioned in the distant past—but always with the caveat that we can't know for sure, because, as I said earlier, behavior doesn't fossilize. These are best guesses. Also, for the sake of simplicity, I'm going to speak of these groups in the past tense because many of these cultures have ceased to be pure hunter-gatherers, though there are still some that continue to practice the traditional way of life.

easily become convinced that the stranger is not a human at all, but an animal, a pathogen, or a demon of some sort. There are many tragic instances of this sort of dehumanization in action. But my favorite lighter example comes from the Korowai people of West Papua, Indonesia. Their word for foreigner—*laleo*—has acquired two meanings. The first is "foreign humans." And the second: "dead nonhuman monsters." I can say this is a "lighter example" only because the Korowai trade peacefully and enthusiastically with outsiders and take pride in their ability to attract guests.

We can think of greeting rituals, then, as a response to both ingroup favoritism and the lesser minds effect. When encountering a stranger, we have a tendency to believe they lack, say, the same willpower as we do, or a full scoop of brains, and that worries us. Understandably. "One of the things that make strangers scary is that you don't know what they're going to do," Henrich tells me. "But if we have a shared agreement that we're going to have this ritual every time strangers meet, then we can at least begin with a bunch of practices that say, 'Okay, we're about to have a peaceful interaction, and as long as we follow the ritual, and nobody deviates, then everyone's going to be comfortable.'" He offers an example. "When you would approach Australian aboriginal camps, you couldn't just walk up to the camp, because everyone would go crazy and there'd be a fight," he says. "You had to set up shop far away from the camp, sit with your weapons far away from you, and then wait for them to approach you."

We've seen a recent example of what happens when care is not taken in such an approach. I mentioned the Andaman Islands in the Bay of Bengal earlier. That was where a lone American missionary, John Chau, visited in 2018, because he believed the people on one of the islands—North Sentinel Island—were in thrall to Satan. He approached the beach, and began shouting to them in his own language about the redemptive power of Jesus Christ. They responded by shooting arrows at him. He wrote in his diary, "I felt some fear but mostly was disappointed they didn't accept me right away." He shouldn't have been surprised. This is an inadvisable way to introduce yourself to members of a traditional society. It cost him his life.

By successfully executing a greeting ritual, however, strangers can show self-control and intelligence, and demonstrate that they are not a threat, and could in fact be a boon. It is a highly structured, closely observed process to safely defuse tension among strangers, encourage familiarity, and hopefully forge a relationship. In other words, it's the howdy door from the chimp facility, but for people.

The ethnographic record features many colorful examples of greeting rituals. In 1932, anthropologist Donald Thomson recounted one scene from Cape York in northern Australia.

> Three men, each carrying a bundle of spears, spear-thrower and fire stick, appeared out of the scrub to the north of the camp. Although their approach was at once observed, causing an under-current of excitement in camp, no apparent notice whatever was taken of the men, who approached slowly to within about 40 feet of the northern fringe of the camp, where each squatted on the ground a few feet apart, placing his weapons in front of him. . . . Not a word was spoken, and apparently no notice whatever was taken of their presence for about 10 or 15 minutes. Then a "big" [older] man left the camp unarmed and strolled casually towards the man on the left, scraped a shallow depression in the ground close to him with his foot, as a native does before sitting down, and then squatted on the ground about a yard away from the visitor. . . . Still not a word was spoken. They did not even look at one another, but kept their eyes downcast.
>
> After a few minutes had elapsed, the old man of the camp spoke a few words in a low tone—inaudible to me where I stood a few yards away—and the other replied in the same casual way. Still neither looked up—lest he might betray to the watching camp the slightest interest or emotion. At length the old man called the single word *Bat* (fire) and a boy brought out a small piece of smoldering wood which he handed to the old man from the camp. This fire

the old man then placed on the ground between himself and the visitor to whom he had spoken. In former times this no doubt concluded the ceremony, but on this occasion a tobacco pipe was lighted and handed to the visitor. A second man now left the camp, strolled casually over and spoke to the man at the other end of the line, making a present, which was reciprocated.

Four decades later, the Australian anthropologist Nicolas Peterson wrote of this and similar rites: "Throughout the continent, failure of a visiting person or party to announce its presence to the local residents is taken as a prelude to an act of hostility and provokes the likelihood of aggression from the territory occupiers," he wrote. "Once the person or party has been through the rite of entry, however, they have equal access with the hosts to the everyday resources of the territory."

In 1934, anthropologists Viktor Lebzelter and Richard Neuse observed another ritual among the San (then known as the Bushmen) in the Kalahari Desert.* "If two armed Bushmen who are strangers approach each other, they disarm at first sight before they greet each other. When a Bushman comes to a village or to a farmhouse, he will put down his arms at a certain distance and sit down to wait patiently, if need be for hours, until he is questioned."

In 1957, the American anthropologist Lorna Marshall gave a sense of what that conversation might be like in a book drawn from her time among the !Kung people of the western Kalahari: "Their word for stranger is *ju dole. Ju* means *person, dole* means *strange* or *harmful*—one word for both concepts, in the !Kung language, as though they were a single concept." Nevertheless, she found that it didn't take much to turn a bad person good. "When a !Kung meets a stranger and finds that he has the same name as one of his kin . . . he is reassured and feels a sense of belonging." Writes Marshall:

---

* The San are not considered *pure* hunter-gatherers, as they have had interaction with pastoralists for one thousand years, but the approach they take to greeting rituals is similar enough to hunter-gatherer groups that I'm including it here.

Gao, the brother of !U, went on an errand for us to Khadum. Khadum is about 115 miles north of Gautscha and
about 40 miles north of Cho/ana where we were staying at
the time. He had never been to Khadum before, and the
!Kung Bushmen who lived there at once called him *ju dole.*
He was in haste to say that he had heard that the father of
one of the people at Khadum had the same name as his
father and that another had a brother named Gao. "Oh,"
said the Khadum people, in effect, "so you are Gao's
!gun!a" [which could mean namesake, or simply a person
who had the same name] and they took him to their fire
and gave him a present of edible gum.

Some greeting rituals were more rambunctious, involving ordeals
or games that look more like hazing, serving the duel aims of welcoming a stranger and establishing his worth as a potential confeder-
ate. My favorite account dates to 1885, when anthropologist Franz
Boas published a memorable account of greeting rituals among the
Canadian Inuit of southeastern Baffin Island.

If a stranger unknown to the inhabitants of a settlement
arrives on a visit he is welcomed by the celebration of a
great feast. Among the southeastern tribes the natives ar-
range themselves in a row, one man standing in front of it.
The stranger approaches slowly, his arms folded and his
head inclined toward the right side. Then the native strikes
him with all his strength on the right cheek and in his turn
inclines his head awaiting the stranger's blow. While this is
going on the other men are playing at ball and singing.
Thus they continue until one of the combatants is van-
quished.

The ceremonies of greeting among the western tribes
are similar to those of the eastern, but in addition "boxing,
wrestling, and knife testing" are mentioned by travelers
who have visited them. In Davis Strait and probably in all

the other countries the game of "hook and crook" is always played on the arrival of a stranger. Two men sit down on a large skin, after having stripped the upper part of their bodies, and each tries to stretch out the bent arm of the other. These games are sometimes dangerous, as the victor has the right to kill his adversary; but generally the feast ends peaceably.*

On the rare chance that a hunter-gatherer did bump into a stranger outside of the proper channels, there was still a way to avoid strife. The American anthropologist, historian, and geographer Jared Diamond, author of the book *Guns, Germs, and Steel,* explains how these encounters might be handled. "[A tense situation] can be resolved by the two of you sitting down, each of you naming yourself and your relatives and exactly how you are related to them, and continuing in an effort to identify a relative in common, such that the two of you would have some relationship to each other and wouldn't have grounds to attack each other." This, Diamond writes, could go on for "several hours." If no connection is made, he says, you had two options: fight or flight.

When human societies grew in population and complexity, greeting rituals endured, though in an altered form. Once people settled into villages and mastered agriculture, attracting new members became both a practical advantage and a mark of prestige for leaders. Some even claimed to possess magical powers to attract strangers. "Economically a newcomer is an asset to the tribe," anthropologist Otto Friedrich Raum wrote of the Zulu people in southern Africa, in 1972. "He not only increases numbers, he may add to its wealth in goods, in offspring, in specialized knowledge and skill. . . . Strangers

---

* Writing of this greeting ritual in 1977, anthropologist Julian Pitt-Rivers wondered, "Is it not likely that the right to defeat the executed stranger existed . . . only to be waived, establishing the fact that subsequent to his defeat, he 'owed his life' to his conqueror? The fact would surely find some social recognition in a kind of bond; when one has fought for one's life against someone, lost and been spared, one can hardly resume the relationship of mere acquaintances." Like how military service, team sports, and disasters can bond strangers together in a profound way, so could this ritual.

were welcome since their arrival helped to differentiate society, giving it a wider range of personality and interests." They just had to be
rendered safe, first. Among the Zulu people, a stranger was seen as
simultaneously strong and weak. They were strong with mysterious
and potentially dangerous foreign influences, but also weak because
they weren't one of *us*. So the greeting ritual needed to reconcile the
threat with the opportunity they presented.

"The entry of a stranger into a [village] can be compared with
passing over a succession of barriers," wrote Raum. A stranger arrived at the gate and saluted. A boy was sent outside to find out where
they came from. The boy then went back inside and conveyed this
information to the leader. On the leader's word, the boy led the
stranger inside, where he was assigned to a hut, sometimes the boys'
residence. "He may not leave the hut assigned to him," writes Raum.
"If he does he is suspected of being mad."

The anthropologist Harriet Ngubane wrote about a version of this
process she observed in the Nyuswa Reserve later, in 1977: "During
this period the local people have an opportunity of observing [the
strangers] and deciding whether they are 'dangerous' or not, and also
whether they can be assimilated into their social life. Only after the
period of probation, and when the people in the immediate neighborhood have indicated their acceptance of the strangers, can they
build their own homes. Once this is done they get a local practitioner
to strengthen them and their homestead with local medicines in
order to make them fit into the new environmental situation."

But note the themes among all these rituals: rules, respect, time,
meaningful contact, and some measure of commonality, however
slight. When you met a stranger, you understood what you were
supposed to do, and you did it. In doing so, you demonstrated a measure of predictability, familiarity with the broader culture, and respect for the would-be hosts.* By following these rules, and sitting,
sometimes unarmed, for hours, or even allowing yourself to be

---

*   And basic manners. Otto Friedrich Raum, who studied the Zulu, was lauded in an obit-
uary for showing how "ritualised behavior helps to distinguish a polite person from an im-
polite person."

punched in the face repeatedly, you, the stranger, also demonstrated self-control—evidence you were an unlikely agent of chaos, that you possessed all the desired human characteristics, that you had a mind in full and were therefore safe to admit.

Let's return to the interaction I had at the library. When I initiated contact with the man, I didn't just shove my laptop in front of him and say "Watch this." I deliberately gave off a calm and predictable vibe. I made eye contact, but I didn't glare. I politely and quietly asked permission to enter his space—physical and psychological—and use his resources, leaving it to him to decide whether to grant it. Of course, I figured he'd say yes. People always do. As with many hunter-gatherer groups, permission is always asked, and always granted.

In granting me access, a reciprocal relationship was formed. That obligated me to return the favor if the situation required. Which I did. But even if I didn't, maybe it wouldn't deter the man from helping someone else at another time. We mentioned the concept of indirect reciprocity earlier. Maybe he just considered his kindness a coin in the cosmic favor bank that would be repaid later, by someone else, a person or some supernatural force or other. Maybe, being an ultra-cooperator, he didn't really think about it at all. Human behavior often starts out as a practical response to a problem and, if we do it enough, over time encodes in our genes and becomes something we just do without really thinking about it.

I haven't seen the man since, and I may never see him again, but for a moment we formed a little *us,* treating each other as honorary kin: tens of thousands of years of human history culminating in that one tidy and thoroughly unremarkable moment between two perfect strangers in a public library. The fact that these things happen in a city of millions, among strangers who look different and speak differently, and the fact that they happen frequently enough that we take them for granted, is evidence of an achievement that surely, even in our moments of hopelessness, we'd do well to appreciate.

Which we will now do, on a very, very, very long train ride.

Chapter 7

Meet the Murderer and the Man from Another Dimension

In which I ride a train for forty-two hours in an effort to get better at talking to strangers, and, in the process, make friends and learn about both the benefits of leafy greens and the exciting possibilities of interdimensional travel.

Somewhere near the border of California and Arizona, in the pre-dawn light, two men are talking about cabbage. One is tall, tan, a strapping guy in a flannel shirt with the look of a rancher. I'll call him the Rancher. Probably midsixties. The other is an older Chinese American man. He's reading a book called *The Plant Paradox*. I'll call him the Vegetarian. It's five-thirty in the morning, and we're all awake because that's when, for reasons no one has been able to adequately explain, Amtrak has decided to serve breakfast on this train. I'm numbly drinking coffee while staring out the window of the observatory car, watching the dim contours of the scenery scroll by, as scrubby Arizona yields to California in the early morning light.

The Rancher wanders over, glances at the Vegetarian's book, and takes a seat next to him.

"Are ya into science?" he asks.

The Vegetarian says yes, he is. The Rancher asks what the book is about, and the man explains it to him. It's about the dangers of lectins, he says, which are plant-based proteins found in many fruits and vegetables. This segues smoothly into a conversation about fasting and diet. The Vegetarian has been a vegetarian for years, he says—since he retired. He fasts regularly, too. I horn in and ask if fasting makes him ornery. A large, bearded guy behind me hears my question and pipes up, "You bet I'd be ornery! I need my meat, man!" The Vegetarian nods and says yes, it does make him a little tired when he's doing it, but he's never felt better on the whole.

The Rancher considers this, narrows his eyes, and asks: "What do you think about cabbage?"

"Cabbage?"

"Yeah, cabbage."

"Cabbage is good."

"*Really?*"

It's May 2019, and I'm on this train—some forty-two hours from Chicago to Los Angeles—because in my quest to get good at talking to strangers, I wanted to find a situation in which it was the norm, but in a venue that's less structured than my experiences at Conversations New York. If you're looking for a context in which talking to strangers is pretty much obligatory, America is a good bet. It's unusual among Western nations in its general chattiness, which has always been one of my favorite things about it—even in a deeply fraught historical moment like the present. Only in America would the cliché "never met a stranger" be considered so flattering, so desirable, so virtuous, that it would appear in countless American obituaries every single day.

In his 1971 memoir, the great British actor David Niven recounts a cruise he took as a young man. "The crossing was my first confrontation with Americans en masse and I found it a delightful experience," he wrote. "Their open-handed generosity and genuine curiosity came as something of a shock at first. What a change, though, to be asked the most searching personal questions in the first few minutes of contact, or to be treated to a point-by-point replay of the life of a stranger. What a difference as an unknown foreigner to be invited to sit at a table of friends or to join a family."

So it was decided: I'd do this exercise in America. But where specifically in America should I go? That's where the train came in. I'd read novelist and travel writer Paul Theroux's 1975 book, *The Great Railway Bazaar,* which is largely an account of talking to strangers while riding trains halfway across the world. After one fruitful exchange, Theroux writes, "The conversation, like many others I had had on trains, derived an easy candor from the shared journey, the comfort of the dining car, and the certain knowledge that neither of us would see each other again." I had also recently happened upon a magazine story about taking the train across the country, in which the writer observed that train people are "individuals for whom small talk is as invigorating as a rail of cocaine." Sign me up.

There was something deeper that appealed to me, though. Americans are bewitched by trains. Trains transformed America, and in exchange, Americans are transformed by trains. I had been corresponding with one such person, an American musician by the name of Gabriel Kahane. After the 2016 U.S. presidential election, Kahane had become downcast about the country. So he set out to spend two weeks on trains to get out of his bubble and spend time with his fellow Americans. In effect, he wanted to talk to strangers—strangers in the sense of people he didn't know, but also people from whom he'd become estranged culturally and politically. The journey resulted in his acclaimed 2018 recording, *Book of Travelers.*

"It was absolutely transformational," Kahane told me. "It mostly reinforced my belief that the digital lens through which we interpret the national mood is deeply skewed. Not that we don't have serious, life-and-death ideological differences, but that those differences are so much easier to navigate when you're dealing with someone as flesh and blood, rather than as a digital, glowing, faceless avatar." Kahane says the experience forced him to confront his biases about people in the other parts of the country—though politics seldom came up. He found most of the conversations he had with people naturally revolved around family—around the love people have for their families and the sacrifices they make for them. "If anything," he says, "it gave me faith in humanity."

That was good enough for me. I booked a sleeper cabin on Amtrak's cross-country train, the Southwest Chief. On departure day, I take a cab to LaGuardia Airport. A nice lady at the newsstand asks me where I'm going. I say Chicago, but from there I'm actually getting on a train to Los Angeles.

"Oh my. How long is that?"

"About two days," I tell her.

"Why don't you take a plane?"

"Because I've always wanted to do this, and I figured out a way to do it for work."

"I don't understand," she says. "Why don't you take a plane?"

"It'll be fun!" I say.

She looks at me.

"It's an adventure! I'll meet new people!" I say. "There will be great views! I'll have a bed!"

"Hotels have beds."

"Look, you're not going to change my mind on this."

She laughs and wishes me good luck. I board a flight to Chicago, where on a moving sidewalk I encounter a man with a large and oddly shaped plastic case. I follow my curiosity, as Gillian Sandstrom advised.

"What is that thing?" I ask.

"It's a dead body," he says. Then he pauses. "I'm kidding. It's a stand for a trade show."

Hours later, I step onto a very large train at Union Station, find my cabin, and away we go.

As the train eases into motion and the journey gets under way, the conductor, a natural performer of Colombian extraction, makes two announcements to the residents of our two-story sleeper car: "The coffee is hot, fresh, strong, and Colombian. And so am I." And then: "There is no Wi-Fi on this train. They took it away two months ago. So you'll have to talk to each other. I hope you like each other." As he ticks off the rules and amenities of the sleeper car, travelers are already circulating, sticking their heads into various cabins, introducing themselves, asking, "Are you our neighbor?"

My hopes for this trip are immediately realized. The beauty of traveling by long-distance train is that strangers mingle without hesitation or self-consciousness. It is a completely fluid social environment. Like hunter-gatherer society, the model is fission-fusion. People mingle, meet, and introduce the people they meet to other people. What's more, the awkwardness people tend to feel at the prospect of talking to a stranger is dialed down. You are invited to talk by your presence on the train—that's the social norm—and you always have a good opener: "Where you headed?"

People are almost always game to talk. You don't have to apologize or offer some kind of excuse for talking to someone. Passengers are constantly either having conversations or joining conversations already in progress. If you hear something interesting to you, you can just politely sidle up. This sort of wide-open sociality, I'd wager, has to do with a few factors. First, a lot of these people are from the South and the Midwest, where people talk to strangers. Second, we're all in the same metal container, which means you quickly come to recognize one another on sight. And third, unless you're part of a foursome, you're going to be eating all your meals with strangers. If you're me, and you're alone, you're going to walk into the dining car, and you're going to be waved over to a table, and then you're going to talk.

My first dinner was with a retired couple, Penny and Bill, from South Carolina. They were traveling to California to see Bill's brother. Bill's a retired navy officer, and his job has taken them all over the world. Penny tells me they have moved twenty-nine times. Once they had made plans to travel to Nova Scotia for vacation, when Bill told her it was off—they were going to Paris instead. Penny was delighted, until he told her it was for good. Then she was shattered. She didn't want to move again. She didn't speak the language, which was hard for a born talker like Penny. "My mother used to say, 'Penny, stop talking and eat!'" she tells me. "My teachers used to say that on my report cards: *'Penny is always talking!'* It's just who I am!"

Having a dog helped in Paris, she says. It was an incidental similarity, and it broke down barriers among her and strangers. She had started saying hello to a man she came across while walking her dog, Muffin. One day he said, "*Bonjour*—your dog, what is her name?" She said her name was Muffin. He said, "*Non, non, non!* Her name is . . . Croissant!" Thereafter, every time they met he'd say, "*Bonjour,* Penny! *Bonjour,* Croissant!" After that, things got better. Since then, everywhere Penny goes, she asks dog owners what their dogs' names are. It's a surefire way to meet people, she says.

We talk and talk, and she tells us all about their adventures, including the time they ended up helping a friend birth sheep on a farm in England. As she's recounting the tale, she struggles to remember a word. She asks Bill, "What is a male sheep called?"

"A goat."

"It's not a goat!" she says.

"Hey, I don't know," he exclaims. "I'm a navy man!"

As we talk, I can't believe my luck. All their moving around has made Penny very good at talking to strangers. After all, if she didn't talk to strangers, she says, she'd never be able to meet people and find a sense of community. One of her techniques, she tells me, is, when people say "How are you?" she doesn't say "Good." She says, "I'm great and getting better every day." When she asks them how they are, and they say, "Good," she says, "Are you really?" And then they just talk. "People *need* to talk," she says.

We talk for two hours—about Amtrak food, about life, politics, anything. The conversation just wends easily along. I find them fascinating and lovely. Twice Penny calls me "a national treasure," which, not to put too fine a point on it, but: *It's about goddamn time someone figured that out.* Our fourth fellow diner, a fit, tan middle-aged woman, doesn't have much to say, however, except that immigrants were overrunning California as part of what she believed was a criminal conspiracy. She was born in England, she says. She wears a T-shirt that reads LOVE.

That night, we're told that the train is being taken out of commission due to flooding in Kansas. At midnight, we're herded off the train and onto buses and driven three hours through the dead of night. Even then, people are chatting, at least initially. The people behind me, after the usual getting-to-know-you chitchat, realize that *they were both hit by the same tornado*. After a couple of hours, though, people get tired and our bus falls silent. A tall, jangly man walks up to the front and says something to the driver, then turns, walks back, and takes his seat. Twenty minutes later he's back up there again. This time the driver snaps, *"Sir, take your seat."* The other passengers exchange glances. Twenty minutes after that, we pull off the highway, into a gas station parking lot that is full of police cars. The jangly man stands up, walks out, and surrenders himself to the cops with barely a word. He had asked the driver to speed up, we learn later, because "there are some people I have to kill in California."

The next day, the man, who quickly became known as "the Murderer," is the talk of the train. Over a Bloody Mary lunch with a retiree from Indiana and two younger Kentuckian women, we gaze out the window and talk about the fearsome emptiness of the American West rolling by the windows of the dining car. The man says this is nothing. He's recently started teaching an adult education class about the size of the universe, he says. He pulls out a quarter, slaps it on the table, and says, "If our solar system is this quarter, our galaxy is the size of the continental United States." We start talking about the sensation of awe after that. And when the train stops in the middle of the New Mexico desert, someone at another table goes, "Uh-oh, what now?"

"I'm not sure, but there are a couple buses parked outside," I joke.

"And one of them's driven by the Murderer," says one of our companions. "He's waving at us!" She waves back.

The rest of the trip rolls along like this, drifting in and out of conversations, some casual, some deeper and more personal—with a social worker, a dairy farmer, an art teacher, and others. Most people are middle-aged or older, but not all; probably three-quarters are white. But everyone mingles for the two days we spend together, rumbling across the western half of the country. The ample time and magnificent scenery make people comfortable and unselfconscious. After a day or so, I feel like I'm learning to have a conversation again. Just sitting back and letting it go where it goes. A collaboration, not a competition. But what takes place on the train feels settling and restorative. It makes the complexity of others undeniable. Everybody is pretty good company. Everyone's story is a pretty good story. They are familiar enough to be relatable, but different enough to be interesting.

Which brings us back to cabbage. After the Rancher and the Vegetarian exhaust the topic of fasting, the Rancher and I fall into conversation. There's something about him, something about the way he speaks, that is intriguing to me, something eccentric that doesn't match his looks. I ask what he does, but he dodges the question. These days, he says, "I think. Maybe too much."

"What do you think about?"

After telling me repeatedly that his opinion doesn't matter, he starts in on something. He says he had a thought early this morning, in fact, while staring out the window of his cabin. He said he's long believed in the existence of other dimensions, and increasingly believes they might be closer to us than we think. He says as we passed a freight train going in the opposite direction this morning, something took hold of him. He says he noticed that in one sense, the freight train was blocking his view. But if he squinted, he could still see the moonlit desert through the gaps between the train cars. He says he imagined this passing freight as the other dimension, full of unknowable cargo, passing so fast we don't even see it; we just see our own world through the gaps between its cars.

"Perhaps then," he says, "perceiving another dimension is simply a question of speed." He wonders if it could be possible to slow down the mind enough to perceive this other dimension passing before our eyes. He takes comfort in knowing it's there, but he's still happy to have a few feet between it and us. "I wouldn't want to be walking around outside and end up in front of it," he says, and chuckles.

He then goes quiet, and I get to thinking that I feel the same way about strangers: vessels of unknowable cargo, containers of whole universes, silently passing in front of us day after day, and us unaware. Some traditional island cultures believed this literally—that strangers are visitors from other dimensions lying beyond the known horizon. In a sense they're right. They are. And we can go our whole lives without even seeing them if we don't learn to look.

The man and I gaze out the window of the observatory car as day breaks over the California desert, and he says that only on a train can you have such thoughts, and then he gets up and walks away before I can ask him his name.

Chapter 8

How Humans Came to Rely on the Kindness of Strangers

In which we learn that being hospitable to strangers wasn't an exception in deep history—that it was a sacred law that laid the groundwork for human civilization, and breaking it got you turned into a bird by the gods.

Two guys walk into a village. They're dressed like beggars, and they're going door-to-door to make sure people are being nice to strangers. One is Jesus Christ, Son of God, in the Christian tradition. The other is Saint Peter, his right-hand man and the rock upon which his church is built. Jesus and Peter arrive at the house of an old peasant woman and beg for some bread. She gives them some crumbs. Jesus gives her another chance. He miraculously causes the cake in her oven to grow larger, giving her more food to share. She stiffs them again. At this point, Jesus and Peter decide they have seen enough, and they turn her into an owl.

This is a European folktale from the Middle Ages, but other versions exist. In a variation that appeared in Baltic countries, Jesus and Peter punish the miser by forcing her to raise two snakes as foster children. In another version, this one Scandinavian, she is turned into a woodpecker. In Germany, they turn her into a cuckoo.

These stories aren't just Christian, nor are they limited to Europe or the Middle Ages. A Moroccan version, which also turned up in Spain, Russia, and Turkey, features the Prophet Muhammad in the beggar role. His rich host refuses to kill a sheep for him, and instead boils a cat. Muhammad responds by reviving the cat and turning the man into an owl. In a Native American folktale, it's an old woman and her grandson who are turned away by stingy townspeople. They punish the misers by turning them and all of their children into, you guessed it, birds.*

In the Japanese folk tradition, the stranger—*ijin,* or "different person"—often appears as a tinker, a foreigner, a beggar, or some other kind of vulnerable outsider, but in reality is a god, a priest, a prince, or someone else endowed with magical powers. In one such story, a Buddhist priest named Kōbō Daishi arrives in a village where water is scarce. He's dressed like a beggar, and he begs for a cup. A woman travels a great distance to a well and brings water back for him. To thank her, Kōbō Daishi strikes his staff against the ground, and a spring of water bubbles forth. In the next village, where water is plentiful, Kōbō Daishi is rejected. This time he strikes the ground in anger. The wells dry up and the settlement fails.

In the West, the ancient Greeks are perhaps most famous for promoting the idea that gods reside in strangers. Strangers were said to be protected by Zeus, who was both the father of the gods and the god of strangers. He frequently took up the wandering beggar guise to make sure people weren't mistreating strangers. In *The Odyssey,* the epic Greek poem written in the eighth century B.C., a former charge of the hero Odysseus encounters his former master after a long separation. The man doesn't recognize Odysseus, but still he extends hospitality. "You must eat something, drink some wine, and tell me where you are from and the hard times you've seen," he says. "All wanderers and beggars come from Zeus." In *Laws* in 360 B.C., Plato warned, "He who has a spark of caution in him, will do his best to pass through life without sinning against the stranger." That spark burned for millennia, entering folk traditions around the world. In

---

* At a certain point, while reading these stories, you begin to wonder if this is just where birds came from.

his song "Stranger Blues," the American bluesman Elmore James sang, "Well, I wonder how come they dog a poor stranger so / Yes, I wonder how come they dog a poor stranger so / And they all should remember / They gonna reap what they sow."

We saw in the previous chapters that we became who we are in large part because we learned to cooperate with strangers. We developed the capacity for honorary kinship, which allowed us to treat genetic strangers as family. We developed a capacity for indirect reciprocity, which allowed us to forge critical relationships with other bands. We developed cultures in which simple ornamentation signaled that the stranger was in fact one of us, and we devised greeting rituals to safely interact with them. All of these developments allowed *Homo sapiens* to scale the *us* to dimensions that would have beggared the imaginations of their own distant ancestors.

That brings us to the next great evolutionary leap in our life among strangers, our next social renaissance: hospitality. Like honorary kinship, hospitality is something that started out as a practical solution to a novel problem and in time proved so integral to the success of humans that it eventually became simply part of our morality, something we did without thinking, something encoded in our genes. "One thing that's clear is that humans know and do hospitality pretty much as extensively as they know and do kinship, or exchange, or gender," says Andrew Shryock, an anthropologist at the University of Michigan who specializes in hospitality. "It's something that evolved with us, as us," he adds. "My own hunch is that human sociability is impossible without hospitality."

The tradition of hospitality toward strangers is, of course, more than just folk stories by and for people who seem to really hate birds. It has lived in practice for thousands of years. In 1906, Edward Westermarck, a well-traveled Finnish philosopher who is considered one of the founders of sociology, published a book called *The Origin and Development of the Moral Ideas,* in which he examined dozens of traditional societies that extended generous hospitality to strangers. "The stranger is often welcomed with special marks of honor," Westermarck observed. "The best seat is assigned to him; the best food at the host's disposal is set before him; he takes precedence over all the members of the household; he enjoys extraordinary privileges."

There was such prestige attached to hosting the stranger that people would compete to attract them. Among the Arabs of Sinai, Westermarck wrote, "If a stranger be seen from afar coming towards the camp, he is the guest for that night of the first person who describes him, and who, whether a grown man or a child, exclaims, 'There comes my guest!'" Westermarck found that the concepts of hospitality and the supernatural were intermingled in many cultures. The stranger represented another dimension, in all its graces and terrors. He wrote:

> Among the doctrines held up for acceptance by the religious instructors of the Iroquois there was the following precept: "If a stranger wander about your abode, welcome him to your home, be hospitable towards him, speak to him with kind words, and forget not always to mention the Great Spirit." The natives of Aneiteum, of the New Hebrides, maintained that generous hospitality would receive the highest reward in the Land of the Dead. The Kalmucks believe that want of hospitality will be punished by angry gods. The Kandhs say that the first duty which the gods have imposed upon man is that of hospitality; and "persons guilty of the neglect of established observances are punished by the divine wrath, either during their current lives, or when they afterwards return to animate other bodies," the penalties being death, poverty, disease, the loss of children, or any other form of calamity. In the sacred books of India, hospitality is repeatedly spoken of as a most important duty, the discharge of which will be amply rewarded. "The inhospitable man," the Vedic singer tells us, ". . . lives not, though he breathes." According to the Vishnu Purána, a person who neglects a poor and friendless stranger in want of hospitality, goes to hell. On the other hand, by honouring guests a householder ob-

tains the highest reward. "He who entertains guests for one night obtains earthly happiness, a second night gains the middle air, a third heavenly bliss, a fourth the world of unsurpassable bliss; many nights procure endless worlds. That has been declared in the Veda." It is said in the Mahabharata that "he who gives food freely to a fatigued wayfarer, whom he has never seen before, obtains great virtuous merit."

There were few limits placed on hospitality in many of these societies. If the man who killed your brother asked for hospitality, you had to grant it. And if someone came to kill your guest, you had to defend him, even with your life.

Andrew Shryock tells me that in many cultures hospitality and religion are not just related. They are inextricable. "Hospitality developed into and alongside religion," he says. "It's hard to say if hospitality derives its power from its sacredness, or if it lends its power to the sacred." In other words, are we religious because of hospitality? Or are we hospitable because of religion? It's impossible to say. Shryock has spent years studying Arab hospitality—*karam*—research that led him to the Balga tribes of Jordan. To the Balga, Shryock wrote in 2012, "a house without guests, without the spaces necessary to take them in, and without the materials needed to prepare food and drink, is not only weak, it is shameful." Hospitality is a kind of deep faith there, he writes, "'a burning in the skin' inherited 'from the father and the grandfathers.'" One Balgawi man told Shryock, "*Karam* is not just a matter of food and drink. Hospitality is from the soul; it's from the blood."

The depth of the obligation was such that the Bedouins there were said to occasionally host the stranger with a zeal that could tip into a kind of madness, specifically, *hiblat al-'arab*—"the Arab madness"—in which a person overcome by the spirit gives everything away to guests. Shryock spent years searching for one particular Jordan Valley folk story in which a man gave away his children to a stranger because he had nothing more valuable to offer. There were more such tales bearing the same message. In the way a zealot could lose everything in his quest for the face of God, so, too, can the *karim*—the hospitable man—draw too close to the ruinous ideal of total hospitality when met with the face of a wayfaring stranger.

Today when we think of hospitality, we usually think of the private hospitality industry, which hosts weary travelers for a fee, replacing conversation with Wi-Fi, and the lavish spreads of old with rust-colored coffee and those clammy, shrink-wrapped muffins served in the lobby between seven and nine A.M. But for our distant ancestors, hospitality to strangers was something else entirely, a daily practice elevated to a supernatural plane, fashioned into an inviolable law enforced by gods and priests and anyone else with the power to make you pay dearly for mistreating a stranger.[*]

Which leads to our next question: Why?

The Greeks get a lot of credit for hospitality—called *xenia,* from the root *xenos,* meaning "stranger." Our words xenophobia and xenophilia derive from this. But the Greeks didn't invent the tradition. It goes much further back. How far we don't know, exactly, but archaeological evidence suggests hospitality as we now understand it may have begun in earnest some ten thousand years ago, around the time of the agricultural revolution, when the hunter-gatherer lifestyle commenced its long decline. Like cooperation, honorary kinship, and greeting rituals, hospitality in its earliest stages likely wasn't just a nice thing to do, or a virtuous thing to do. It was an effective thing to do. People did it because it worked.

The University of Cambridge archaeologist Martin Jones studies

---

[*] Sometimes the supernatural power lies in the hands of the host, too. In a 1951 study of the Toraja of what is now South Sulawesi in Indonesia, Nicolaus Adriani and Albertus Christiaan Kruyt turned up this gem:

> It has sometimes happened that strangers behaved rudely and laid out a field in the territory of another tribe without having asked for permission to do it. This is done by persons, among others, who know that the owners of the land cannot stand up against their tribe and thus will avoid unpleasantnesses. "But then we curse the people [said one villager] . . . and then our ancestors come as mice to eat up their rice and maize, so that there will be nothing to harvest."

the flow of goods and food and culture across great distances around the time that humans began to settle down and farm. That period, he has written, left a great deal of evidence to show that human beings, always a mobile species, suddenly began going farther afield, covering greater and greater distances. Archaeologists have found shells that traveled the entire length of the Euphrates River, some 1,740 miles, and obsidian, the gleaming black igneous rock used in ornamental blades, in a trail connecting central Turkey to southwest Asia. Those distances might mean little to us today, but for their time they were extraordinary, even for a species that has traveling in its blood.

According to Jones, hospitality made this possible. Humanity had begun its shift from hunting and gathering to farming, and from a nomadic lifestyle to a settled one. Once communities began to form, they could be used effectively as transit hubs for traveling strangers. In putting down stakes, Jones writes, these settlers "were creating a fixed human landscape that enabled a new kind of mobility for travelers, over considerable distances. These new landscapes of permanence and mobility generated new kinds of social encounter, sometimes between complete strangers." Today we have cities and towns, hotels and Airbnbs, and airports and bus terminals to facilitate long-distance travel; back then, these fledgling settlements served that purpose.

Basing his argument on ancient DNA analysis, Jones believes that these wayfarers were mostly men. More specifically, they were men at loose ends—"surplus" or "exported" males. When hunting—traditionally men's work—started to give way to farming, Jones believes these men simply didn't have that much to do. In today's world, an abundance of surplus men, especially younger ones, can be trouble. "The behavior of young surplus males also follows a broadly predictable pattern," write political scientists Valerie Hudson and Andrea den Boer, who have studied the problem. "Theory suggests that compared with other males in society, [they] will be prone to seek satisfaction through vice and violence, and will seek to capture resources that will allow them to compete on a more equal footing with others." Ten thousand years ago, however, perhaps because videogames and white nationalism had yet to be invented, these men hit the road. Jones believes they became a legion of wanderers and traveling salesmen, carrying with them status objects like decorative shells, tools, and weapons, as well as foods like chickpeas, figs, beans, and different types of wheat, from settlement to settlement, across great distances of extraordinary diversity. "Their migration to new territories became an influential driving force in the peopling of the modern world," Jones writes.

A thousand years or so later, with sprawling social networks established, people traveled in order to find a place to settle down, bringing with them domesticated animals, new farming and building techniques, and new cultural and spiritual beliefs. Social networks grew, innovation quickened, new people met, and populations mixed, forming even larger and larger social networks. What began as intimate encounters among individuals in time formed into a tradition, and that tradition, writes Jones, became the "cornerstone of civilization."*

It's obvious why hospitality is a good deal for travelers. You travel from place to place, and people lavish attention on you and give you free food and lodging. But what's in it for the hosts? They already have a home, they have food, they have clothing—why share with some random stranger? He could be dangerous. Why let him in? Edward Westermarck wondered the same thing in 1906: "That a stranger who under other circumstances is treated as an inferior being or a foe, liable to be robbed and killed with impunity, should enjoy such extraordinary privileges as a guest, is certainly one of the most curious contrasts which present themselves to a student of the moral ideas of mankind. It may be asked, why should he be received at all?"

---

* I am aware of the counterargument here: that human civilization is an ecological catastrophe, humanity is a cancer upon the Earth, and we'd all have been better off if we'd just stayed as hunter-gatherers forever. I am sympathetic to these arguments, and concede they are not wholly without merit. Nevertheless, while human civilization has a lot of work to do to meet its own promise, I remain fond of it. Some of my most favorite people, I find, are people.

There are a few potential answers to this question. First, there's a charitable explanation: The hosts might have seen a stranger in need, and perhaps they felt something—empathy, or at least sympathy. In especially harsh climates, say the Sinai desert, to deny hospitality to a stranger was tantamount to murder. The stranger was standing right here in front of you, murder was bad, and therefore it was up to you to keep him alive. If he did die, sure, maybe nothing happened. But then again, maybe your god becomes angry, or maybe your neighbors shame you, or maybe he has friends just over the horizon who might want to avenge him. Better to risk hospitality.

But hospitality wasn't just about risk management. A stranger was a potential ally. In the case of the ancient Greeks, for instance, the Mediterranean region was so lawless that any opportunity to form a relationship with someone from somewhere else was seen as something you'd have to be a fool to pass up. In lieu of centralized states, these relationships provided contacts, news, and potential alliances that made travel through the Greek world possible. You'd host someone from somewhere else, and later, you have somewhere safe to stay when you need to travel. And if you developed a reputation as a good host, others may come to you, presenting the potential for more relationships that secured your place in the world and shielded you from the buffeting winds of an otherwise ruthless age. It was that important. For the Greeks, "every man regarded it as his privilege and inviolable duty to receive and entertain any stranger who applied for hospitality," writes historian Oscar Nybakken. "A stranger was almost always welcomed immediately upon arrival; to delay the welcome was a disgrace to the host."

There's a scene in *The Odyssey*—sometimes known as the Greek bible—that perfectly captures this mind-set. When Odysseus and his men encounter the Cyclops, they request hospitality. The Cyclops responds by calling Odysseus a ninny, says he's not afraid of Zeus because his people are more powerful than any god, and then eats several of Odysseus's men. Odysseus replies with near-comic exasperation. "You are mad. After this, will any traveler come to see you?" The idea being that even if you were a literal one-eyed monster who had everything you needed and feared no god, you'd still have to be insane not to want strangers to come and stay with you. That's how valuable they were.

Again, hospitality didn't flourish because hosts had become convinced of the essential goodness of humanity. They didn't necessarily believe people were good, or trustworthy, or interesting, or fun to hang around with. If anything, it was kind of the opposite, as suggested by the Latin word for "guest"—*hostis*—which means both "stranger" and "enemy." Hospitality served the purposes of alleviating fear and seizing opportunity in an unstable environment. People felt deep ambivalence when a stranger appeared because the stranger represented the unknown, and the unknown represented both a threat and an opportunity. A threat, because they could kill your family, rob you, or otherwise sow chaos in your life or the life of your village. And an opportunity, because who knows what they know? Who knows what they have? Who knows who they are?

By extending hospitality, you took that fear, brought it inside your house—literally domesticating it—and plied it with food and drink and a place to sleep. In doing so, you eased your mind and came to know the individual. The philosopher Nietzsche argued that hospitality was a way of "paralyzing the hostile in the stranger," but it may have been as much about paralyzing the fear in the host. You'd sit with this person, eat, look each other in the eye, talk—for hours, quite likely, given that they didn't have iPhones to stare at numbly— and in so doing, you'd defuse the tension.

Once that occurred, a small *us* could form, and something special could happen. At that moment, "fearful strangers can become guests revealing to their hosts the promise they are carrying with them," wrote the Dutch theologian Henri Nouwen in 1975. That promise could be friendship, or an alliance, or a trading partnership, certainly. Maybe he can tell you where he found water, or give you some seeds for a new crop, or reveal a farming technique. Maybe the gift he's providing is a knife, or decorative beads, or even a joke, a song, a funny story, or just some good company to break up the monotony. And if you ever travel to his neck of the woods, he will repay the favor. That is the beginning of the sort of indirect reciprocity we saw in hunter-gatherer bands. And reciprocity is "the cement that holds any society together," argued the great anthropologist Julian Pitt-Rivers. "Once you have exchanged something, you are related."

But something much deeper than favors or entertainment can be exchanged in these interactions—something that brings us closer to the heart of our little project here. Philosophers, anthropologists, sociologists, and theologians for the past century have argued that there are far more profound and intangible benefits to hospitality toward strangers, beyond just obtaining information or securing alliances. "The arrival of a stranger breaks up the eternal recurrence of daily events and opens the door to the extraordinary," writes the German social anthropologist Florian Mühlfried. "The stranger is thus attributed the power to break up the familiar."

Thomas Ogletree, a former dean of Yale Divinity School, put it this way in 1985:

> To offer hospitality to a stranger is to welcome something new, unfamiliar, and unknown. . . . Strangers have stories to tell which we have never heard before, stories which can redirect our seeing and stimulate our imaginations. The stories invite us to view the world from a novel perspective. The sharing of stories may prove threatening, but not necessarily so. It may generate a festive mood, a joy in celebrating the meeting of minds across social and cultural differences. The stranger does not simply challenge or subvert our assumed world of meaning; she may enrich, even transform, that world.

In most places, particularly in the West, this sort of hospitality has largely ceased. Governments have taken up part of the job through welfare programs, public housing, shelters, formal immigration channels, and asylum for refugees. The private hospitality industry has picked up some of the slack for domestic travelers with resources. Yet, Andrew Shryock—the anthropologist who studied the Balga in Jordan—tells me that he believes that the rise of huge, complex societies like ours "has created hospitality problems we've not yet been able to define, diagnose, or fix." Industrialized countries continue to take in new people, immigrants, and cultural strangers, as many societies always have, but what we've lost with the decline of personal hospitality is *contact*.

In general, citizens don't sit down with these new strangers, don't meet them. Some do—some volunteer, or work for organizations in their communities that help settle newcomers. But for the most part, the state has taken over the role, and that has rendered these newcomers mere abstractions in the minds of many citizens. Bi Puranen, a Swedish researcher, pointed out to me the contradiction in her own country, which has accepted many Middle Eastern refugees and also experienced an intense backlash. "[Sweden has] taken in more refugees than any other country, per capita," she writes in an email. "But is that hospitality? Very few have been invited to a Swedish home."

Hospitality is about overcoming fear in order to unlock the opportunity the stranger represents, and vice versa. But without that contact, the fear is more difficult to paralyze. We are naturally wary of strangers, and with the right prodding, our biases against them can be activated, our imaginations can run wild, and we can come to think of them as subhuman. We're likely not going back to a time where it will fall to individuals to host strangers passing through town, but there remains a basic human instinct to provide and receive hospitality, to host and connect with new people, stemming from millennia of practice and a faith that it will not only be okay, but that our hospitality will be repaid multifold. What do we do with that instinct?

To answer that question, you and I are going to take a trip to Los Angeles, where there is a street corner with our name on it, and a slightly mortifying experience ahead.

Chapter 9

How to Listen to Strangers

In which, through an experience marbled with light horror, we discover that even listening to strangers can have a powerful effect on us, and on them, alleviating loneliness, enhancing belonging, and paving the way for understanding.

I'm standing on a street corner in Los Angeles holding a crude cardboard sign with *Free Listening* scrawled across it, next to a man named Ben Mathes, waiting for someone to come talk to me. Mathes is an actor, acting coach, and—apropos of our purposes—the founder of an organization called Urban Confessional. Urban Confessional encourages people to make their own crudely drawn cardboard signs and stand in heavily trafficked locations offering themselves up as listeners to anyone who wants to talk. I had read about Urban Confessional, and frankly reacted with skepticism and perhaps a touch of light horror at the prospect of standing in broad daylight on a busy street with a crude sign inviting random strangers to come spill their guts to me. Nevertheless, I contacted Mathes, who invited me out to L.A. to go listen to strangers with him. I got off the forty-two-hour train ride, caught some sleep, and went to meet him for breakfast.

What would possess a person to do this—to stand out in public, vulnerable and exposed, and offer themselves as receptacles for whatever random strangers want to unload on them? In Mathes's case, it was a crisis. He grew up in Georgia and came out to California in 2005 to get his master's degree in acting from the University of California, Irvine. He won some roles—acting in *American Sniper* and working as a dialogue coach in the Russell Crowe vehicle *Robin Hood,* as well as some other films and TV shows—and he taught on the side, which he liked enough to launch his own acting studio. He got married at twenty-six. Things were good.

"So how did Urban Confessional start?" I ask him over breakfast.

"I got divorced," he says. "Where all good stories start."

Divorce, as it is wont to do, deposited Ben Mathes at the bottom. But he wasn't hopeless. He'd done volunteer work in the past, and his father runs a nonprofit that does mission work overseas. "I knew that serving others had a restorative effect on the person doing the serving," he says. So he started looking for ways to be of use. One day in May 2012, as he was headed to his acting studio, a homeless man approached him and asked for money. Mathes didn't have any on him, but an impulse seized him. He suggested maybe they could pray together.

"I'd never done that," he says. "But I did." He can't say why exactly. It wasn't a conversion attempt; he wasn't trying to save the guy's soul. It was just a simple ecumenical prayer of well-being, a kind of "free prayer," Mathes says. They prayed, and quite unexpectedly, Mathes felt like he communed with the man, like they had dropped everything and were simply there for each other, just for a moment.

They parted ways after the prayer. But the feeling stayed with Mathes. "I thought, *How do I get this again? What would be the closest thing to free prayer? And I thought, Well, maybe free listening.*" He walked into his studio that day and told his students he was going to go out on Thursday to offer himself up to strangers as a free listener. A couple of them joined him. On the first day, they had one woman who came over and said some pretty profound things, followed by another one who laughed at them. "Free listening?" she said. "No one's listened to me in thirty years. Why would *you* do it?" And she walked off.

Mathes, however, was hooked. He went out every day, for four hours a day, for a year, as he gathered the broken pieces left in the aftermath of his divorce and formed what would become Urban Confessional. As he did it, he also noticed that the sessions seemed to have a profound effect on the people he was listening to. Once you allayed their suspicions that you were selling something, or a Scientologist, or trying to convert them, or that this was some kind of social media play, they really opened up. Mathes found it helped him, too. "It would be clever of me to think that I learned everybody else was in a bad place, too, and I felt solidarity with their suffering," he tells me. "I did, but mostly it was really nice not to focus on me for a little bit."

Others began to join, and as Urban Confessional grew, Mathes developed some simple guidelines for volunteers based on his own experiences. The first was to understand that this isn't about you. It's not about being validated by all the people who want to come talk to you, or having your specialness recognized. "It only stings if you *need* them to come talk to you," he says. You become a servant, a conduit for others.

Next was the idea of "imbalanced conversation," also known as the 80/20 rule. Free listeners are discouraged from talking about themselves more than 20 percent of the time. Then came "empathetic agreement," which means that the listener seeks to understand what the other person is saying, not counter a viewpoint they feel is incorrect or try to solve their problems for them. That means asking open-ended questions like "Why do you feel that way?" and not offering opinions or advice, or arguing, or judging. Fourth, listeners practice "nonverbal attentiveness," which means making eye contact, nodding, saying "uh-huh" and the like, and, most important, not checking your phone. This shows the speaker you are paying attention.

Finally, there was "respecting the silence." When someone pauses, you don't jump in and fill the space. Let them think. Let them sort it out. It's simple. It's also much harder than it seems.

Mathes claims no clinical expertise in any of this; he just developed this method from his own experience. But his instincts are keen.

A substantial body of research has arrived at many of the same conclusions—dating back to one of the fathers of clinical psychology, Carl Rogers, who believed that empathic listening could heal individuals, alleviate social problems, and end war.

More recently, two prominent Israeli business professors who specialize in listening, Guy Itzchakov and Avi Kluger, argued in the *Harvard Business Review* that the best way for managers to become good listeners is to do just what Mathes is recommending: Either "give 100% of your attention, or do not listen." "Do not interrupt." "Do not judge or evaluate." "Do not impose your solutions." And "Ask more (good) questions," which is to say, ask questions that help the speaker better articulate what they're telling you. Researchers have found that people who feel listened to have a stronger sense of well-being, and feel less anxious. They feel freer to speak their minds without fear of rejection or repudiation, which makes them less defensive and more likely to speak truthfully.

Carl Rogers argued that when people feel comfortable, and are asked open-ended questions, they gain the opportunity to more deeply consider what they are actually saying and what they believe, because they don't feel the need to be defensive. This helps them more clearly elaborate on a thought or an experience, which allows them to understand and remember it more clearly, which results in them being more self-aware by potentially revealing complexities or contradictions they hadn't been aware of previously. Paradoxically, being listened to well actually makes you a better speaker and a better thinker: calmer, more clearheaded, nuanced, and self-aware.

When Urban Confessional's volunteers take to the streets, they stand in pairs, a rule Mathes created in order to help the volunteers feel safe, but also because having two people to talk to makes the experience less intense initially for the speaker. When the speaker comes over, the volunteers put the sign away, so people don't feel self-conscious or stigmatized. To others, it looks like you're just three people talking on the street. Obviously, nothing is recorded, so when the conversation is over, it is gone. It lives in the memories of the participants and no one else. It won't be processed by Google and sold to an advertiser. It won't turn up when some competitor or ideological foe or some other malefactor is rooting for dirt in the depths of your Twitter feed to wound you. It's ephemeral, truly; it's up and gone in the air.

The benefits of this exercise, however, are real. Mathes and his students and friends did free listening for years, and no one really noticed until somewhat recently. Alerted to rising rates of reported loneliness by the likes of U.S. Surgeon General Vivek Murthy—who said in 2016, "Despite the ubiquity of social media, we are facing an epidemic of loneliness and social isolation," which could also seriously damage sufferers' physical health—researchers, activists, and Western governments started looking for ways to attack the problem. That led some of them to Urban Confessional. The organization went viral, and national, and global. Mathes started getting queries from people all over the world asking how they could get involved. There are now Urban Confessional affiliates in more than fifty countries.

One of those interested parties was Dr. Sarah Tracy, a celebrated professor of human communication at Arizona State University. She was becoming increasingly concerned about the lack of face-to-face contact she was seeing among her students. She believed a life spent communicating digitally was eroding the sort of basic social skills previous generations took for granted. She saw students becoming more isolated, struggling to connect with others. One even confessed to her that she avoids ordering pizza from places she has to call, because talking to the stranger on the other end of the line stressed her out.*

Research bears out Tracy's concerns. One study by the American College Health Association found that more than half of college stu-

---

* Incidentally, I happened upon a story in a local paper in Massachusetts about Danielle Crafford, a woman who had become a successful builder. She attributed part of her success to her father's efforts to get her used to talking to strangers. "My dad made me call every Friday night the pizza delivery guy," she said. "I hated calling people. I hated talking to people on the phone. . . . And my dad would make me. He was like 'You need to learn how to talk to people.' And he made me call the pizza guy."

dents report being lonely. A large-scale 2018 survey by the health insurance company Cigna found eighteen-to-twenty-two-year-olds reported higher levels of loneliness than all other age cohorts. Sixty-nine percent of them believed people around them were not really with them, and 68 percent felt no one really knew them well. Other generations fared much better for a simple reason: "Those who engage in frequent meaningful in-person interactions have much lower loneliness scores than those who rarely interact with others face-to-face," the study's authors concluded. This lack of contact can do more than make people lonely. It can damage you as a social animal. Another study reported a 40 percent drop in empathy among college students over the past thirty years—face-to-face contact being key to the formation of empathy.

Dr. Tracy had heard about Urban Confessional and thought that it could be a valuable tool to help her students. She decided to assign free listening to help teach them to listen, and, more important, to get more comfortable connecting with other strangers offline. "People assume that [listening] is naturally cultivated, but in today's age, it isn't," she tells me. She believes that free listening provides a way for students to experience "the extreme reward that is available by simply being open to and hearing others' viewpoints and stories—without the need or expectation that they say anything much in return, or have a quick judgment," she writes in an email. "They also learn that other people oftentimes feel as alone and disconnected as they do—and this in itself helps attend to feelings of loneliness. And they get clear on how infrequently they truly invite others—especially strangers—into their worlds, and how difficult it is to listen without resistance coming up over and over."

One of her students was Nikki Truscelli, an irrepressible California native who recently earned her PhD in communication at Arizona State. When Truscelli heard about free listening, she thought, *Whatever this is, I have to do it.* She started free listening around campus and loved it. "It's uncomfortable," she says, "but once you start doing it, I almost feel like there's, like, this natural sense that this is what we're supposed to do." She also thought it could be helpful to students. ASU is one of the largest universities in America, and Truscelli had begun "noticing how little connection really is taking place" among the kids, she says. "Do my students even know how to talk to each other?" she wondered. "I don't know." So Truscelli began incorporating free listening into her own classes.

"I've always made it optional, but my students who have done it have had these life-changing experiences," she says. "The stories that I've heard from some of them—just, like, 'I had no idea that there's other students who are also suffering from anxiety, or are super depressed, or also really homesick, or who had a friend who committed suicide,'" she says. "Or maybe they just had a nice conversation with their professor that they've never had before. It creates this really special space—but more so, it creates a community. I just wish we were in a place where we didn't need the *Free Listening* sign."

In 2018, Ben Mathes talked to Tracy, Truscelli, and some other scholars about the possibility of doing a study on free listening to get a better understanding of what exactly is happening when people do it. One of these scholars was Cris Tietsort, a PhD student and friend of Truscelli's. He and a colleague, Kyle Hanners, created a study in which they enlisted fourteen participants, all eighteen or nineteen years old, and had them do free listening weekly for five weeks and report back on how it went.

The responses fell into a few distinct buckets, says Tietsort. One was that students considered free listening "a weird, new thing." They never just stand around campus, quietly, off their phones, noticing. They realized "they rarely are very observant of their surroundings," Tietsort says. Second, they're accustomed to having control in interpersonal interactions, online and in person. "Students don't have uncontrolled conversations," he says. "They don't start conversations with others; they aren't used to quiet, aren't used to being ignored and being vulnerable." One even told him, "I never talk to someone unless I *want* to talk to them." So standing there and relinquishing control over an interaction was unsettling for many of them.

Once they got past that, though, the effect was profound. One student reported that after strangers confided in her, "they were noticeably a lot happier—or if they weren't happier, they were just a little more relaxed." Another said it made him feel like a "public servant." Another felt like he'd given a "gift" to the community—which hearkens back to the practice among traditional societies to exchange gifts when interacting with strangers. Some students who prided themselves on being bold and opinionated realized that by dominating conversations, they were actually shutting them down, cutting off all the potential unexpected insights, stories, and surprises that the conversation might have yielded. Some who were disturbed by silence in a conversation realized that by jumping in to fill it, they were preventing the conversation from going deeper. By hanging back and letting the other person find whatever it was they were trying to say, the conversation unfurled naturally. "It was really good just to keep my trap shut a little more just so I could really understand these people," said one young man.

Tietsort let me take a look at the data—with all identifying information stripped out. One student's experience was particularly representative. We'll call her Bree. "It was definitely very, very intimidating," she recounted. "Just standing was already weird. Holding the sign was weirder. And then being alone—the first time, I don't think anyone even came up to me for the first, like, twenty-five minutes. So it just felt a little bit degrading." But then people came, and they started to talk, and Bree found she liked it. She realized she had "never had a time in my life" when she wasn't busy, or talking, or on her phone. "I found it kind of peaceful," she says.

The more she did it, the stronger the effect it had on her. "I mean, this might've been just for me," Bree says, "but I came back, and every time, I was like, 'I have faith in humanity now.' If I was not having a great day, it made me feel a lot better. I don't know if that had to do with existing in this space or, like, maybe it was just also an opportunity to interact with random people that you don't normally. Like sometimes if you're, like, in an elevator with someone, you'll have a small conversation—it's weirdly satisfying when you're doing something or waiting for something, and someone actually starts up a conversation with you. Like, who does that anymore?" She told the researchers that she considers herself a good listener, generally, but she's an outlier among her peers in that regard. "I have friends that don't even like listening in general," she says, especially if someone has something heavy to share. "I have friends that are like, 'Oh, it just makes me uncomfortable. I just avoid it at all costs.' And I was like, *'How do you connect with other people?'* "

Even introverted students reported that they found it easy to do free listening once they got past the initial anxiety. Several who had been afraid they'd have nothing to talk about with strangers were taken aback by how, by relinquishing control, the conversations just happened organically, and often went deep quickly. Some said it made them more connected and empathetic, and countered stereotypes they'd held about other people. One student said he used to walk into a lecture hall and think, *There are people here,* but now he walks in and says, "There are *people* here." One student reported that by listening, "I feel like I learned how to have a conversation."

Back in L.A., Ben Mathes and I finish breakfast and walk out to find a suitable street corner to free listen—a prospect that, if I'm being honest, I am not particularly relishing. I ask questions and listen for a living, of course, but usually shielded in the identity of a journalist, working within rules and parameters set by the process of interviewing someone. I'm not just some guy holding a cardboard sign in the street. I'm also highly susceptible to embarrassment, I should add. I cannot overstate this. Not that I have to, because when I do get embarrassed my ordinarily bone-white face turns a deep and mortifying red. But in order to free listen effectively, you have to strangle that part of yourself. It's not about you. It's about being open and welcoming. The thinking goes that if you're open, people will sense it, and they'll be drawn to you.

"So what's the opener here?" I ask Mathes, as we take our position on the street corner. "If someone walks over and says, 'What is this bullshit?,' what do you say?"

"A lot of people will say, 'Why are you doing this?' " he says. "And we say, 'We're doing it for you.' And that's usually enough to blow their minds, in a real way. Or they'll just start weeping right there. I've had that before. Some people just cannot get their mind around

the idea that somebody would be doing something with no expectation of return. And I love that. It's my favorite thing ever." He nods
to a sports car pulling over in front of us. The youngish guy inside is
craning his neck to see what the sign says. Then he's getting out of
the car and walking over.

"Here we go," Mathes says.

"What are you guys doing?" the guy says. "What is this? I've
driven past, like, three times and I had to ask."

"We're here to listen," Mathes says.

The guy can't believe it. He's delighted. He tells us he recently got
sober, and what we're doing reminded him of Alcoholics Anonymous, the chance to speak freely to a sympathetic audience. He says
AA helped him far more than doctors or therapists. He says he's late
for something but he wanted to check us out. But then he lingers. He
just keeps talking. We hear about the drinking and some related job
difficulties, how he and his wife struggled for years to conceive and
were finally successful, but then two more kids came right on the
heels of the first one, and now he's worried three may be too many
kids. He laughs. He talks for a while longer, then gives Ben his card
and says he might want to go out and do this, too. He seems ener-
gized by it. He thanks us and goes.

A woman comes by and asks if we're social workers. She says we
should look into volunteering for the city. They have people who do
this, she's done it herself, she says, and it's vital because "people can
commit suicide when they feel like they have no one to talk to."

A guy in a '62 Cadillac convertible rolls up to a red light shortly
after, scrutinizes us, and yells out the window, "I want to talk about
my transmission!"

Finally, toward the end of our session, a tall older guy walks up
and asks us if we think God has a name. I bite. This leads to a long
speech about the Jehovah's Witnesses. Ordinarily this would be my
cue to find somewhere else to be, but I hang in and ask some clarifying questions. The man says he was born Catholic, but he recently
studied with the Witnesses and it's cast everything into an apocalyp-
tic peace and clarity for him. He's retired, he says. But he doesn't
want to talk about work. He wants to tell us about Jehovah.

He talks and talks, and as I listen, I begin to wonder about the source of his zeal. I ask if he's married, and he tells us he was, but his wife died a few months earlier. He chokes up at the memory, and tells us he was lost until he found the Witnesses a month ago. He says he takes great comfort in knowing the world is going to end soon, and he's amazed that no one else around sees it like he sees it. He says when resurrection comes, the Bible says the first shall be last and the last shall be first. That means Abel, slain by his brother Cain in the Bible's first killing, will be last to be raised; but more important, the man tells us, it means he will be raised before his wife, which is good, he says, because he needs to catch her up. He needs to tell her what she missed. "There's so much," he says, through tears.

He thanks us repeatedly, shakes our hands, and goes. Mathes looks at me like, *See?* And he's right about one thing. Once you get past the awkwardness, it's remarkably easy. Yes, it's hard to keep your mouth shut, to not jump in, particularly at a time when we're all conditioned to jump all over anyone we disagree with on pressing matters ranging from nuclear diplomacy to avocado toast. But when you show that openness, people just come to you. You ask them open-ended questions, and they talk, and you listen, and they talk more. And it was actually freeing, not having to worry about having something smart or funny to say. I came away pleasantly spent, but feeling a kind of high. A strange feeling of grace, which of course is a state of giving more than you receive.

I ask Mathes how the experience has changed him, how it's affected his perspective on the world. "I mean, you do this long enough, really, you can't stand on the street without coming to tears at some point," he says. "Watching everybody, everyone is really so sweet. They're really wonderful. *Really.* I think that was a shift in my perspective. It's overwhelming. Listening, by nature, takes us to sensitive subjects. That'll heal you. It healed me, I think."

Afterward, I wondered if the buzz we got from this—from having an intimate conversation while looking each other in the eye—had something to do with our scary little buddy, oxytocin—the bonding molecule. Could talking to a stranger trigger the release of oxytocin? I asked Larry Young, who directs an oxytocin research laboratory at

Emory University. He told me he believes it's possible, especially if there is real eye contact. "One of the purposes of looking into the eyes of another is to make them feel a positive connection with you," he says. "And if you're good at that, then you're probably causing oxytocin release in others, and that would make them feel more likely that you are part of their group." Touch can have the same effect, he says, as long as it's appropriate to the situation and not creepy or assaultive, not that I was touching anyone.

But can just *talking* trigger the release of oxytocin? "I think if they're talking about something that really makes them feel like they have a sense of connection with each other, that they're in the same group, I would hypothesize yes," Young says. I ask him if the weird sense of relief I feel after a positive interaction with a stranger might be associated with oxytocin. He says that it could be, because oxytocin is anxiolytic, meaning it reduces anxiety. "Oxytocin does induce a sense of calmness and relaxation," he says. "When you see a mother nursing, she has a sense of calmness about her. And that is from oxytocin."

There's a peculiar thing that happens after you do free listening. First, you do actually feel better. At least I did. Certainly I felt relieved, because the experiment worked. But I also felt lighter, and like the students in the free listening study, I felt a bit calmer, more present, more open, and, yes, a little better about the world. It felt like a slight chemical high, and maybe it was: oxytocin doing its work.

But I also felt like something else was happening. People who study listening often use words like "availability," "openness," and "holding space" to describe what they do. When people do free listening, they are stationary, and total strangers approach them with trepidation and are welcomed, and after a brief period of awkwardness and uncertainty, their defensiveness eases. They become comfortable, and they begin to talk, and in so doing they lighten their burdens and give the listeners a glimpse of lives beyond their own horizons, and news of other worlds. Remember what the scholar Nikki Truscelli said: "Once you start doing it, I almost feel like

there's like this natural sense that this is what we're supposed to do."
Maybe we are. Maybe it feels as good as it does because we are satisfying something fundamental, something in our blood, burning in our
skin, something stamped indelibly upon our natures, which has been
so long neglected. Maybe we're practicing hospitality.

A Quaker theologian by the name of Parker Palmer defines hospitality as "inviting the stranger into our private space, whether that be
the space of our own home or the space of our personal awareness
and concern. And when we do so," he continues, "some important
transformations occur. Our private space is suddenly enlarged; no
longer tight and cramped and restricted, but open and expansive and
free." That certainly applies to free listening. We had exchanged
things, these people and me. Maybe that made us related, and maybe
that's why I felt more connected to the world. I don't know what it
was. But I do know that for a couple of days after I stood out there
with that sign in Los Angeles, people would just start talking to me.
On the street, in stores, on the subway. It was the strangest thing.
Over breakfast Mathes had predicted this would happen: "You're
flexing that openness," he said. "And then you can't go anywhere
because people talk to you."

After our session, I hail a Lyft to get across town to see a friend.
The driver starts right in. He tells me I'd better buckle up because this
is his first day and he doesn't know what he's doing. "Really?" I say.
And he starts laughing. "Are you kidding? Do I look like a rookie?
This is Hollywood! And I know it like the back of my hand!" He's
stout, maybe late fifties, not from here. I decide to try free listening
on him, honoring the 80/20 rule, asking open-ended questions. Sure
enough, in minutes he's unfurling a tale of woe stretched across two
countries. He was successful in his home country, he says. He had his
own business, and he was giving his family the life he always wanted
for himself as a kid growing up in poverty. Then his fortunes turned.
The business started to falter.

At first he tried to hide it. Partly because he was embarrassed, and
partly because he was afraid his family wouldn't understand having
to pare back on all the niceties he'd provided them. He thought they'd
be ashamed of him. He started lying to his wife when she'd begun to

sniff out that something was off. The bleeding continued and the business finally came crashing down. It took with it nearly everything he had. His marriage barely survived the fallout. He was so ashamed of himself, he says.

These days, though, he's feeling better. He's driving to scrape up some money to start a new business. His kids are smart and healthy. He feels good. He thinks things are just about to turn around for him, and he says he'll be ready for it this time. He sees life more clearly now, he tells me. He says calamity revealed it to him. He says Steve Jobs had all the money and adoration in the world, but he's willing to bet that Steve Jobs would have traded it all for just one more day on this earth with his family, outside in the California sunshine.

Chapter 10

The God of Strangers

In which we learn of an era characterized by fear, plague, chaos, and hatred—that isn't actually our own—where we expanded our groups to unprecedented dimensions and developed a faith in strangers that covered half of the world.

Ben Mathes is a man of faith—in a lot of ways, really—and when he created Urban Confessional, he was inspired by a prayer, a simple act of communion between himself and a struggling man. They were strangers to one another, divided by status and circumstance and a thousand other factors, but for a moment they became honorary kin, guest and host, sharing something profound: their humanity, their sorrows. Out of that moment came an organization that has helped a lot of people by, in effect, lowering barriers between them, by creating a new *us,* if only for an instant. In that sense, free listening is akin to religion. And the story of religion is the story of strangers.

Abraham was a stranger. In the book of Genesis, God told the spritely seventy-five-year-old to "Get thee out of thy country, and from thy kindred, and from thy father's house, unto a land that I will shew thee." Abraham left his hometown, the Sumerian city of Ur, and embarked on 115 years of strangerhood, in the process laying the

foundation for what would come to be known as the three Abrahamic religions: Judaism, Christianity, and Islam.

He lived in Hebron for some time—in the present-day West Bank—
but he was a resident alien there. When his wife Sarah died young, at
127, Abraham couldn't buy a burial plot. He had to appeal to his social betters, "the people of the land," to authorize the purchase.
Standing before them, he opened with a simple statement: "I am a
stranger and a sojourner with you." Throughout the Bible, we hear
that again and again. "And the land is not to be sold in perpetuity, for
all land is Mine, because you are strangers and sojourners before
me," God tells the Israelites. "For we are strangers before you, and
sojourners like all our forefathers," the Israelites tell God. "Hear my
prayer, O Lord . . . for I am a stranger with thee, and a sojourner, as
all my fathers were," King David tells God. But Abraham got there
first, and when he delivered the line, it worked. They granted him
the right to buy the plot. He buried Sarah there, and then he was
buried there, and people have been fighting over Hebron ever since.

The secular knock against religions, especially against big, monotheistic ones, is that they are divisive. That they take the inborn
human capacity to dehumanize members of other groups and super-
charge it with the belief that one is acting on express orders of the
divine. This is an especially popular argument among godless savages
in major cities—a subset of the population that includes yours truly.
And there is of course a good deal of historical evidence to support
it, both in the scriptures and in the world. I am not a man of faith,
and this is the reason why.

Nevertheless, I've come to think about mass religions differently.
Taken together, I see them as an extraordinary human achievement.
An unprecedented leap in our capacity to increase the *us* to include
millions of strangers. And I find a lot of wisdom in the texts that can
show us the value of strangers, and help us learn to live together with
greater numbers of different people.

After all, people didn't need religion to justify carnage. Remember, archaeologists have uncovered evidence of mass murder dating
back to ten thousand years ago, six thousand years before the emer-
gence of the Abrahamic religions. Douglas Fry, the anthropologist

who studied violence in hunter-gatherer societies, noted that this sort of wholesale carnage emerged after the advent of agriculture, when people settled down and societies became more populous and more complex, more hierarchical, and less egalitarian. In other words: when people had status, and stuff to protect, and land to defend. Humanity was not waiting for a banner emblazoned with a cross or a crescent to license mayhem. Mayhem not only preceded the monotheistic religions; mayhem brought them into being. Mayhem was the reason they were invented.

As humanity drew closer to the Common Era—c.e., formerly known as a.d. for *anno Domini, the year of the Lord*—empires rose and crumbled before anyone reverently uttered the names Jesus or Muhammad. In the twelfth century b.c., the Greek, Hittite, and Egyptian empires all collapsed. Historians once believed that pillaging "sea peoples" did it—sailors from Crete and Anatolia who arrived from the Mediterranean and rampaged across the Levant, sacking villages and towns. Modern historians aren't so sure. "The sea peoples may have been a symptom of the catastrophe rather than its cause," writes the religious historian Karen Armstrong. "Climactic or environmental change may have led to extensive drought and famine that wrecked the local economies, which lacked the flexibility to respond creatively to the disruption."

Whatever the cause, the aftermath was pure chaos: violence, social instability, mass migration, privation, alienation, inequality, and human suffering on an immense scale. Life had become intolerable, populations were migrating and mixing and clashing, and these humans needed to find a new way to be, to bind people together, to help deal with the pain of being alive. And for many, this way came in the form of religion.

Believers grasp the power of religion intuitively. In its simplest sense mass religion offers consolation and belonging; it marshals order out of chaos and tempers our fear of the unknown—be it strangers, death, God, fate—with ritual, service, and community. But even scientists have underscored the social importance of religion. The anthropologist Joe Henrich, whose work has turned up a few times in this book, described it as "a technology for scaling up human societies." It was a way to get ever greater numbers of people to accept strangers as honorary kin and cooperate. We know by now that humans have long been able to transform strangers into honorary kin with language, or through culture or ritual, and work with them, sacrifice for them, and care about them as though they were family. Religions—especially Western ones—accomplished that on an immense scale, and they did so by addressing many of the things that kept people apart: tribalism, diversity, density, and disease—all the vexations that came with a life lived among an ever-shifting multitude of strangers.

In fact, researchers have found a connection between the size of a population in a society and the types of religious belief that developed from it. A 2019 global survey led by Oxford's Harvey Whitehouse analyzed data for 414 societies over the past ten thousand years. They found that once societies hit about a million people, moralizing gods appeared. That could be the Christian God, for instance, or something like karma: a force that watches over people, rewards good deeds, and punishes antisocial ones.

On one level, such a force functioned as a kind of celestial surveillance system for societies that had gotten so big that it was no longer possible to keep tabs on everyone. On a deeper level, though, the rise of major religions helped alleviate a novel kind of social strain. The authors of the study believed that these creeds helped sustain empires that consisted of members of many different ethnicities—people who otherwise might have been at constant war with one another—by creating a new mode of belonging that cut across tribal boundaries. They made a bigger tent that could accommodate different social, cultural, ethnic, and racial groups, and scale up trust in strangers without requiring people to spend time getting to know them. Religion provided a way to live surrounded by people you don't know without feeling alone.

This is its genius. "Religions seem to know a great deal about our loneliness," argues English philosopher Alain de Botton. "Even if we believe very little of what they tell us about the afterlife or the supernatural origins of their doctrines, we can nevertheless admire their understanding of what separates us from strangers and their attempts to melt away one or two of the prejudices that normally prevent us from building connections with others." De Botton cites the Catholic Mass as a template for bridging differences and crossing boundaries. "Those in attendance tend not to be uniformly of the same age, race, profession or educational or income level," he writes. "They are a random sampling of souls united only by their shared commitment to certain values. The Mass actively breaks down the economic and status subgroups within which we normally operate, casting us into a wider sea of humanity."

In this chapter, I'm going to focus on Western religions. No question there is plenty in the Eastern traditions about living with strangers. Versions of loving-kindness meditation—which requires the meditator to send out good wishes to family, friends, and strangers alike—appear in Confucianism and Buddhism. Confucius had a number of teachings that touch upon our project here: Among them, "Don't worry that other people don't know you; worry that you don't know other people," and "Ideal people are universal and not clannish. Small-minded people are clannish and not universal." Hinduism and Buddhism both teach that there are no real strangers, that every individual is an indispensable part of a whole, that we are nothing without each other. For early followers of Buddha in particular, this was a radical idea in a time governed by a caste system.

But I want to focus on the Western faiths here, because their origins reflect our own historical moment. Arvind Sharma, a professor of comparative religion at McGill University, breaks down the difference between Western and Eastern religions this way: "The religious communities constituted by Western religions are typically constituted by culturally different groups of people, who may be considered the same because they subscribe to the same creed. The religious communities of the Eastern traditions typically consist of constituencies of culturally similar people, who are prepared to let others adhere to different creeds." The Western religions, in other words, were formed by heterogeneous people—strangers—living in a time of crisis, not unlike our own.

I am well aware of their abuses, as I said. I grew up Catholic in Boston. While I saw the good of it—the community, the charity— my local archdiocese is now most famous for operating like a criminal organization. But the founding stories of Western religions can get us closer to understanding why we should, and how we can, live among strangers. To begin, let's visit that whirlwind of flood, blood, and pox, of hungry whales and talking foliage, that braying and galloping horror that so scarred me as a boy: the Old Testament.

When I told a friend I was rereading the Old Testament for what it says about strangers, she replied, "Let me guess: It says 'Kill and eat all of them.'" And yes, there is indeed a great deal of stranger killing (though mercifully little stranger eating). This was a reflection of the times in which the Bible was written. It was "wartime literature," writes the Catholic scholar James Carroll. "The violence of the Bible . . . came from the world the people who wrote it lived in. Sheer violence was their one absolute."

Hidden within these stories of wrath and conquest, of cities leveled and multitudes consigned to earth and sky by spear and fire, however, there is, surprisingly, a tender place reserved for strangers in the Old Testament. Some of them, anyway. These strangers are catalysts for action and agents of influence, and without them the story of the Bible simply does not happen.

Let's go back to Abraham. In Genesis, Abraham offers hospitality— there it is again—to three strangers. They turn out to be angels speaking for God. One promises that Sarah, then ninety, will have a child. That would be Isaac, one of the patriarchs of Israel. The other two angels notify Abraham of the impending destruction of the wicked city of Sodom. Abraham urges them to spare his nephew Lot and his family, the lone righteous outliers in Sodom. The angels agree, and head to Sodom to warn Lot, posing again as strangers in need of hospitality. Lot hosts them generously, but the mere presence of the angels drives the Sodomites into a frenzy. A mob of men demand Lot turn them over. Depending on the interpretation, the cardinal sin of

the Sodomites is either sexual deviance (they want to rape the angels), or a failure of hospitality (they want to rape the angels), but in
either case, their antics seal their fate: Sodom is leveled.* Later, in the
New Testament, when Christ warns his followers "be not forgetful
to entertain strangers, for thereby some have entertained angels un-
awares," you can almost smell the smoke and putrescence arising
from the ruin of Sodom.

In the book of Exodus, we find the Israelites enslaved in Egypt.
There, another prophet, Moses, sees a stranger mistreating a fellow
Israelite and kills him. Fearing for his life, Moses flees, and, wandering in the land of Midian, he comes upon seven sisters being harassed
by shepherds, and he protects them. The girls go home and tell their
father, Jethro, a Midianite priest, who insists they find Moses and
bring him home for dinner. It doesn't matter that Moses is a stranger,
an Israelite. They ask Moses, and he agrees to come. He stays. He
marries one of Jethro's daughters, Zipporah. They have a son.

Looking back over his life since the killing, Moses reflects, "I have
been a stranger in a strange land." Thus, he names their son Gershom,
meaning "stranger in a strange land." Jethro, however, though a cultural stranger, proves pivotal in the story of the Jews, because he acts
as a wise adviser to Moses, helping him succeed in his mission to lead
the Israelites out of slavery. Scholar Christiana van Houten argues
that Jethro epitomizes "a certain type of Biblical stranger, in which
the *them* isn't the opposite of *us,* but instead the complement of *us.*"
He's the stranger who helps us, makes us better. Without these strangers the exodus never happens, and the Israelites never escape bondage
in Egypt, and the whole story pretty much ends there.

Of course, the Old Testament is brutal on the many non-Israelite
strangers its heroes encounter on their march to the Promised Land.

---

* It's worth noting here that Lot responds by offering his two virginal daughters to the
ravening mob, which is seen as the "righteous" move. Later, after Lot's wife is turned into a
pillar of salt, the daughters, holed up in a cave above the wreckage of Sodom with their old
man, get him blind drunk and have sex with him to get pregnant. They are successful, and
the town of Moab, Utah, is named for one of their offspring, a fact that should probably be
brought to the attention of the local tourism authority.

These strangers are defined solely by their membership in their re-spective groups. They are endowed with no trace of humanity. In the book of Joshua, a grisly, genocidal affair, the Israelites, now led by Moses's successor Joshua, cross the River Jordan and enter Canaan with the intention of exterminating the people of the seven nations therein. They are acting on God's orders, who, in the book of Deu-teronomy, told them to "Cast out the many nations before thee. . . . Smite them and utterly destroy them; thou shalt make no covenant with them, nor shew mercy unto them. . . . The Lord thy God shall deliver them unto thee, and shall destroy them with a mighty de-struction, until they be destroyed."

Several of these nations are indeed destroyed with the very might-iest of destructions, the campaign playing out as a numbing litany of violent death, void of sympathy: Joshua took Makkedah and killed its king and people. Joshua took Libnah and killed its king and peo-ple. Joshua took Lachish and killed its people. Joshua killed Horam, king of Gezer, and killed his people. Joshua burnt Ai and made it a heap forever. "And the king of Ai he hanged on a tree until eventide: and as soon as the sun was down, Joshua commanded that they should take his carcase down from the tree, and cast it at the entering of the gate of the city." One could be forgiven for seeing in Joshua a clear template for the thousands of years of religious violence to follow. Swaths of this book read like something found in the notebook of an emotionally disturbed teenage boy. Theologian L. Daniel Hawk wrote of it: "For many readers in an age haunted by violence—often sponsored, sanctioned, and sanctified by religious ideologies—this is an ugly, repugnant story that scarcely deserves retelling."

And yet, it does deserve retelling. Because even amid the carnage, strangers play a key role. When we read about the strangers in the various Canaanite cities as a bloc, they are smashed and killed with-out compunction. But when we actually meet them, as individuals, the tone of Joshua shifts. The characterization becomes more com-plex. The strangers become people. They play against type, they sur-prise the Israelites, they even help them. Yes, the Old Testament revels in the slaughter of strangers, but it also tells a story of a move-ment that simply would not have happened without strangers. It has our human ambivalence toward strangers—our fear of them and our need for them—splashed across every page.

Take Rahab. When Joshua sends his spies to Jericho to case the city prior to the Israelite invasion, they wind up in the house of Rahab, a prostitute. As luck would have it, Rahab's house is attached to the exterior of the famous wall of Jericho. That she is both a prostitute and a Canaanite are two strikes against her. And yet Rahab ends up being unflappable, loyal, and quick on her feet. Word gets out that spies are in the vicinity, and the king of Jericho demands Rahab turn them over. She tricks the king's men, hides the spies, and provides them with valuable intelligence: that the locals are terrified and will present no meaningful opposition. Armed with this information, the spies leave, the Israelite army advances, and, circling the city seven times with the Ark of the Covenant, sounds its trumpets, levels the walls, and kills all the inhabitants, save for Rahab and her family. The scholar Adriane Leveen sums up the irony of this: "The first encounter between the Israelites and a stranger in the book of Joshua is one highly favorable to a harlot who becomes nothing less than a savior to the people of Israel. . . . Rahab, not the Israelites, sets in motion the implementation of God's plans."

There are more stories like this—in which a stranger or strangers are met, engaged, recognized as fully human, and thus spared a grisly end. L. Daniel Hawk sums up the dynamic nicely: "As long as the people of the land remain faceless, they may be killed with little remorse," he writes, "[but] recognizing the humanity of others makes killing a far more unsettling enterprise."

Another unexpected feature of the Hebrew Bible—especially to those of us who recall it as a fervid, xenophobic bloodbath—is the presence of the *ger*. The *ger*, generally referred to as "stranger" in English translations of the Bible, is a non-Israelite living among Israelites, a resident alien. He is different from a foreigner, who was a pure outsider. In the Hebrew Bible, the *ger* is accorded far better treatment than the masses of faceless strangers that Joshua's army puts to the sword. These strangers are granted many of the rights of Israelites, as long as they uphold local rules—no incest, no blasphemy, no worshipping strange gods—and they follow the purity laws that apply to all Israelites, like washing up properly after handling dead animals or humans, and not partaking of blood.

In return for following the local statutes, the *ger* is accorded many of the same rights as an Israelite. The *ger* has access to the justice system; the *ger* gets to rest on the Sabbath, can make offerings to God, and can celebrate Passover, if circumcised; a *ger* can be bought as a slave by an Israelite, but an affluent *ger* can also buy an Israelite as a slave. As God said to Moses in the book of Leviticus, "Ye shall have one manner of law, as well for the stranger, as for one of your own country: for I am the Lord your God."

There are also some *ger*-only privileges, which are more of a mixed bag. Israelites cannot charge one another interest on a loan, for instance, but can to the *ger;* If a farmer is harvesting his crop and drops some food on the ground, he must leave it for the *ger* to eat; same with grapes in a vineyard—though he can sell either to a foreigner. If an Israelite finds meat from an animal that died on its own, he or she can't eat it; instead, "thou shalt give it unto the stranger that is in thy gates, that he may eat it; or thou mayest sell it unto a foreigner."* These laws serve to emphasize a boundary between Israelite and *ger*. Israelite will remain Israelite, with all the rights and privileges that implies, and *ger* will remain *ger,* with access to the justice system, reasonably warm relations with the majority, and all the free roadkill they can stomach.

So how is this not a form of apartheid? How is a situation in which a majority imposes permanent second-class citizenship upon a vulnerable minority a leap forward? Three reasons. One, this sort of arrangement was virtually unheard of in its time. While laws governing special treatment for orphans and widows appear in Mesopotamia— perhaps most notably in the law code of the great Babylonian king Hammurabi—scholars have found little to suggest that care for alien strangers specifically, like the *ger,* was mandated in the law. That doesn't mean it was just open season on these people before—it might have been, though the tradition of hospitality was well established by

* LOL.

then, as we know. It just means that the moral concern for these strangers didn't necessarily merit being enshrined in written law. The *ger,* and the legal status conferred upon them, was new. And in that sense, it was progress.

Second, the significance of the *ger* is also rooted in empathy and personal experience. Unlike regard for orphans and widows, which a person can muster without necessarily having been an orphan or a widow, some scholars believe that the Old Testament placed such an emphasis on treating strangers and sojourners well because the Israelites knew what it was like to be a stranger. It's a point God makes repeatedly in the book: "Thou shalt neither vex a stranger, nor oppress him; for ye were strangers in the land of Egypt," he says in Exodus 22—adding just one chapter later, "Also, thou shalt not oppress a stranger: for ye know the heart of a stranger, seeing ye were strangers in the heart of Egypt." The Israelites knew what it was to be a stranger—they had been enslaved far from home, they had suffered and starved and wandered the wilderness, and, theoretically, that endowed them with a capacity to be empathetic to the plight of other strangers. The *ger* represented an expansion of a believer's circle of moral concern beyond the limits of tribalism. It encoded in law protection for people who are not *us*. In humanity's time among strangers, this was an achievement. One that could be built upon.

Then came Jesus Christ. The world he was born into was also a mess. Especially the cities. "The cities of the empire were incredibly disorganized," writes sociologist and religious historian Rodney Stark. And the density of human life in those cities was inconceivable to modern sensibilities. One city, Antioch, had a density of 117 people per acre. That's 8.5 more people per acre than Manhattan had in 2010. But Manhattan is a vertical city. In Antioch, few buildings were taller than five stories. Antioch was a pit of suffering. Construction was shoddy. Tenements were crammed with people. Building collapses were frequent. There were catastrophic fires, often caused by indoor cooking stoves. There were earthquakes and rampant homelessness and poverty. Whatever sewers the city did have were open, and soap had yet to be invented. As Rodney Stark notes, these urbanites must have "lived in filth beyond our imagining."

And there were strangers. Because the Roman Empire was united by long-distance trade and imperial activity, Romans were able to travel to a degree the world had never before seen, and they moved and they mixed. We talk about diversity today as though it's unprecedented. It is not. The Roman world "was a proper melting pot," wrote historian Ramsay MacMullen. "If we imagined the British empire of a hundred years ago all in one piece, all of its parts touching each other so one could travel . . . from Rangoon to Belfast without the interposition of any ocean, and if we could thus sense as one whole an almost limitless diversity of tongues, cults, traditions, and levels of education, then the true nature of the Mediterranean world in [the era] would strike our minds."

This influx of peoples was good for cities. Partly because it allowed a vibrant traffic in goods and ideas, but also, on a darker note, because the death rate was so high and they needed to maintain population levels. "Greco-Roman cities required a constant and substantial stream of newcomers simply to maintain their populations" at the start of the Christian era, writes Stark. "As a result, at any given moment a very considerable proportion of the population consisted of *recent* newcomers—Greco-Roman cities were peopled by strangers." Living in such conditions triggered these strangers' instinct to close ranks, and cities fractured into ethnic enclaves that openly fought and frequently rioted. It was hell, and death was all around, and it made denizens wonder if they were witnessing the apocalypse.

Jesus came out of Galilee—a motley, rowdy place in its own right, largely out of the reach of Jerusalem, with a mix of Jews, Samaritans, Greeks, and Syrians living shoulder to shoulder with one another. It was the last place the elites would expect the Son of God to come from. Sort of like the messiah coming from New Jersey. Jesus arrived in Jerusalem and started preaching a radical gospel that addressed three things: Life is terrible, God is the answer, and people need a way to live in a world populated with strangers and riven by tribal conflict. This meant loving your neighbor—an idea based on Jewish law, but expanded to include everyone—not just resident aliens like the *ger*. He appreciated that this is hard. "If you save your greetings for your brothers," Jesus says, "are you doing anything exceptional?" No. Caring for your family, your tribe, your neighbors—that's fairly easy. But caring for strangers, sinners, and outcasts: That takes work.

You recall how Zeus often posed as a stranger to ensure people were behaving themselves and being hospitable. Jesus adopted that mantle, telling his followers that whatever they did to the lowest among them, they did *directly* to him. "I was hungry and you gave me food, I was thirsty and you gave me drink, I was a stranger and you welcomed me, I was naked and you clothed me, I was sick and you visited me, I was in prison and you came to me," he said. "Truly, I say to you, as you did it to one of the least of these my brethren, you did it to me."

Most famously, Jesus told a story about a Samaritan—a member of a group the Jews hated—helping a Jew. The inversion is a genius stroke, and shows a keen understanding of psychology. Believing that *my* group is decent enough to help an outsider is easy. It's in-group favoritism. We're the good ones. We're moral. But forcing people to reckon with the possibility that their enemies could behave morally and help them in a time of need is a demand to appreciate and honor the complexity of strangers. Remember what we said about dehumanization: We have a tendency to underestimate strangers, to blind ourselves to their richness, their inner lives, and we have a capacity to do terrible things to them when the situation calls, to harry them and slaughter them without a thought of their humanity. Much of what Christ taught is a hedge against that. Not only were the strangers not subhuman; they were actually stand-ins for Jesus. And thus, like Zeus, they carried the power to punish and reward.

It was more than just words. After Christ's death, the success of the church was built on ministering to strangers. Early Christians created "a miniature welfare state in an empire which for the most part lacked social services," the historian Paul Johnson writes. In 362, the emperor Julian wrote a letter complaining about how the Christians were making Rome look bad with "their benevolence toward strangers." In another letter he wrote, "The impious Galileans support not only their poor, but ours as well, everybody can see they lack aid from us." Julian would be Rome's last pagan emperor before the empire converted to Christianity in 380.

In many ways, Christ's teachings were a solution to the problems of the city. "To cities filled with the homeless and impoverished, Christianity offered charity as well as hope. To cities filled with newcomers and strangers, Christianity offered an immediate basis for attachments," writes Rodney Stark. "To cities torn by violent ethnic strife, Christianity offered a new basis for social solidarity. And to cities faced with epidemics, fires and earthquakes, Christianity offered effective nursing services."

The Jews of the Old Testament were strangers and sojourners, enslaved in a foreign land and made to wander the wilderness for decades, rootless. The people in the time of Jesus were strangers and sojourners, always moving, mixing, struggling in a cruel, capricious world that had ceased to make sense. Jesus was a stranger, an immigrant, an outsider. But that mutual recognition, that we're all strangers, that we're all adrift and afraid, created a new form of social solidarity. A newer, more expansive *us*. And that made it possible—and still makes it possible—for Christians to comfortably have meaningful contact with those who otherwise might have been permanent strangers. "They can become a pilgrim people, finding new companions in their life-journey from every race and nation and from every social stratum," writes Thomas Ogletree, the former dean of Yale Divinity School. "Since all are strangers, no one is a stranger anymore." What resulted from that was the biggest single community of strangers yet devised. That is still true today, when 2.3 billion humans identify as Christians, a third of the planet.

Islam, too, is a religion of strangers. It draws much of its DNA from the story of Abraham, who Muslims consider the first Muslim. In the Old Testament, before the birth of Isaac, Abraham's wife Sarah is unable to procreate. She offers Abraham her servant Hagar as a surrogate. Abraham takes her up on the offer, and Ishmael is conceived.

This is where the traditions begin to diverge. When Abraham and Sarah have a child of their own, Isaac, Sarah becomes convinced that Ishmael is a bad influence, and banishes Hagar and Ishmael into the desert. When food and water run short, Hagar panics and beseeches God for help. God tells her to lift the baby up. She does, and water springs forth from the earth, forming a stream called Zamzam. Birds, detecting water, begin to circle overhead. Bands of strangers see the birds and approach, asking for water. Hagar trades it for food and supplies. According to the Islamic tradition, out of that exchange rises the city of Mecca (a city that was, incidentally, developed into a major trading port by a descendent of Ishmael, Zayd ibn Kilab, nicknamed Qusayy, or Little Stranger).

By the time a successful trader named Muhammad came to prominence in the seventh century C.E., Mecca had hit a slump. Coastal trade routes were stealing its business, and old tribal hatreds flared anew as the broader world was torn by competition between the Roman and Persian empires. After being visited by Allah, who told him to unite everyone under one god, Muhammad set out to do so. He accused the Meccans of being selfish idolators, indifferent to one another as well as orphans and the poor; he accused the elite of being greedy. Naturally, this did not go over well. The Meccan elite turned on him and tormented his followers so grotesquely that even otherwise unsympathetic locals were sickened by the cruelty on display in the streets of Mecca. Muhammad fled to Medina in 622.

There, preaching his gospel, he united the tribes under Islam. But he also took pains to ensure that the locals didn't close ranks against the largely destitute refugees who followed him there from Mecca. "In order to integrate immigrants with the local Muslims, the Prophet declared brotherhood between every immigrant and local Muslim, and he asked the local Muslims to help the immigrants," writes scholar Zeki Saritoprak. "This historical brotherhood in Islam is called *mu'kh't*." It comprised two groups: *Muhajirun* (immigrants) and *Ansar* (helpers). That brotherhood was a form of honorary kinship, and it carried real benefits. Ansar provided housing and food, regardless of means. When an Ansar died, his Muhajirun became his heir. This tradition effectively eliminated racial and tribal strife by making *mu'kh't* more important than familial or ethnic bonds. "One can argue that this declaration of brotherhood can be considered one of the most important and exemplary practices of integrating disparate fragments of society in human history," writes Saritoprak.

While Muhammad united Medina, Mecca continued its slide. Hatred of Muhammad and his followers had united the city for a time, but with the Muslims largely gone, all the tribes turned on one another again. One tribe, Banu Bakr, slaughtered the Khuza'a, who were allies of the Muslims. Muhammad fielded an army of ten thousand, a motley assemblage representing the many tribes of Medina, an unprecedented display of unity among strangers. The king of Mecca saw this force and is said to have wondered, "What kind of army is this?" Muhammad entered the city unopposed, and instead of killing everyone, extended amnesty to anyone who surrendered. "Go your way, you are free," he told them.

In Islam, strangers are a dominant theme. Like Judaism and Christianity, the Koran places kindness to strangers just behind worshipping the one god: "Worship Allah . . . and do good to parents, kinsfolk, orphans, al-Masakin (the poor), the neighbor who is near of kin, the neighbor who is a stranger, the companion by your side [and] the wayfarer." More than that, though, to be a stranger in Islam is in fact a mark of distinction, of holiness, as it is in Judaism and Christianity. "Islam began as something strange and will return to something strange just as in the beginning, so glad tidings to the strangers," Muhammad says. He tells them, "Live in this world as though you are a stranger or a wayfarer." In his case, it means continue on your journey, your true home awaits at the end. In Islam, as in Christianity, as in Judaism—these faiths of strangers and sojourners—the fact of estrangement is the commonality, the source of solidarity. It is a community of strangers who, in worshipping one god, manage to transcend tribal divisions and become like family.

Viewed from one perspective, this sense of permanent strangerhood can lead, and has led, down a dark path. Fanatics come to think that since there is great honor in being a stranger, they should remain strangers; that there is no point in mingling with others, with non-Muslims. That they should throw up walls and man the battle-ments, or aggress against infidels. In the first couple of centuries of the religion, the faith of Islam, like Christianity, twinned with the ambitions of empire, propelling a brutal march across the land, con-structing an unbroken empire stretching from Spain to Central Asia.

I'm not going to get into a debate about the supposed true nature of Islam here. As with the darker parts of the Old Testament, I am aware of the passages that both extremists and critics of Islam point to as justifications for violence. And I live in New York City. I see the good routinely, and I live in the indelible shadow of the bad. No, I'm more interested in what Islam says about uniting fractious societies, what it teaches about how to treat strangers. In the Koran, there are two series of verses, one addressed to believers and one addressed to humankind as a whole. The latter begins with the phrase "O man-kind." "O mankind!" one reads, "We have created you from a male and a female, and made you into nations and tribes, that you may know one another."

This may seem, in translation, to be confusing. After all, tribalism is, by popular definition, a disinclination to know one another. But according to Imam Khalid Latif, the first Muslim chaplain at New York University, and a former NYPD and FDNY chaplain, the root of *know* in this verse—pronounced lee ta'aarifoo—isn't like knowing the answer to a trivia question. It means something more like ac-quaintanceship, or experiential knowledge. "Essentially the verse is saying that we created you in this diversity," says Latif. "It is saying that you and I, coming from seemingly different racial backgrounds, were made into these backgrounds so that we wouldn't just have consciousness of the other, or awareness that we both exist, but so that we would perhaps experientially *understand* each other. That we would get to know one another, which fundamentally becomes a component of humanization."

In other words, in this conception, the presence of different peo-ple is not an aberration, not a departure from some kind of Edenic natural order. Diversity is the point. What's more, it's an opportu-nity. An opportunity to know others, in order to serve others, and an opportunity to get to know yourself more in the process, to discover your true convictions in the context of the world, and the lives of strangers. "[It says] that there's a categorical difference when someone has actually spent time with the other, as opposed to just spending time with a stereotype of the other," says Latif. "And that contact is key."

Muhammad made this point in his final sermon. "You know that every Muslim is the brother of another Muslim," he is said to have remarked. But then he continues: "All mankind is from Adam and Eve. An Arab has no superiority over a non-Arab nor a non-Arab has any superiority over an Arab; also a white has no superiority over a Black, nor a Black has any superiority over a white—except by piety and good action." Today 1.8 billion humans on the planet identify as Muslims, a quarter of the population of the planet.

I mention all this for a couple of reasons, and none of them are an effort to convert you. As I have said, I am a godless savage for whom religion has never made much sense. James Joyce described religion as a net, and, like nationality, a thing to be avoided if you ever wanted to meet your full potential, and I'm inclined to agree with him. That said, I certainly don't begrudge anyone their belief, and I know it can be a great comfort for the faithful, and it can lead in the best cases to caring for others, regardless of who they are. Whatever gets you through is fine with me, as long as it isn't used to bludgeon people you disagree with. To draw from the political scientist Robert Putnam's work on social capital: Religion at its best builds bridges; religion at its worst starts wars.

No, I mention this because in spite of it all, I see mass religion as an extraordinary accomplishment, and, more important, a source of hope. Not hope that there is a god who will salve our wounds, reward our goodness, and settle our scores after we shuffle off our mortal coil. No, for me, mass religion is a source of inspiration because in a time of intense strife and division, human beings were able to figure out a way to belong among what is for all intents and purposes an infinite number of strangers. I recognize this is blasphemy, and I apologize—sort of—but to me religion isn't an end. It's not a finished product. It's just another step, another in a line of social renaissances, that shows that we have a remarkable capacity for bonding with an immense number of strangers, and that we can scale faith in the goodness of others to a near-infinite degree based on what in reality are a few small commonalities: following a book, saying a prayer, donning certain garb, and following some basic ethical precepts like not stealing and being kind to strangers. To me, it is progress. If an American Christian can feel immediately comfortable in the company of a Sudanese Christian they have never met before, shouldn't it be possible for any American to feel comfortable in the company of any Sudanese stranger?

The most pressing problems facing the Greco-Roman world at the time of Christ, and the Arab world at the time of Muhammad, were twofold: a crisis of need, and a crisis of belonging in a world populated by strangers. The crisis of need arose partly from the lack of centralized institutions: law enforcement, welfare agencies, medical services, shelters, etc., the absence of which has inspired previous social renaissances. The crisis of belonging was not dissimilar to our present predicament. Society had become strange. Strangers were pouring in, and when strangers pour in, it can cause us to lose our bearings. We define ourselves in the context of our world. When the world changes, it puts our understanding of ourselves under stress and it upsets our relationship with the world we live in. When that happens we have two options: Try to restore the past, which never works, or figure out a new way to belong. Religions taught many humans a new way to belong that transcended their tribes and ethnicities and races. I don't believe religion alone will get us to the finish line. There's too much historic conflict among them. The boundaries have hardened. To get where we need to go, we need a new social renaissance. We need to talk to strangers.

And yet we aren't, and we don't. For all the good that talking to strangers can do—from the personal level to the civilizational—there are just as many forces aligned against our having these simple, powerful interactions. They can be something as insidious as the lesser minds problem, or as dark and complicated as sectarianism and prejudice, or as simple as a poorly designed public space, or the pace of life in a city, or, as we'll see, citizenship in the country of Finland. Whatever the reason, this much is clear: If you and I are going to get good at this business, we need first to get a better handle on what keeps us from doing it at all.

Part II

Why *Don't* We Talk to Strangers?

Chapter 11

Strangers in the City

In which we learn that humans invented cities so they could be around lots of new and different people, but then created a bunch of unwritten rules that kept them from talking to one another, which we must now shatter.

In 2011, a man named Hunter Franks decided to walk across America with a friend. They were both young artists in Los Angeles, and they planned to chronicle their journey for a multimedia project called *talking2strangers*. They made it only to New Mexico, but that's all Franks needed to set a course for the rest of his life. "For me, as I started to see how many different stories, and communities, and types of people were out there," he says, "I started to understand that there was value to getting to hear those stories." The experience changed him, altering his perception of the great formless mass that is *other people*. "I started to understand just how kind people are," he says. "There were people that would give us water and food for no reason, who didn't know who we were. I started to really see the kindness of humans."

In 2012, after studying communications and studio art in college, Franks landed a job as a community manager at the mayor's office in San Francisco, in the office of civic innovation, where he was given the freedom and the funding to launch projects aimed at reweaving the city's frayed social fabric. He glimpsed the potential of public projects that combine art and talking to strangers. He saw these projects as a way to combat loneliness and alienation, partly because he observed the effect these interactions were having on him personally. "I figured if I was feeling lonely at times, then other people were also probably feeling lonely at times," he says. "And what I discovered, when I started to do this, was that everyone needs this, badly." With that, his future came into sharper relief.

Franks became a full-time artist in 2013, launching his own organization, the League of Creative Interventionists. He has since attracted a number of prestigious grants and mounted projects around the country. One is Fear Doctor. Franks sets up a booth on a sidewalk—it looks like Lucy's psychiatrist booth from the *Peanuts* cartoons—and people come over and tell him what they're afraid of. He asks them a few questions, and in the end he gives them a "philosophical prescription," usually involving some kind of small action to take—a few deep breaths, or resolving to be more available for someone, or taking a few minutes to themselves, or just calling their mom. It's a way, he says, "of reminding people: *Hey, it's okay. You're here. Fear is fine. It's perfect that you're feeling these things that you're feeling.*"

As with Urban Confessional, the idea of such an endeavor triggers my native skepticism—my kind is not necessarily prone to immediate and total disclosure to strangers on the street. So I ask Franks how he gets people comfortable enough to tell him things. "I didn't need to, honestly," he says. "I think people are just starving to share what's on their minds—particularly the hard things—because we don't have a lot of avenues to do that. I didn't really have to do much." If someone told him they were afraid of snakes, for instance, he'd ask them some open-ended questions, and maybe they'd reveal there was something deeper going on. Sometimes people will admit that at the bottom of it all, they're scared of being alone.

When Franks was in San Francisco, he worked on a project involving a neighborhood with a bad reputation. He created the Neighborhood Postcard Project, in which he collected positive stories from the neighborhood's residents, written on postcards, and then mailed them to people in different neighborhoods—in effect, introducing them to the richness and complexity of a place they may have written off. The results inspired him. Later, he won a grant from the Knight Foundation, which commissions projects aimed at fostering social cohesion, to do residencies in four cities the foundation works with. One of those cities was Akron, Ohio. Drawing on his success with the postcard project, Franks came up with the idea of a huge communal meal. He went to each neighborhood in Akron to identify ambassadors to help recruit guests. Each was asked to offer a favorite recipe, which would be printed on the plates at the dinner for other guests to take home. He learned about a stretch of freeway that was marked for demolition. That became the setting for a long, curved table for five hundred.

When guests arrived, they were seated with strangers from other parts of town. "You would see the well-off older white guy, who is sitting next to someone who looks like they might have some sort of mental challenges, and a person of color who might be low income," says Franks. "You would never have those people sitting next to each other for that period of time in any other contexts." There were moderators spaced out to facilitate conversations and ask questions about issues facing the individuals and the city at large. That means the guests not only had permission to talk, but they had something to talk about—which solves two of the things that prevent strangers from talking, especially strangers of different groups. Plus, since it was a meal, they couldn't really leave. And the longer they talked, the deeper the conversation went. It was a hit. People loved it.

"We want to connect with each other as humans," Frank says. "We need connection to exist on this earth in a way that feels good to us. But there are so many forces that are stopping us from actually doing that." Over the last five years, Franks has focused on external factors that prevent strangers from talking—like segregation, or norms. But more recently he's started to ponder the internal component of it, too. He wonders if he can find more people like him—who feel the way he does and who derive hope from these sorts of interactions—and if those people can in turn show other people the benefits of a life lived like this, until they achieve a critical mass and change the culture. "How do we get enough people to create enough of a movement to where it's just totally the norm to walk down the street and say hi to everyone?" he asks. "It is about creating a world where curiosity and connection rise above fear and isolation. And I think that begins in small, daily interactions, and hopefully weaves its way into all aspects of culture and society."

But this, suffice to say, is easier said than done.

About twelve thousand years ago, humans put down stakes. They became farmers. No longer did they have to travel and hunt large game to survive. They could grow their own food. They could own land in a way that was impossible before, and they could live on it for generations. For many, gone were the days of wandering. "People spent their entire lives in the company of the same people," writes the UCLA archaeologist Monica Smith. "New faces appeared only at the time of marriage or when itinerant peddlers came with their wares. Familiarity was the constant measure of human relations, and strangers were regarded with wariness and misgiving."

Periodically, however, there were these pilgrimages, Smith writes. Residents of small villages would travel to ritual sites, where they could meet and mingle with people from other villages and tribes, trade goods and techniques, and find mates. These were festivals, basically, gatherings for the pleasure of gathering, with the added bonus of maintaining positive relationships with more distant neighbors. "By bringing people together for a shared purpose, ritual places made it possible for people to develop and practice the skills of communication and interaction that enabled them to deal with so many strangers," writes Smith. Those gatherings, and the skills they allowed people to hone, eventually led to the rise of cities, some six thousand years ago. This is humanity's next big social renaissance.

Cities were the first widespread form of human social organization that didn't arise out of pure necessity. "We had everything we needed for a successful life of small-scale farming that would have allowed for population growth to cover the planet, one little village at a time," Smith writes. "Clearly, that simple and straightforward village life wasn't enough for our urban ancestors. [They] wanted plenty of intangible things that they couldn't get out there in the countryside: the thrill of a crowd, the excitement of new inventions and novel foods, and the tantalizing allure of meeting a romantic partner from beyond the confines of the village."

After many millennia of being careful about dealing with strangers—expressed through greeting rituals, hospitality practices, and occasionally violent death from above—humans were entering a mode of existence that not only included more strangers, but was actually *defined* by the presence of strangers. Strangers—meaning people we don't know, as well as people who are different from who we are—were both the substance of the city and its primary reason for being. "A city is composed of different kinds of men," wrote Aristotle in *Politics*. "Similar people cannot bring a city into existence." This was another radical departure from our chimp ancestors. Human beings were now putting themselves into a situation where they would be hopelessly and permanently outnumbered by strangers— a situation, you'll recall, that chimps simply would not abide.

Naturally, this idea was, and remains, disturbing to some, carrying with it nightmare visions of violence and depravity. In the Old Testament, the first city was founded by the bad seed Cain, who murdered his brother. Rome was founded by Romulus, who also murdered his brother. Critics have often accused the city of unleashing a rot across the human character. The philosopher Jean-Jacques Rousseau idealized the simple genius of small-town folks, and decried urbanites as "big city monkeys." "In a big city, full of scheming, idle people without religion or principle, whose imagination, depraved by sloth, inactivity, the love of pleasure, and great needs, engenders only monsters and inspires only crimes," he wrote.

A whole tradition of sociology was pretty much devoted to pointing out all of the supposed mental disorders cities were said to visit upon those with the misfortune of having to live in them—much of it produced around the start of the twentieth century, all of it uneasy with an ascendant individualism.

The sociologist Émile Durkheim argued in 1897 that being surrounded by so many strangers will scramble our brains and lead to calamity. He believed that because urbanites are forced to adjust to each stranger they encounter at any given point—some might call this "having social skills"—their understanding of themselves would inevitably decay, leading to disorder, despair, and finally suicide. The German sociologist Georg Simmel—who in 1908 wrote a brief but influential essay about strangers, defining them as a combination of physical nearness and social remoteness—conceded that the city can be exciting, but also argued that living in it requires a "thousand individual modifications" to one's personality, and the sheer onslaught of stimulation leaves urbanites "blasé," emotionally numb, "indifferent to all things personal," and able to relate to others only as "numbers" in a math equation.* But this mind-set is understandable, Simmel argued, because if urbanites felt for everyone around them the way small-town people did, "they would fall into an unthinkable mental condition."

In 1938, Louis Wirth echoed Simmel, arguing that while being "a most favorable breeding ground of new biological and cultural hybrids," cities made intimate friendships impossible and led to human relations that are "largely anonymous, superficial [and] transitory." While graciously conceding it was in fact possible for city dwellers to attain friends, those friendships were strictly "regarded as a means for the achievement of our own ends."

Despite the prospect of having one's identity scrambled and capacity for genuine human connection destroyed, when cities were invented six thousand years ago, humans took to them immediately. Certainly, they presented economic opportunities, then as now. But as Monica Smith writes, something else was afoot, too. "It's as though there was a pent-up capacity for all of those things that had somehow been encoded in our collective consciousness, just waiting for an opportunity to burst forth." What was that pent-up capacity? Let's unpack it.

We know that expanding our social networks is in our nature. That's part of the appeal of the city: more people. But there's also

---

* You'll recall from chapter 2 what the psychologist Juliana Schroeder said about people in cities treating one another as objects. Simmel got there a century earlier.

something more personal, more intangible, that might have driven us into the gates of the city—where more than half the world's population now resides. It's a concept in psychology that comes from an influential American psychologist by the name of Arthur Aron: It's called self-expansion.

Aron's idea is that a person does not have a wholly fixed identity or set personality. There are no impassable walls between who I am and who you are. Instead, he believes, "each self is largely a product of multiple relationships throughout the life span." That means that as we grow, and meet more people, and engage in more relationships, we change. Maybe the core of who we are remains stable, but as we move along through our lives, we take a little bit from all the people we've had meaningful interactions with, and that helps us become more complex. Think of a person in terms of rivers. Water is water, but water also takes on the character of the riverbeds that it runs across. In a way, humans are the same.

"To the extent we include another in the self, we take on the resources, perspectives, and identities of that person," Aron wrote in 2013. "The other person then informs who we are, enhances the tools we feel we have at our disposal, [and] shapes how we see the world." Aron calls this process "expansion of the self." It mostly comes from close relationships, but it can be achieved via many sources—acquaintanceships, books, travel, and personal experience, and, Aron tells me, it "should apply to strangers as well." He theorizes that it is one of human beings' strongest drives—meaning we naturally seek out opportunities for expansion.

That drive to expand the self could have been the pent-up capacity for city living that Smith describes. It may have been a force behind honorary kinship and hospitality as well. Perhaps all along, if the circumstances allowed, we've wanted to interact with new people as a means of expanding not just our networks, but ourselves. We just needed ways to feel safe while doing it. And once cities were invented, they delivered those opportunities on an unmatched scale. That's their power. "Cities can be badly run, crime-infested, dirty, decaying," writes the urban sociologist Richard Sennett. "Yet many people think it worth living in even the worst of them. Why? Because cities have the potential to make us more complex human be-ings."

My friend Billy Giraldi captured this nicely in his book *The Hero's Body,* in a passage about leaving his hardscrabble New Jersey home-town: "I left for reasons people have always left small towns: not because I didn't value it, but because I believed my development waited elsewhere." My favorite writer, the Argentine author Jorge Luis Borges, rang this bell, too: "I am not sure that I exist, actually," he once said. "I am all the writers that I have read, all the people that I have met, all the women that I have loved; all the cities I have vis-ited." Perhaps this is the "unthinkable mental condition" Simmel warned us against.

The irony of the city, then, is that it throws us into the company of hundreds of thousands or millions of strangers, and then, subtly or not so subtly, indicates that we're not supposed to talk to them. That's the social norm that Gillian Sandstrom was concerned about, and the effect that Nicholas Epley and Juliana Schroeder observed in their sub-way experiment: members of a hyper-social species, in a tight space, not saying a word because they've come to believe no one wants to talk. How did that happen?

You may have heard of Stanley Milgram. He was the American psychologist who did those infamous experiments in which partici-pants seemingly shocked total strangers to death just because a man in a lab coat told them to. Fortunately, he also conducted a number of other important studies less likely to haunt the nightmares of high school students. These examined how humans live with strangers in an urban setting. Milgram's experiments ranged from sending stu-dents out to ask strangers on the subway for their seats with no justi-fication (the students were mortified to ask; most commuters gave up their seats), to trying to figure out how many people on a sidewalk needed to be looking up before other people stopped and looked up, too (4 percent stopped when one person was looking up; 40 percent stopped when fifteen people were looking up).

But for our purposes, Milgram's big idea is *overload.* He argued that, like a computer, there is only so much information a human being can process before they begin to melt down. How do we cope with overload? he wondered. Milgram believed that we regulate our "inputs." We manage how much we pay attention to, how much stimulation we take in. Strategies for regulating inputs can range from staring blankly ahead, or scowling to deter people from talking to us, to keeping most of our daily interactions fleeting and superficial. To do this, we develop "scripts"—things we can say to acknowledge the other person, while also subtly signaling we're not interested in talking. We offer a curt "How's it going?" to a cashier even though we don't care, aren't listening, and aren't looking at them. "Fine, how are you?" they reply, with the same indifference.

Lyn Lofland, another influential twentieth-century sociologist who did a great deal of urban fieldwork, observed a number of methods people employed to regulate inputs. "If in a seated or waiting situation, have some prop to look at such as a book or a magazine or a letter," she wrote. "Concentrate one's gaze on inanimate objects.... If one wishes to gaze about, gaze at surrounding persons only below the neck." If something seemed off, Lofland observed that people either fled or acted as if it was completely normal so as to avoid giving other people permission to talk to them about it.

The social norm against talking to strangers can also be reinforced by velocity. If you're out for a leisurely stroll, you're more likely to actually see other people, notice things, and maybe say hello. But leisurely strolls are less common in bigger and more affluent cities, which tend to move faster. Researchers since the 1970s have found positive correlations between average walking speed and the population size and wealth of a city. So big, dense places like Tokyo or London may have a faster pace of life, making citizens less prone to spontaneous interactions, whereas smaller cities and towns will move at a less breakneck pace. Some argue this happens because in such places time is money. Stanley Milgram believed that sensory overload was triggering a flight reflex. Whatever the reason, it results in fewer opportunities for interactions with strangers.

Now, none of this is to say that city dwellers are totally blind to other people in big cities. On the contrary, they're generally very aware of one another. They just have more subtle ways of showing it. This brings us to our next big idea, which comes from another influential twentieth-century urban sociologist, Erving Goffman. Goffman's contribution is something called civil inattention. Civil inattention is the silent ritual that takes place between two strangers passing on a city street. Contrary to what more alarmist thinkers believed about life in cities, Goffman observed that passersby are not completely and heartlessly indifferent to one another. Many are simply being courteous by not talking. It's less an expression of callous indifference than it is a peculiar form of cooperation: helping one another cope with overload.

A person extends civil inattention in a couple of ways. They might move to the side to give someone space to pass. Or they might make brief eye contact or give a quick nod, and then look down.* As with greeting rituals, civil inattention is a form of ritual politeness that arises in part from ambivalence. "By according civil inattention," Goffman wrote, "the individual implies that he has no reason to suspect the intentions of the others present and no reason to fear the others, be hostile to them, or wish to avoid them. . . . He has nothing to fear or avoid in being seen and being seen seeing, and that he is not ashamed of himself or of the place and company in which he finds himself."†

Lyn Lofland argued that there is something even more meaningful communicated with civil inattention. She believed that it "implies that one understands [the stranger] to possess a basic level of humanness, [and] that one admits them into the human family, that one accepts their claims to the rights of citizenship." It's a check against dehumanization and the lesser minds problem. That's to say, civil inattention is important for the health of a city. It is a subtle but power-

---

* You'll recall the thing that inspired Gillian Sandstrom's research was realizing that she kept looking down after making eye contact with strangers while walking along the street. That was civil inattention.

† That's not to say everyone's humanity is recognized, in a city or anywhere else. Goffman also noted that it can be denied in the cases of the disabled and members of minority groups, who, he observed, were sometimes stared at with lurid interest, fear, or hatred.

ful way to bond citizens together, bond cities together, and establish shared humanity. And yet, if I'm being honest, the more I looked for it, the more I realized that it's kind of rare. In my experience, there's seldom eye contact, no quick nod, no flash of recognition of one another's humanity. There is virtually nothing. Why? To help answer that question, I'd like to introduce you to a man named Cliff Adler.

Cliff Adler is a cabbie in New York who has been driving for more than four decades. A great character and conversationalist, Adler has observed a marked shift in the way his fares interact with him in recent years. "People were different" when he started, he told me over breakfast one morning. "They were usually more than amenable to talking," he says. "You'd look up and you'd say, for example, 'Do you follow the Yankees or the Mets?' And they would talk to you: 'Well, I'm a Yankee fan,' or 'I'm a Met fan,' because this, that, and the other. They were raised in the Bronx, or their uncle this, and their father that. And we'd talk about it." Adler takes a sip of coffee. "And I'm a diehard Mets fan, so sometimes I actually let the Yankee fans live— although a little more often than not, I just stop the cab, drag them outside, and throttle them."

You recall that the Epley and Schroeder study we discussed included an experiment in which people talked to their cabdrivers, and reported liking them and enjoying their rides more. Adler tells me that these days, that is a rarity. Fares get into the cab on their phones, bark out an address, and stay on their phones for the duration of the ride. "They're definitely not as friendly or open," he says. "They don't say good morning or good afternoon—nothing." Sometimes it'll be an hour ride to the airport, "and not a peep." They arrive at their destination, pay, and leave. "You say, 'Thank you, have a good day,' and not a word. Not a squeak. They just take their stuff and leave," he says. "You're done with, you're a machine."

What does he say when that happens? I ask. How does he feel? What does he do?

"I just go into another world," he says, shrugging. "I don't know how else to put it."

Erving Goffman referred to magazines and newspapers as "screens." He said that they functioned to deter unwanted contact when in public. Since then we've developed a lot more options involving literal screens that accomplish this goal. We can steer most communication to email or text to remain in control of the interaction; we enter our names on do-not-call registries so strangers don't pester us with sales overtures; we can shop on the internet and order delivery via apps, and when we do go into a store, we can gravitate toward the self-checkout machines; we can wear earbuds and stare at our phones almost constantly while out in public. All these may be strategies for coping with overload,* but our reliance on them can erode our ability to interact with people in real life, because they allow us to shuffle through our days with very little human contact at all. We saw in a previous chapter that college students struggle with talking face-to-face with people they don't know. Some experts speculate that the lack of interaction is a driving force behind the loneliness epidemic, because the erosion of social skills makes it harder to meet new people.

Please be assured that this is not another tirade about how technology is ruining everything special about humanity. I'm a bit of a Luddite for sure, but I also know that technology can be a lifeline for marginalized people, or people living in far-flung places who can't find supportive communities at home, for one. As one study on social media used by transgender individuals—led by Yuliya Cannon at the University of Texas at San Antonio—concluded, "Social media has become a platform for establishing social ties, receiving education, and sharing of resources that may not otherwise be available to individuals on the margins of society."

Likewise, technology can provide access to new ideas and perspectives offered by strangers in other cultures and other lands, which can be very enriching under the right circumstances. Those connections,

---

* One could argue that we're replacing one load of stimulation with a much larger one. A 2009 study by Roger Bohn and James Short and the University of California, San Diego, found that people consumed 400 percent more data in 2008 than they did in 1980. That number has continued to climb, steeply.

if made in good faith and in a spirit of curiosity—and not, for example, in an effort to rekindle the flame of Nazism—can be profound and inspiring. Remember that one of Gillian Sandstrom's experiments was conducted over digital platforms, and it still resulted in participants feeling happier, more connected, and more optimistic about the world. Organizations like Living Room Conversations offer other promising opportunities (although moderated) for people to talk to strangers about heady topics online. I've done some, and they were challenging, enjoyable, and edifying.

Still, researchers have also found that technology can harm our ability to connect in the physical world. The mere presence of a smartphone in a social situation can be deleterious, because it leads to what psychologists call *absent presence*. You're there, in other words, but you're not *there*. One study, led by psychologist Ryan Dwyer, found that participants instructed to keep their phones on the table during dinner with family or friends reported enjoying the meal less than participants asked to keep their phones in their pockets because they felt more distracted. Another study by Georgetown's Kostadin Kushlev made pairs of strangers spend ten minutes in a waiting room. Half had their phones. Half did not. While 94 percent of people without phones chose to interact with the stranger, that number dropped to 70 percent for those who had phones. What's more, people with phones smiled 30 percent less. In a 2019 study and review of the literature, Kushlev and his colleagues concluded that "smartphones may lead people to miss out on the emotional benefits of casual social interactions by supplanting them altogether. . . . We find that smartphones consistently interfere with the emotional benefits people could otherwise reap from their broader social environment." Survey data back this up. A 2015 Pew poll found that almost half of young people between eighteen and twenty-nine report using their phones to avoid interacting with other people.

Smartphones and social media have been shown to be addictive: technologies that dispense little jolts of dopamine that can hook us and make using them compulsive. That explains part of the attraction. But there's another explanation for why they took such a hold on us so quickly, which is relevant to our quest here. According to what is known as the *principle of least effort,* humans tend to follow the path of least resistance. Since interacting with strangers in person is cognitively demanding, and involves, at least to some degree, not being in control of the conversation, people tend to gravitate naturally to digital communication. The convenience offered by phones saves time and helps smooth some interactions. But the more you communicate like this, the less social you become offline, and the more anxious you become about talking to someone you don't know. Suddenly, you're living in a city, surrounded by millions, and only ordering from restaurants that are on Grubhub because the prospect of placing a phone order with a stranger at the pizza place is simply too daunting.

This collective absorption into personal technology has also altered the character of public space. In 1989, the sociologist Ray Oldenburg wrote a highly influential book called *The Great Good Place,* which examined what he referred to as "third places"—public gathering spots, like beloved bars, coffee shops, or hair salons. Oldenburg believed they were essential to the well-being of individuals and the cohesion of cities and towns. At their best, he found, third places unite neighborhoods by giving locals a place to meet and mingle as equals; they serve as "ports of entry" for newcomers—a place to learn about their new homes and make connections and friends and maybe find work; in times of hardship, they can become staging areas for relief efforts or places to heal collectively.

"Nothing contributes as much to one's sense of belonging to a community as 'membership' in a third place," Oldenburg concluded. "It has to do with surviving and, indeed, *thriving.*" Oldenburg was lamenting the disappearance of these places as many Americans retreated to the suburbs in the 1980s, resulting in lifestyles that, "for all the material acquisition and the seeking after comforts and pleasures, are plagued by boredom, loneliness, alienation, and a high price tag." Suffice to say, this trend created a less than ideal situation, "as public life is populated with strangers more than ever before [and] as strangers frighten us more than ever before," Oldenburg wrote.

In the intervening years, many people have moved back to cities, but technology is still denying them the critical benefits of third places. Over drinks one night, I asked Joaquín Simó, a renowned mixologist and the owner of a cocktail bar called Pouring Ribbons, located in New York's Alphabet City neighborhood, what had changed about the business since he started out. It was simple, he said: People don't talk anymore—specifically young people. "It's generational," he says. "Twentysomething kids will sit down, order something, and then retreat back to the safety of their phones. They're lost. And it's weird because I used to go to bars to meet people." Simó says about fifteen years ago, many local places started getting rid of TVs, which had the effect of encouraging conversation. "That worked for about twenty minutes," he says. He pulls out his iPhone and waves it. "Then this thing happened, and it put a huge dent in people's willingness to interact with the people around them. And that sucks."

Today, when he recruits employees, Simó looks for someone who is conversationally adept, who has interests outside of cocktails, and things to say. He places great stock in this aspect of the hospitality business: connecting with strangers. But it's a struggle. The norm is hardening. When someone tries to talk to someone else today, it's often met with mystification, awkwardness, or fear. Simó believes this stems from a failure to understand the nature of a bar, or, for that matter, the nature of a city. "Your personal space terminates when you walk into a public space," he says. "You shouldn't be upset that someone came into your bubble, because you're in public. I feel the bubble has become very sacred to people."

There are other factors that serve to keep us apart even when we're sharing physical space. Take the wealth gap—a serious problem in modern cities. A series of laboratory experiments have found that when affluent and nonaffluent people are paired in conversations, the affluent will interrupt more, monopolize the conversation, and fail to show signs of "nonverbal attentiveness"—nodding their heads, making eye contact, saying "uh-huh," or any of the other subtle ways we show people we're paying attention to them.

In 2009, Michael Kraus and Dacher Keltner, psychologists at the University of California at Berkeley, conducted a study in which more affluent students were paired with less affluent students and told they'd be simulating a job interview. They'd spend five minutes getting to know each other, and then they'd be interviewed jointly by the experimenter for a fictitious job.

The latter part was a sham. What the psychologists really wanted to see was the getting-acquainted portion. For this, they gave the participants a list of questions such as "How would you describe yourself?" to get the conversation going, and they monitored the session for signs of social engagement (nodding, eyebrow raises, laughter, and gazing at the partner) and social disengagement (self-grooming, fidgeting with a nearby object, or doodling). They found that participants with higher socioeconomic statuses showed significantly less engagement, and those from lower statuses showed more. (Also, they found that women were more engaged than men.) Kraus and Keltner enlisted more volunteers to observe these discussions, too. And although these observers were not aware of each participant's socioeconomic status, they were able to accurately judge it just by watching them.

In a follow-up study, Kraus, Keltner, and a colleague conducted another experiment to see how accurately people of different classes could judge a stranger's emotions. The participants of lower socioeconomic status were better at it than more affluent participants. Why? Kraus and Keltner suggest it's a matter of having to be more reliant on others and responsive to one's environment when you lack means. You have to be more aware of potential threats and potential collaborations. You have to be present in the world. And being present in the world often means dealing with strangers in the flesh. People who are more affluent have less of an immediate need to develop that skill.*

This is admittedly a generalization. It's not to say that wealth makes everyone antisocial; businesspeople are often highly social—because they need to be in order to meet new clients, build networks, and gain exposure to new ideas, for instance. And there are caring,

---

* And I say this as a middle-class man who works from home. I could literally go weeks without talking to anyone outside my family if I wanted to.

friendly, and engaging people in any class. But that antisocial tendency is there, generally speaking, for the wealthy. It can keep them from enriching their own lives by talking to strangers, and it can also deny them a more complex understanding of the lives of others— lives that become increasingly abstract in a time of great inequality. A lack of meaningful contact between the top and the bottom of a society can lead to stereotyping and dehumanization, and that can lead to bad policy and, ultimately, the fraying of societies. "Those without status are all but invisible," wrote the English philosopher Alain de Botton in 2011. "They are treated brusquely by others, their complexities trampled upon and their singularities ignored."

Here's an example. I was in a Whole Foods in my neighborhood not long ago. It was a Sunday afternoon, and the place was positively overrun. There was an air of light panic, as if the customers, overwhelmingly white, overwhelmingly affluent, and almost invariably clad in luxe gym uniforms, were jockeying for the last plane out of Casablanca. In the face of this chaos, one cashier stood like a beacon: She was smiling, chatting with customers, joking around, making observations. Really working to make a connection. Or at least she was trying to. The customers, when they did tear their eyes from their phones, all looked at her like she was a talking ostrich. They didn't seem to know what to do with her. Some were annoyed; some just smiled tensely. Clearly they wanted her to be an object, a service module. But she wasn't. She was a person in full, and she kept trying.

When I got up to the front of the line, I told her she should get combat pay for working Sunday afternoons at this place. Her smile faded and she told me she'd rather they install a therapist in the back room. I asked her what the shrink would tell her. She told me, "He'd say: *These are not your friends, and this is not your fault.*" And there it was: the complexity of a stranger, trampled, her singularities ignored, denied simple connection in a city of millions. And she was not alone.

Chapter 12

Why Are We So Afraid of Strangers?

In which we learn how a zippy little rhyme turned us into a nation of paranoids, undermining our capacity to trust, our willingness to interact with strangers, and perhaps even our ability to heal from actual trauma.

The Semai people live in the mountains of central Malaysia. They are horticulturalists, and fear pervades every aspect of their lives. "Dangers of all sorts are ubiquitous in the Semai world," wrote anthropologist Clayton Robarchek in 1979. "They fear strangers, supernatural beings, storms, and animals; virtually everything in their culturally constituted environment is viewed as actually or potentially threatening."

For the Semai, laughing at a butterfly, or even uttering the word for dragonfly, is an invitation to calamity. Major storms are often believed to be punishment from the god Ngku for some *terlaid*—or affront—likely perpetrated by a Semai child, whose hair will be cut off and burned at the peak of the storm in the hopes of appeasing Ngku. "Often, hair from all the children is burned just in case they may have unknowingly committed some *terlaid* offense," writes Robarchek.

The children are trained to be fearful. "To keep their children safe from kidnappers, Semai taught their children to fear strangers," wrote anthropologist Robert Dentan, who lived among them on three separate occasions, between the late sixties and the early nineties. When an unfamiliar person—Semai or not—appears in the hamlet, mothers snatch their children away, crying, "Afraid! Afraid!" "They tell their children hair-raising tales about what will happen if Semai fail to protect one another from strangers. . . . Semai adults think that children need to learn to fear, to flee friendly strangers, to trust no one and nothing not already intimate."

That fear persists into adulthood. It often manifests in beliefs in bogeymen—human strangers who have taken on a supernatural dimension. "In the area where I worked, the bogeymen were . . . Malays, Chinese, Indians, or even strange Semai who, it was said, came to collect Semai heads that would be buried to ensure the success of construction projects undertaken by the outsiders," Robarchek recalls. "The Semai name for these bogeymen, *mai kahanoh kuui,* translates literally 'cutting-off-head strangers.' "

The Semai are devoutly nonviolent, but anthropologists suggest that their pacifism, like their xenophobia, is the result of trauma: years of violent persecution at the hands of their powerful neighbors, the Malays, who enslaved and slaughtered them, kidnapped their children, and looted and burned their homes well into the twentieth century. Those horrors have since ceased, but the fear has not. It is encoded in the culture. It has *become* the culture.

Here's another story, one that Westerners will find hits closer to home. In 1981, a boy named Adam Walsh was abducted from a shopping mall in Hollywood, Florida, and murdered, by Ottis Toole, a man posthumously discovered to be a serial killer. Adam's head was discovered in a ditch on the side of the road, and his body was never found. In 1984, Adam's parents, John and Revé Walsh, cofounded the National Center for Missing and Exploited Children (NCMEC), and John Walsh rose to prominence as the host of *America's Most Wanted,* a popular TV show that ran for more than two decades.

That same year, their son Cal Walsh was born. The center has been a part of Cal's life from the beginning. "They were pulling paper clips out of my mouth as I was crawling underneath the tables as a little boy," he tells me. When he stopped trying to eat the office supplies, they put him to work stuffing envelopes. "I grew up watching my parents channel their anger and their emotions over my brother's kidnapping, disappearance, and murder," Walsh says. He watched his parents lobby for legislation to protect children, and raise money to fund the center's work, and he watched his father become very famous for his work on television.

I asked Cal what it was like growing up in the shadow of his brother's murder. What was his childhood like? "I think most people would assume that after what happened to my brother, my parents wouldn't let me or my other siblings even out of the house," Walsh says. "And that just wasn't the case. We lived a very normal childhood." There were rules, of course: Don't put your name on your backpack, don't talk to strangers, don't get in strange cars—all that stuff that anyone who grew up in the 1980s and early '90s had branded into their psyches, but "they weren't overbearing with that," he says. "I think my parents understood that children can't be locked away in the home—that they need to get out into the world, and experience it, and grow. And part of that is social exchanges and interactions."

Walsh eventually went to work as a producer on his father's show and other shows, which he still does. But six years ago he also came back to the center to work. Today, he's the father of a young child, and he has tremendous admiration for his parents' fortitude. They could have retreated from life, become embittered against humanity. But instead, "They believe that most people are good." I ask Walsh how he keeps himself sane while doing the work he does, and he says that while his job can be unrelentingly dark, it also puts him in touch with the best of people, in the form of the strangers who voluntarily help the center recover missing children. "To see all the people who come in and support the work that we do—that's how you're able to keep your head above water: There are so many good people," he says. "There really are so many good people."

Walsh was a kid at the peak of the stranger-danger panic in America and beyond, a white-knuckled period in which children were inundated with dire warnings about strangers—the NCMEC featuring prominently among voices pushing these messages. There were the scary videos, the ominous pamphlets about shady vans and free candy, the local cops brought into schools to warn kids about all the ghastly surprises strangers had in store for them should they even momentarily relax their guard, and, throughout, that relentless messaging: *Don't talk to strangers. Don't talk to strangers. Don't talk to strangers.*

It didn't matter that there was virtually no evidence to justify poisoning the minds of children against *literally everyone in the world they hadn't met*. Or that according to the U.S. Department of Justice, kidnappings by strangers represent "an extremely small portion of all missing children." For instance, in a one-year period ending in 2011, strangers were responsible for just 65 child abductions, while some 258,000 reported abductions were committed by family members and people known to the victim.* It was a classic moral panic, a perfectly combustible cocktail of fierce parental love, natural ambivalence toward strangers, declining social trust, and a media happily overhyping isolated incidents to drive up market share.

Throughout, voices of reason were few and far between. When they were raised, they were ignored, as is usually the case when humans succumb to moral panics. In a 1986 review of a book about keeping children safe, one writer noted, "While pointers such as these are fine, the book fails by putting so much emphasis on protecting children from outsiders, when most child abuse occurs in the home at the hands of frustrated parents, angry boyfriends and jealous stepparents. When is someone in public office going to admit that, for the most part, the problem is in our families, instead of pretending the perpetrator is waiting in the dark shadows to snatch our young?"

This was not strictly an American phenomenon, either. It spread all over, data be damned, warping people's sense of threat. As one researcher put it in an extensive review of Canadian press coverage, "In every instance where the media provided tools or tips on how

---

* Strangers do commit a larger percentage of *total* crimes against children, but that number is still low: only around 10 percent.

parents should keep their children safe from abduction, there were zero references to protecting children from parental/familial abductions or seeing the warning signs of parental/familial abductions. The media only provided tips and strategies for how to keep children from being snatched up by 'The Stranger.'"

For members of my generation, the stranger-danger panic reads like eighties kitsch. But this messaging was so prevalent, and these fears were so pervasive, and that rhyme so fiendishly zippy, that political scientists Laura Nishikawa and Dietlind Stolle have suggested that it may have actually eroded an entire generation's ability to trust other people. Over the past generation, the levels of social or *generalized* trust among young people in America, and across much of the West, have fallen to historic lows. Older generations have become less trusting as well, but the young have plummeted the most. Drawing from surveys with some fourteen hundred children and interviews with their parents, Nishikawa and Stolle found that even parents who believed people are essentially good raised their children to fear strangers. "Our investigation shows that ingrained parental fears of strangers' child abduction and abuse often override their own value system when it comes to teaching children how to behave with strangers." As with the Semai, the fear has become the culture.

Because a person's ability to trust others is formed to a great degree in childhood, Stolle argues that "these parenting values may have lasting consequences on the generalized trust of generations to come." Sure, it may seem sensible to teach a child to be very careful around people they don't know, but a sense of social trust opens you up to a wider variety of social relationships and experiences and professional opportunities. "How many social or economic opportunities do we miss by simply being afraid of strangers?" the authors wondered.

Every year, researchers at Chapman University in Orange, California, conduct a nationwide survey to try to understand what Americans fear the most. Part of that is aimed at unpacking stranger danger. In the 2019 edition, only 7 percent of respondents reported that they are afraid of strangers as a generic category, placing strangers below zombies, ghosts, and of course clowns. But respondents are far more afraid of being killed by a stranger than by someone they know (29.7 percent to 21 percent), and far more afraid of being sexually assaulted by a stranger than by a familiar person (27.1 percent to 19.2 percent). Yet, as with crimes against children, the vast majority of murders and sexual assaults are committed not by strangers, but by people known to the victims.

According to data from the Centers for Disease Control and Prevention, in 2016, 85 percent of murders in America were committed by people the victims knew. Thirteen percent were committed by strangers. More than half of the women murdered in America were killed by a current or former intimate partner or a spouse; 6.8 percent were killed by strangers. Women were more likely to be killed by their own parents (8.2 percent), or their own children (9 percent), than to be killed by strangers. And men are twice as likely to be murdered by an acquaintance or a friend (35.2 percent) than by a stranger (16.8 percent). We see the same pattern in terms of sexual violence. According to a 2017 survey by the CDC, 19.1 percent of sexual assaults against women, and 18.6 percent of sexual assaults against men, were committed by strangers. The rest were committed by people known to the victims, especially current or former lovers or spouses. None of this is in any way meant to downplay the suffering experienced by the victims of these crimes and their families, nor to shrug them off as statistically insignificant. It is just to draw attention to the uncomfortable reality that the biggest threat to us doesn't come from strangers. Far from it.

An analysis of the Chapman University fear survey data, kindly performed for me by a talented Chapman graduate student named Muhammad Karkoutli, provides more revealing insights. Of the people who expressed fear of strangers, 73.5 percent are female; 28.6 percent of them were eighteen to twenty-nine years old, and 30.9 percent were thirty to forty-nine. Older Americans are considerably less afraid—which fits with Stolle's argument about stranger danger warping the children of the 1980s and '90s. People with less education are significantly more likely to fear strangers, as are people who make less money, with those making under twenty thousand dollars a year being the most fearful of any income group.* Among white Americans, 48.8 percent are fearful of strangers, whereas just 24.4 percent of Black Americans are. Finally, Americans who own a home are two and a half times more likely to fear strangers than are Americans who rent. Religion, region, and political party affiliation have no statistically significant impact on fear of strangers, although independents report being more afraid of strangers than Democrats and Republicans.

There are certainly conditions in which a fear of strangers is wholly justifiable. You could be in a violent or unstable place. You could be in a militant theocratic state, where one might be easily marked as a heathen and a pestilence and targeted for extermination. You could be gay in a land with high levels of homophobia. You could be a racial minority in a virulently racist culture. Or you could live in a totalitarian country, like East Germany under the Stasi, where neighbors were encouraged to denounce wayward neighbors to the secret police. The historian Timothy Snyder, drawing from his deep study into twentieth-century totalitarian movements, pointed out that the success of despots often hinged on turning neighbors, friends, and family members into strangers. "When friends, colleagues, and acquaintances looked away or crossed the street to avoid contact, fear grew," Snyder writes. Fanatics, cultists, and fundamentalists often do something similar, warning their followers to avoid contact with others. This is because, as we know, contact with different people expands us, and changes us, and complicates our identities and our perception of the world, which is a grave threat to demagogues peddling a simplified vision of who we are, who they are, and how the world must be. As the theologian Martin Marty puts it, "Members of intense groups erect boundaries, create distance between themselves and others. Not always because the stranger is abhorrent but because she may be beguiling."

---

* Lower income people are also, if you recall, more attentive in conversation, and more adept at reading the emotions of strangers, than more affluent people. Again, we see the connection among friction, ambivalence, and sociality.

Generally speaking, though, outside the context of conflict, you can see how stranger-danger messaging can form an insidious loop. We're conditioned from early childhood to believe that strangers are dangerous. As a result, we don't talk to them. If you recall, Gillian Sandstrom found in her study that paired students for online conversations during COVID-19 that talking to strangers actually increases social trust. That means that a moral panic has damaged our ability to trust other people, and the solution proposed by those who peddled the panic is to avoid doing the very thing that will help rebuild that trust. It's a hell of a cycle.

Which made it all the more inspiring, and heartening, when I encountered someone who had been talking to strangers as a way of coping with real, and not imagined, trauma.

I've said before that there seems to be something infectious about talking to strangers, even paying attention to strangers. There's something about the energy you give off when you do this sort of thing that draws people into your orbit. After I started trying to talk to strangers more, I found that situations just presented themselves. The morning I got back from my free listening adventure in L.A., a guy on the subway looked at me and said, "Hey, you look good today." Not in a lascivious way, just an observation. I thanked him, and we talked pretty much the whole time. Later that day I went down to get on the subway and found myself standing right next to a college kid wearing a T-shirt that said "I Talk to Strangers." Sure enough, he did.

Anyway, in one of these instances, I was heading home in my neighborhood, and I caught a glimpse of a woman walking down the street carrying a tote bag that read "Ask Me About the Book I'm Reading." I caught up to her. "I'm sorry," I said, "but I saw your bag. Can I ask you: *Does it work?*" And she said yes, people talk to her all the time. I asked her where she got it, and she said it was from a friend of hers who runs a popular Instagram account called Subway Book Review. The friend interviews random strangers on the subway about what they're reading.

I went home, looked it up, and emailed the woman, Uli Beutter Cohen, to see if she'd get coffee with me. She said yes.

On the appointed day, Beutter Cohen walks in—tall, voluble, funny, and direct—and after we get a couple of coffees and find a table, she sits down and begins. "I have a very clear mission," she tells me. "A mission to disrupt the evolution of separation. That is what I'm here for."

Beutter Cohen is thirty-nine years old. She was raised an only child in a tiny, tight-knit village in Germany. Her mother was born in a refugee camp during World War II. Her father was born in Germany at the end of the war. Her parents responded to their trauma in divergent ways. Her father was protective and focused on providing security for his family. In contrast, "my mother is exuberant, needs to connect with the world, always talks to strangers, and would take me on trips to the library in the city, making sure we'd go the long way so that we could see more people on the street and have a chat," Beutter Cohen says. "If my dad could have had me under a glass dome, just so he knew that I was okay, he would've been a happy man. He loves me more than anything, so his inclination is to protect me."

Seeing these two modes of living, she says—of one person being most content keeping the outside world at bay, and the other needing human connection like a person needs food and water—was formative. Beutter Cohen breaks these down between security and safety. Her mother found safety in human connection she says, meaning she felt seen and accepted. And her father found security in maintaining a border between a small, well-defined *us* and the sprawling, unknowable *them*. It's obvious which approach Beutter Cohen would ultimately choose. "I opted very clearly for a life that's not security-driven," she says, "for the connected life." At twenty, she packed two bags and left for America.

After graduating college with a media degree out west, Beutter Cohen moved to New York City in the fall of 2013, and started Subway Book Review a couple of months later. "It started out of self-interest," she says with a laugh. "I wanted to connect with the city. . . . I was excited to find the other dreamers and artists and the

people who give this city its soul." As with Nicholas Epley and Juliana Schroeder, Beutter Cohen's work was inspired by the subway.
"To me it was a sacred space where people were gathering, every day;
they had to stand still; it was like this churchlike experience, where
we come together," she says. "A train can be super loud or super
quiet. Sometimes you close your eyes and feel like you're all by yourself, and then you open your eyes and there are hundreds of people
standing around, together in silence." She pauses, and adds with a
gesture: *"Amazing!"*

When she rode the train, she found herself drawn to the people
reading books. She figured they were the dreamers, the critical thinkers, the creators. She wanted to meet these people. Drawing on her
training as a filmmaker, her experience in improv comedy, and the
insights she gained from watching her mother talk to everyone, she
started asking people what they were reading. And despite the grave
injunctions against talking to people on the subway, she found that
the vast majority were interested. "I can tell you that eighty-nine
percent of the people—maybe even ninety percent of people, if I can
be so bold—are so excited that I see them, that I'm willing to listen
to them, that they have a space where they get to tell their story on
their terms, and are so happy to have a conversation with a rando like
me," she says. "They feel appreciated, and they often say thank you
to me after, which is mind-blowing, because I'm like, 'You just gave
me a gift.' They're like, 'No, no, you gave *me* a gift.'"*

Beutter Cohen had no system for initiating these encounters in the
beginning. She just looked for people reading interesting books and
talked to them. She developed stranger mojo herself. "If you are curious and open, you'll get a feeling for who wants to connect with
you," she says. She looks for people who make eye contact, or maybe
someone who looks like they're having a good day, though bad days
also attract notice. "A young man was sobbing on the subway the
other day," she recalls. "Did I go over to check on him? Of course I
did. I said, 'Are you okay?' And he said, 'I'm having a really bad day,'

---

* Which recalls the Arizona State University student in the free listening experiment who
said he felt like he'd given "a gift" to the community.

and I said, 'You can do this. You're not alone,' and he nodded, he took it in."

Beutter Cohen doesn't consider this strictly a nice or fun thing to do, but a moral obligation. "If you live in a city, if you're part of any community, it is your responsibility to be awake in that community and to understand the people you share an environment with. Otherwise we're totally fucked," she says. And that sense of moral obligation and the optimism to act on it is hard-won. She tells me she has anxiety that can be paralyzing at times, and is treating it in therapy. She tells me she has days when she feels no hope, where she feels like she can't leave the house, when she cannot identify with the society in which she lives.

"And I want to say this," she adds. "Like many people, I have had traumatic experiences with strangers, namely men. But the interactions in the underground, however surprising they may be, they don't make me feel like I'm putting myself at risk. Of course I see all kinds of crazy stuff on the subway. But having had negative experiences in life shouldn't stop us from going out there and trying again," she says. "And by 'trying again' I mean trying to trust people. Just because one or two people have tried to destroy you doesn't mean that all other people want to destroy you, too."

The work, she says, "has led me to understand that I have the choice to say that all these beings around me are part of my human family." When you choose that route, she says, "Your life changes tremendously—and it will come with incredible pain, because you will understand your place in the world, which can be eye-opening in a painful and also in the most exhilarating way. Because that choice comes with the responsibility to take care of—and to love—other people and yourself."

She's not prescribing this to everyone. "I fully understand that some trauma survivors can't get past that point, and may feel that it's really not on them to try again. They need to be proven first by society, that it's a trustworthy society. And I completely respect that, too." But for Beutter Cohen, Subway Book Review "is my daily affirmation that most humans want to be good. I ask one question: 'What are you reading?' and then I turn on my tape recorder and I listen," she says. "It is so freaking healing. It's like someone hugging you on the inside, and it combats that feeling of isolation in a way that really no other thing does. That's many years of doing this: tried and tested and true."

In 2018, the National Center for Missing and Exploited Children made an announcement. It was retiring the term "stranger danger" and opting for a more nuanced and practical approach that reflects the data. "While these things do happen, and of course we see them at the National Center, we know stranger abductions are rare," Cal Walsh tells me. Warning against all strangers does more harm than good, he says, because "if the child is in a dangerous situation, it's likely that it's a stranger that would come to their aid." That could be a security guard, a firefighter, a mother with children, or someone else who a kid could be relatively assured—based on outward cues— was trustworthy. They still warn kids not to engage with a stranger who asks them for help, or touches them. But they have realized that to warn children to never talk to any stranger cuts them off from potential helpers. That's why "stranger danger" had to go. "We're trying to empower children to make safe and smart decisions," says Walsh. "Not scar them for life."

Chapter 13

How Fear of Strangers Can Make Us Friendly

In which we learn that, in the past, the things that led to places becoming friendly were not so friendly at all.

All right. So what do we know? We know that interdependence made hunter-gatherer groups more sociable among themselves and eventually with other groups. We know that greeting rituals and hospitality were evolved to reconcile the threat strangers pose with the opportunities they present (and that all bad people, in the end, are turned into birds). We know that we're wired to favor our groups, but also that our definition of *our group* is flexible. We know that we're predisposed to like people with whom we have something in common, even if we have no idea who they are and even if it consists of little more than wearing the same baseball cap. We know that cities can bring us together with countless strangers, but they can also create social norms that keep us apart. We know that talking across group boundaries can make us anxious, and we know that the relentless messaging about stranger danger that several generations were clobbered with has warped our sense of threat and possibly harmed our ability to trust.

But what about cultures? What about regions, or countries? How does a place become friendly or hostile toward strangers? How did these cultures come to be? These are our next big questions.

We talked a little about trust in the last chapter. When I started researching this topic, I thought friendliness toward strangers may have something to do with trust—specifically the idea of generalized trust, which we touched upon a little earlier. Generalized trust is measured by a question created in 1948 by the German political scientist Elisabeth Noelle-Neumann, which is used in the annual World Values Survey, a mammoth global-data-gathering effort aimed at tracking social and political changes around the world. "Generally speaking," the question asks, "would you say that most people can be trusted or that you need to be very careful in dealing with people?" People who pick the former are high trusters. People who pick the latter are not. *Generalized trust* is different from *strategic trust,* which is when we rationally calculate the potential upside and downside of trusting someone. And it's different from *particularized trust,* which is when we trust family and close friends.

Really, it means trust in strangers, and cultures that have high levels of it enjoy a lot of social benefits. "Trusting people are more likely to volunteer their time, to give to charity, to be tolerant of others, and to support policies that both promote economic growth and that provide support for the less fortunate," writes political scientist Eric Uslaner, one of the leading authorities on trust. "Countries with more trusters have better functioning government, more redistributive policies, more open markets, and less corruption." This is not to say high trusters are somehow soft, or agents of moral relativism. They expect everyone to participate in the community and play by the rules, regardless of group. They just give others the benefit of the doubt and operate in good faith in the short term.

Who are these high trusters? Generally speaking, people in rural areas score lower on generalized trust, as do people from largely Confucian countries, like China, which stress the primacy of family bonds over other relationships with friends and acquaintances. Countries with a legacy of communism, with their decades of personal experience with corruption and totalitarianism, are low trusters.

Men, older people, those who are less educated, those who are unemployed, members of minority groups, and religious fundamentalists also tend to score lower on generalized trust.

Where does generalized trust come from? That's a tricky question. On a national level, general trust has been loosely correlated with gross national product, negatively associated with levels of segregation, and strongly correlated with Protestantism, but no other religion. But all those factors lag behind one key factor in terms of importance: optimism. Eric Uslaner has tied generalized trust most closely to optimism—the sense that the future will be good, and one has a reasonable amount of control over their fate. Optimism is derived, Uslaner and many others have found, from income equality, which is the strongest determinant of general trust in a society. That's not to say everyone makes the same money in a high-trust society. It is to say that the system is fair, the government is not corrupt, crime is low, and everyone is granted, to the extent possible, equality of opportunity. "When some people have far more than others, neither those at the top nor those at the bottom are likely to consider the other as part of their 'moral community,'" writes Uslaner. "They do not perceive a shared fate with others in society."

Another influential political scientist, Ronald Inglehart, offers a similar argument: the evolutionary modernization theory. Inglehart, who oversaw the World Values Survey for years, writes, "When survival is insecure, people tend to close ranks behind a strong leader, forming a united front against outsiders." When people are comfortable, they move away from this defensive mind-set and toward values more tied to individualism. These individualistic cultures, which bloomed in the post–World War II era, feature an aversion to violence, a disinclination to fight for one's country, the promotion of tolerance for out-group members, freedom of expression, openness to new people and new ideas, a knack for collaboration, equal participation in government, and commitment to genuine democracy. On the other hand, a decline in security triggers what Inglehart calls the authoritarian reflex—the tendency to close ranks, expel or oppress out-group strangers, and hunker down. Like Uslaner, Inglehart concludes that inequality is the greatest threat to a self-expression society. And just like generalized trust rankings, Protestant northern Europe ranks at the top of the list for self-expression and secular-rational values. Therefore, I believed from the outset that cultures that had high levels of generalized trust would be the ones in which people would be inclined to talk to strangers. That to me seemed like the first piece of the puzzle.

But according to American biologists Randy Thornhill and Corey Fincher, there is another powerful factor that can determine a culture's openness toward strangers, which is kind of related to generalized trust: rates of infectious disease. Before early humans colonized more northerly latitudes, they largely inhabited hot, damp places near the equator. These places were, and are, associated with a greater threat of infectious disease—a source of sickness and death. The presence of infectious disease occasioned two adaptations in early humans. First, our physical immune system, for obvious reasons. But more relevant to our current project: our *behavioral immune system*. This is a set of behaviors designed to manage our exposure to infectious diseases by, in essence, managing our exposure to strangers. So in places with high parasite threat, people avoid strangers, and they avoid wandering too far from home for fear of encountering these strangers and the diseases they may be carrying.* This is known as parasite-stress theory.

Thornhill and Fincher found that people in areas with high parasite stress tend to show a set of distinct characteristics that people in cooler, drier latitudes do not. They exhibit higher levels of xenophobia against out-group people, who they perceive as contaminated or unclean, which leads to disgust and dehumanization. People in areas facing high parasite threat are neophobic, distrusting new things, new ideas, and new people, suspecting that they are all potential transmitters of disease. They are also more conformist, more introverted,

---

* We saw flashes of this during the COVID-19 crisis, in which everyone, but Asian people in particular, was met with wariness, fear, and sometimes outright hostility, due to the suspicion that they were carrying the novel coronavirus. A 2020 study by psychologist Ashley Whillans of Harvard Business School confirmed that Americans and Canadians consistently and significantly underestimated the risk of contracting COVID-19 from friends and family, and overestimated the threat posed by strangers.

and more nepotistic, favoring those closest to them. History abounds with episodes in which people are prompted to think of out-group strangers as pathogens. When Nazis isolated Jews in ghettoes, they hung signs bearing messages such as "Plague! Entry Forbidden!" on the gates. In America, in 1962, when the late congressman Elijah Cummings was eleven, he was part of a group that attempted to integrate a public pool in Baltimore. He was met by an estimated one thousand white people carrying signs reading "Keep Our Pool Germ Free," and beaten savagely, leaving him with a facial scar he'd have the rest of his life.

From an evolutionary perspective, though, parasite fear makes sense. When the threat of infectious disease is high, the costs of being sociable with total strangers—a fatal disease—would outweigh the benefits—which, write Thornhill and Fincher, include "gains through intergroup trade, new and better ideas, and larger and more diversified social networks for marriage . . . and other social alliances." The problem is, a parasite-stress response can be triggered even when the real threat is low. Germophobes, for instance, tend to show these characteristics regardless of whether they live in a place with a high risk of infection, Thornhill tells me. Others may behave more like people under parasite stress if they're simply made to *think* about infectious disease. Such cues, Thornhill and Fincher write, can "cause people to immediately adopt personality features, values, and behavioral avoidance that reduce contact with strangers and new experiences."

In 2010, psychologist Chad Mortensen led a study in which participants were divided into two groups. One was shown slides containing pictures and information about germs and infectious diseases. Another was shown photos of conventional-looking buildings. Afterward, each participant was asked to write about a time they encountered something similar to what they had seen in their respective slideshows. Finally, after a thirty-minute break, they were asked to complete two questionnaires—one a personal inventory aimed at measuring extraversion, agreeableness, conscientiousness, neuroticism, and openness to experience, and another one measuring their perceived vulnerability to disease. Participants who watched the disease slideshow reported being less extroverted, less open-minded toward new people and new experiences, and less cooperative.

Save for more recent events, the threat of infection in the West is far lower than it was before rapid advances in immunology in the middle of the twentieth century—in fact, Thornhill and Fincher have suggested that it was the breakthroughs in disease control in the 1940s that led to the sexual revolution, the civil rights movement, and the increase in social permissiveness a generation later in the 1960s. Today, the reason that attempts to cast members of other groups in terms of uncleanliness and disease so often find an audience is because we've evolved to be highly sensitive to the threat of infectious disease.

So, if Protestantism, income equality, low levels of crime and corruption, and low parasite threat are the key drivers of trust in strangers, then it comes as no surprise that the northern European countries are all on the top of the pile. The trust exhibited by these societies is so beneficial that experts have called it "Nordic gold." People in these countries are more likely to regard the strangers around them as fully human, equally deserving of moral concern and trust, and not bearers of disease. Knowing all that, I came to assume that these are the places in which people would be more inclined to talk to strangers.

And as much as it pains me to admit, I was wrong. There actually appears to be an *inverse* correlation between generalized trust and what we—particularly Americans, but others as well—would construe as friendliness. According to data from the World Values Survey compiled by the Organisation for Economic Co-operation and Development, the top trusters in the thirty-five-nation OECD include Denmark, Norway, the Netherlands, Sweden, Finland, New Zealand, Switzerland, Australia, Iceland, Germany, and Canada. The United States is just below average, and Mexico, Portugal, and Colombia all hover near the bottom. Meanwhile, an organization called Inter-Nations conducts an annual survey of expats around the world, in part to rank countries by friendliness. Among the friendliest: Mexico, Portugal, and Colombia. Hovering near the bottom: Denmark, Norway, Sweden, Switzerland, Germany, and Austria. The United Kingdom placed dead last, and Australia proved to be that rarest of birds: high trust *and* friendly.

I asked Bi Puranen, the Swedish researcher and one of the heads of the World Values Survey, how this could be squared. How could high-trust places be less friendly and low-trust places be more friendly? She acknowledged the paradox. "People from the Middle East are quite low on generalized trust and especially low on trusting strangers, people with another religion, and people of another nationality," she told me. "But anyone who has traveled a lot in the Middle East knows that they're extremely hospitable to strangers. On the other hand, the Scandinavians are the most trusting, but we're not very hospitable."

Now, please understand that I'm not saying Canadians, or Finns, or Germans are hostile. Just that they tend to be less outgoing than, say, Italians. And the reason why high trusters tend to be less gregarious is as simple as it is counterintuitive: They don't have to be. We have seen time and time again how friction makes us social. In efficient high-trust societies, friction is minimal. Central institutions handle the things that in less-well-functioning places often fall to individuals. In low-trust countries, however, people can't rely on institutions to take care of them. They have to be more sociable—with friends and strangers alike—in order to get by. This friendliness isn't driven by a love for all, but out of a need to cope with the chaos, instability, and threats affecting life in an unstable environment. We've seen this before in fictive kinship, greeting rituals, and hospitality. Here again, a form of friendliness arose as a practical way of coping with the difficulties of life.

I'll give you a good example. In 2019, Yuna Blajer de la Garza, a sociologist at the University of Chicago, published a paper on *viene-vienes* in Mexico City. These are informal car parkers—in essence, freelance valet parkers. "In interactions with *viene-vienes,* it is considered normal to exit one's vehicle in one of the largest cities in the world, hand the keys to an unidentified individual standing on a street corner, and expect to retrieve the car later," she writes. Blajer de la Garza studied this informal trust economy because it seemed so unlikely in a place like Mexico City—which I have been to and adore, but which also has a high crime rate, endemic corruption, runaway inequality, and low levels of social trust. And yet, people there entrust their cars to strangers. And it works.

The combination of factors that allowed this system to take root is complicated, involving class dynamics, corrupt law enforcement, and, more simply, a strong demand for such services. But, as Blajer de la Garza writes, the combination of inefficiency and dysfunction made contact between people necessary, which allowed members of different classes to not only interact but trust one another, and even develop relationships of a sort: "Ultimately, the hundreds of [these] exchanges that happen every day in Mexico City are among the many pieces that keep a massive city with corrupt institutions from falling into chaos."

These days, however, the *viene-vienes* are giving way to technology, in the form of parking meters. "Middle-class drivers—especially younger generations—have applauded the change, which has made parking a car as efficient as it is impersonal," she writes. But "as efficient as parking meters are . . . they reduce the spaces in which rich and poor are made to interact with one another and gain awareness of each other's struggles and privileges."

After I read her paper, I contacted Blajer de la Garza to ask what she thought about the differences between generalized trust in northern European nations and friendliness in Latin America. I asked her why places where generalized trust is low can be in some ways friendlier than places where trust is high. Her response comes down to social friction, and is worth quoting at length:

> Norwegians don't really have to rely on people being or not being trustworthy because the state functions so smoothly. . . . Those institutions end up making trusting strangers completely unnecessary and irrelevant. Hence,

you end up in a situation in which you simply do not need others to go about your day—it feels more efficient (it probably is), but I do think that it carries a social cost.

Mexico is a mess of a country (I was born and raised there and I love the place, but it is a mess), yet it would be quite difficult for you to find many people who tell you that they feel lonely. . . . Even if you tried to be alone for a long period of time, you probably would not manage: You need to interact with others for everyday exchanges, you need to address them, to ask for help, for directions.

This is even the case when doing bureaucratic paper-work: Everything is so convoluted that you are constantly hoping to find someone who will extend a personal favor to you and guide you. And even the shared frustrations at the inefficiency of the state can produce a sense of close-ness.

Here's another example of how friction makes us friendly. Consider the American South, famous for its friendliness and hospitality.* According to a theory by psychologists Dov Cohen and Richard Nisbett, the South is "a culture of honor." Cultures of honor form in the absence of strong central institutions, like courts or police; they are unstable, and they are characterized by aggression and territoriality. (This is not specifically a southern phenomenon. Cultures of honor appear around the world.) In the South, the culture is believed to have been formed by an eighteenth-century influx of Scots-Irish and

---

* This is not saying that everyone in small towns is friendly. I once said hello to a grizzled-looking character in a bar in Bandera, Texas—"the cowboy capital of the world"—and was told, "I don't speak Yankee." And I am highly conscious of the added leeway I get as a six-foot-tall straight white guy, despite my northern handicap. The reception I might get in a small town anywhere may not apply to, say, a young Black man, a Muslim, or an LGBTQ individual.

Scottish herders from lawless borderlands in northern Ireland and the Scottish Highlands. Because law enforcement was weak both in their homelands and in their adopted region, the men needed to show a willingness to kill anyone who tried to steal their animals. Even mere insults were repaid with violence, for fear of appearing weak and thus vulnerable. From that willingness grew their reputations—their "honor."

"Cultures of honor, which rely heavily on aggression and male honor, are common adaptations among populations living in stateless regions and that depend upon easily stolen herds," writes the economist Pauline Grosjean, in a study citing the culture of honor as the reason why the murder rate in the South between 1980 and 2007 is nearly three times higher than the North—a disparity driven largely by white homicides in instances where honor came into question. Grosjean believes this modern trend arises out of the needs of those early herders. "In the absence of third party law enforcement, aggression and a willingness to kill can be essential to build a reputation for toughness and deter animal theft."*

The culture of honor declines in the presence of stronger central institutions, and its effect is waning around the world. But elements of it persist today. In a series of studies, Cohen and Nisbett gathered northern students and southern students—all men—and placed them in situations where their honor would be insulted. In one, participants were bumped by a large male experimenter in a hallway and called "asshole." The southern students were angrier about being insulted. The northerners thought it was funny. In another study, participants in a classroom were subjected to heckling and derision by an experimenter posing as a fellow student. Tested afterward, the southerners showed much higher levels of testosterone and the stress hormone cortisol than the northern participants. "Although unin-

---

* Here, I have a patriotic obligation to quote another gifted philosopher, the country singer Willie Nelson, in his classic "The Red-Headed Stranger": "The yellow-haired lady was buried at sunset / The stranger went free, of course / You can't hang a man for killin' a woman / who's tryin' to steal your horse."

sulted southerners were, if anything, more polite than northerners, insulted southerners were much more aggressive than any other group," Cohen and Nesbitt found.

There's a name for this link between politeness and violence: *the paradox of politeness.* As Cohen and colleague Joe Vandello wrote in 2004, "Violence and friendliness are usually thought to be opposites. Congeniality, hospitality, openness, and warmth are often assumed to preclude aggression and mayhem. What is frequently missed, however, is how often these two polar opposites seem to go together. . . . Violence, or the threat of violence, can create a society where friendliness, congeniality, and politeness are the norm."

Again, this is in no way limited to the South. The politeness paradox turns up in many traditional societies in Asia, the Middle East, the Mediterranean, and Africa. In these cultures, writes anthropologist Alan Fiske and colleagues in a study, people tend to be "extraordinarily afraid of each other" and thus "may act in extremely polite, gracious, or generous fashion, but these social acts may or may not entail corresponding feelings of love, liking, or trust." They do this to prevent spirals of revenge that can follow an inadvertent insult to someone's honor.

None of this is to say that all nice people are nice because they are afraid that not being nice will win them a one-way trip through a plate glass window. Cultural evolution is more complex than that. A behavior that starts as a practical response to a problem can in time just generalize into a way of being. This is called *functional autonomy.* And while definitively untangling the threads that make up a culture is impossible, we can argue that the ritualized politeness that came out of the culture of honor in time became mere politeness and friendliness, and just stayed that way. I ran this idea by Richard Nisbett, an expert on the culture of honor hypothesis, and he replied, simply, "I like this idea a lot."

We can see this process at work in other places as well, in which friction begets friendliness. Take smiling and laughing, for instance. While it's true that people in homogeneous nations show higher levels of generalized trust, researchers have found that people who live in countries that have experienced immigration from a great number of different countries over the past five hundred years are more emotionally expressive, more likely to smile, and more likely to laugh. North America, Central America, South America, and, yes, that rarest of birds, Australia: These are what social scientists call smiling cultures. Researchers believe that they arose in response to a need to communicate with strangers in the absence of a common language and shared social norms. In such a situation, a smile is a way to signal friendliness and a willingness to cooperate.

In one study of eighty-two countries, psychologist Adrienne Wood and her colleagues found that people in historically diverse places are more emotionally expressive and more precise in terms of conveying their emotions nonverbally, than those hailing from more historically homogeneous countries. Another global study, led by psychologist Paula Niedenthal, found a strong correlation between historic heterogeneity and the amount of time respondents spent each day smiling, laughing, *and just feeling good*. This happened regardless of GDP or current levels of diversity. Niedenthal and her colleagues found a similar result analyzing U.S. census data. States that have historically had a larger share of foreign-born residents—including California, New York, North Dakota, Nevada, and Minnesota—report more smiles, laughs, and positive emotions than states that have not.

And this can be infectious. "Smiles may . . . produce positive social experiences and feelings beyond those associated with solutions of immediate problems of social coordination," Niedenthal writes. "In other words, encountering more smiling and laughing people on a daily basis may in itself increase positive [mood]. More numerous opportunities for smiling and laughter could therefore cause more positive emotional experiences."

Again, what began as a practical solution for a common problem—needing to communicate and cooperate with different kinds of people without the benefit of language or shared cultural norms—in time untethered from its original function and generalized into a culture, a way to behave, regardless of circumstances on the ground.

———

When Nairán Ramírez-Esparza came to the United States from Mexico to attend graduate school at the University of Texas in 2001, she experienced a shock. Her friends had taken her to a party. Back home in Mexico, you'd go to a party and hang out with the people you came with, she says, but in America "as soon as we got to the party, all my friends said, 'Let's mingle.' And I was like, *What is 'Let's mingle'?*" Her friends wandered off and just started talking to random people. "It was really, really hard for me, especially as an introvert," she says. "It still is."

She was born and raised in Mexico City, in a country where a tradition called *simpatía* reigns. Cultures that practice *simpatía*—so called by psychologist Harry Triandis and colleagues in a groundbreaking 1984 study—emphasize politeness, kindness, friendliness, respect, positivity, avoidance of conflict, and deference to other people in everyday interactions. Like in a culture of honor, an insult or a fight in a place that practices *simpatía* is very serious: It's considered an assault on the essential dignity of the other person. And like cultures of honor, *simpatía* exists in places that traditionally have not had strong central institutions to secure social harmony from the top down. Thus, the task falls to the individuals to maintain the peace themselves.

Simpatía has wider benefits for society. It can make people more helpful to strangers, for instance. In an experiment spanning thirty-six countries, the political scientist Robert Levine studied "helping behaviors" in cities by having students pose as strangers in need: by pretending to be blind, dropping a pen on the sidewalk, and approaching someone feigning injury and asking for help, or change. The most densely populated places, and places with the strongest emphasis on the family as the key cultural unit—in other words, more traditional, exclusionary places—were the least helpful.

But notably, several of the most helpful cities were in Latin America: "Considering that some of these places suffer from long-term political instability, high crime rates and a potpourri of other social, economic and environmental ills, these positive results are noteworthy," Levine wrote in 2003. There were exceptions—Copenhagen and Vienna fared well—but on the whole, places that explicitly embraced *simpatía* were more helpful to strangers.* What's more, the overall affect of Latin America is decidedly positive. Every year Gallup issues a "Global Emotions" report, which ranks nations by how positive or negative their citizens report feeling on a daily basis. One metric they use is the number of positive emotions survey respondents report experiencing every day. Of the top ten happiest nations in this regard, nine were in Latin America (the other one was Indonesia).

Now, Ramírez-Esparza contends that Mexico ranks higher in terms of *simpatía* than other Latin American countries. And she attributes this to the way in which they were conquered. In Latin American countries, as well as in the United States and Canada, the newcomers came and eradicated the native peoples. In Mexico, with notable exceptions like the Aztecs, many of the native people cooperated, in time blending their traditions with those of the Spanish, leading to hybrids like Mexico's distinctive form of Catholicism. "The ones that agreed with the conditions made by the Spaniards, they were not killed," says Ramírez-Esparza. "And now we are in a society which has come to be very kind, and polite. We don't like to say what we think; we want to keep things smooth."

These days, as a highly respected social psychologist at the University of Connecticut, Ramírez-Esparza is called upon to mingle with

---

* My current home fared less well in terms of helpfulness. Actually, New York fared the worst in the study—yielding one gloriously bilious piece of datum. While performing what is known as a *lost letter test* in New York, in which experimenters leave addressed, stamped letters on streets and count how many are returned, Levine and company got a nasty surprise from a New Yorker. "In many cities, I received envelopes that had clearly been opened," writes Levine.

> In almost all of these cases, the finder had then re-sealed it or mailed it in a new envelope. Sometimes they attached notes, usually apologizing for opening our letter. Only from New York did I receive an envelope which had its entire side ripped and left open. On the back of the letter the helper had scribbled, in Spanish: *"Hijo de puta ir[r]esposable"*—which I discovered when it was translated for me, makes a very nasty accusation about my mother. Below that was added a straightforward English-language expletive, which I could readily understand. It is interesting to picture this angry New Yorker, perhaps cursing my irresponsibility all the while he was walking to the mailbox, yet for some reason feeling compelled to take the time to perform his social duty for a stranger he already hated.

some regularity. It's still difficult for her, so she has to practice. She and her husband will go somewhere with the express purpose of mingling with random people. She introduces herself, they pick up her accent and ask where she's from, and it goes from there. For Americans, this is simple small talk; for Ramírez-Esparza, it's a significant cultural adjustment. "You cannot do that in Mexico. If a person approaches a group of people, they'll think, *Who are you? What are you doing here? Leave us alone, we're talking.*" Of course, they won't be rude because the culture of *simpatía* disallows it. But it'll be a little weird.

That said, Mexicans are intensely social with their friends and families, so American life was a difficult adjustment for her in another regard, too. "What was challenging for me was how isolated life is here," she says. "You basically go to work, come back home, have small talk with your partner and children, and then go back to bed." In Mexico, most time is spent socializing with friends and relatives. "In Mexico, when I go back on the summers, there are always a lot of people to talk to," she says. "People look at you in the eyes, they smile. You feel connected. You feel like you exist."

After nearly two decades in America, she now resides in a kind of border zone. She loves that in America you can speak your mind, which you have to be careful of in Mexico, for fear of offending someone or making someone uncomfortable. "I do hate that," she says. Yet she still has to work hard to overcome a perception—by colleagues and students alike—that she is meek. But then when she goes back to Mexico, she's more outspoken, and occasionally frustrated by the self-restraint required by *simpatía*. She's not sure she can reconcile these two parts of her personality, though she has noticed that she tends toward *simpatía* when speaking Spanish and away when speaking English. The culture she is in determines which way she leans. "I guess I'm some sort of hybrid," she says.

Now, that might make her seem like a sort of nowhere woman, caught between worlds. But the hybrid that she embodies—a person from a culture of *simpatía* living in a pretty garrulous country—is actually the sweet spot in terms of our project here. She has been trained to be polite, self-effacing, and attentive when talking to other people. *Simpatía* in that regard isn't so different from what we've seen in, say, free listening. It's not about you, it says: It's about the other person. So when someone comes to the United States from a culture of *simpatía,* provided they can speak the language, they come equipped with many of the skills we've been trying to learn—skills that can make them pretty ideal conversational partners.

In a series of ingenious studies, psychologists Gloriana Rodríguez-Arauz, our friend Ramírez-Esparza, Adrián García-Sierra, and colleagues saw this firsthand. They had Latina mothers and white European mothers in the Seattle area wear digital recorders eight hours a day for four days to monitor the tenor of their interactions. They found that the Latina mothers showed far more behaviors associated with *simpatía*—appearing modest, likable, and considerate—and talked far more about *other* people than themselves (you'll recall Urban Confessional's 80/20 rule). The mothers hailing from white European backgrounds were lower in *simpatía* and talked about themselves significantly more. The researchers also found that the Latina mothers laughed more and had more meaningful conversations with others—regardless of ethnicity. Ironically, the European women rated themselves higher in terms of *simpatía* behaviors than the Latina women did.

What's more, *simpatía,* practiced in the context of a garrulous, individualistic country like the United States, can also be contagious. In a 2009 study, Renee Holloway, Amy Waldrip, and William Ickes of the University of Texas at Arlington paired up 126 strangers—white, Black, and Latino—for conversations. Half were paired with people of their own ethnicity, and the other half were either white people or Black people, paired with Latino people. First, they found that the Latino conversationalists demonstrated far more behaviors associated with *simpatía:* eye contact, smiling, and laughing. Second, and more interesting, the white or Black participants who interacted with a Latino showed more *simpatía* behaviors themselves than those who didn't. They talked more and made more eye contact, and laughed and smiled significantly more. "Their interactions were better in both of these respects than the interactions that involved only Black and/or White participants," write the authors.

After the fact, the subjects rated their interactions. Those who talked to a Latino person rated their partner significantly higher than those who interacted with a white or Black person. Plus, "Participants who interacted with a Latino partner perceived their interaction as having been more smooth, natural, and relaxed. They also reported their interactions to have been more involving, and they expressed a greater interest in interacting with their Latino partner in the future than did the participants who interacted with Black or White partners."

This wasn't just a one-way gift, either. For their part, the Latino conversationalists enjoyed their time equally. "Latino dyad members reported their interactions to be more smooth, natural, and relaxed (and significantly less forced, awkward, and strained). They also reported their interactions to be more involving and indicated that they felt more accepted and respected by their interaction partner. Finally, the Latino participants reported a greater level of liking for their interaction partners, and felt that their interaction partners liked them more, when compared with the Black and White participants combined."

My point here is this: We tend to assume that friendliness arises from being content and unworried. And sometimes it does. I'm certainly not saying that all friendly people today are performing a rational calculation before flashing a smile at a stranger, nor that friendly people don't trust others, because that's not how most people are. I'm saying that *cultures* of friendliness arose not in spite of fear, chaos, and insecurity, but because of those things, and in response to them, and as a way of fostering cooperation within them. As with honorary kinship, greeting rituals, and hospitality, this friendliness served as a practical way to reconcile our fear of strangers with the opportunities they present, and smooth the way to cooperation and connection in a frightening or chaotic time.

And guess what, here we are again: living in a frightening and chaotic time, where central institutions are weakening and social trust is cratering. Right now life is difficult, messy, contentious, and increasingly motley, and we've come to distrust the strangers around us, the strangers with whom we share a country, and the strangers with whom we share the world. Certainly, we can go on doing what we're doing, digging in, fighting, refusing to interact across the wall rising between us. Or, knowing what we know, we can make the choice to be friendly, to smile, to talk, to listen. Not because we're soft, and not because we lack conviction, but because cooperating with one another is in our best interests, and because we know that friendliness, far from being an expression of weakness, can be nothing less than the antidote to fear. And with that in mind, I invite you to join me on a trip to Finland.

Chapter 14

How to Procreate with Strangers in Finland

In which we dive into a culture in which people famously do not talk to strangers, and meet the famous man trying to teach them how to do it—before it's too late, by god.

"I'm originally from Turkey," she says. "This matters. This is very much related to what I'm going to tell you."

Ceyda Berk-Söderblom grew up in Izmir, a city on Turkey's Aegean coast, where she worked at an arts foundation for fourteen years, producing festivals. She met and then married a Finnish artist, a Swedish-speaking theater director, and in 2015, they moved to Helsinki.

Helsinki is a harmonious place. There is equality, prosperity, culture, low crime, high literacy, and scant homelessness. It is the capital of Finland, the happiest country in the world, according to Gallup, at least based on certain metrics—GDP per capita, social support, life expectancy, freedom to make life choices, generosity, and a lack of corruption. It is comparatively quiet, and it is orderly. Very orderly. So orderly in fact that when I jaywalked, as I often and instinctively do at home when there's no conceivable reason to remain standing on the sidewalk, I suddenly found myself alone in the middle of a major avenue, with Finns on sidewalks on either side looking at me like I had just tap-danced into church wearing a penis costume.

All of which is to say, by many accounts, Helsinki is a kind of paradise. And yet, when Berk-Söderblom arrived from Turkey, her transition was anything but smooth. First were the cultural differences. Being Turkish, she's warm and talkative, where the Finns are famous for their reserve. A small illustrated book called *Finnish Nightmares,* containing a litany of local horrors, is ubiquitous here. Most of these nightmares boil down to having to interact with strangers. One is, "When someone sits next to you on public transport . . . and then they start talking to you." Another is, "When a stranger looks you in the eyes . . . and smiles."* I told a cabdriver there that I was in town to research a book about talking to strangers, and he replied, "In Finland? You do know that we are, like, the most silent people in the world?"

It was a hard culture to fit into for Berk-Söderblom. When she lost her father-in-law, for instance, she was shocked that people didn't come over to offer condolences, as they do in Turkey, but instead left the family alone, giving them space. Even something as simple as having friends over became a source of cultural friction. In Turkey, Berk-Söderblom says, you extend lavish hospitality. "We try to kill our guests by providing food," she says. Finland, however, tends toward potlucks, an approach to socializing she rejects. When people offer to bring food, she always tells them no. "They are my guests, so I should cook," she says. "I should prepare everything." That ancient tradition of hospitality is hard to shake. "It's in your blood," she says.

More challenging, though, was transitioning professionally. "I suffered a lot as a foreign worker," she says. Her credentials were sterling, but it took her a year to find a way to work in the arts scene. Language was the biggest barrier. She spoke mostly English in her old position, but in Finland most speak Finnish (and some speak

---

* One more, apropos of my jaywalking gaffe, depicts someone crossing against the light while another watches from the sidewalk. This nightmare? "When someone's doing something 'wrong,' and staring at them intensely won't make them stop."

Swedish). This is a pressing problem for the nation, which has seen a huge wave of immigration over the past few years, particularly in the form of refugees displaced by civil war. Many of these newcomers in the metropolitan area do not speak Finnish or Swedish, and have thus struggled to find jobs, and, more broadly, a place in Finnish society. "It was a big shock" to a historically monocultural country that lacks the mechanisms to cope with diversity, Berk-Söderblom says. The newcomers' presence was a potential boon—Finland badly needs new workers for its growing knowledge economy—but like in other Scandinavian countries, the strain associated with it has given rise to a nascent white nationalist movement.

So in 2016, as immigrants so often do, Berk-Söderblom opened her own business, MiklagårdArts, after the ancient name for Istanbul, which Vikings traveling to Turkey in the tenth century described as the biggest city they had ever seen. She decided the focus of her work would be on encouraging interaction between Finnish organizations and international artists in the hopes that these dialogues would help ease Finland into its more heterogeneous future, which at this point is unavoidable. As part of this effort, she contacted a man named Theodore Zeldin and invited him to come to Helsinki and teach people how to talk to strangers.

On a rainy Friday afternoon in September 2019, Theodore Zeldin sits in a chair onstage before a sparse, scattered audience of mostly women at the immaculate new Amos Rex museum in Helsinki. Eighty-seven years old and thin, with a cloud of gray hair and a slight avian caste to his features, Zeldin is clad in gray trousers, a blazer, and a navy sweater. After being introduced, he stands up. He speaks softly but urgently. "I have come here not to give you things, but to ask you questions," he tells the attendees. "Because what interests me is what's going on in this country." He pauses. "You are the most happy people in the world. This *cannot* be true. There are many prizes you have won. And that makes me wonder what are you going to do next. And I need to find out."

Zeldin is an English historian most famous for *A History of French*

Passions, his two-thousand-page emotional history of France, considered a revolutionary masterwork of European history, first published in 1973. He has been a professor at Oxford University. He has advised presidents, cabinet members, and CEOs. More important to our purposes, though, he has devoted his life to speaking to as many strangers as he possibly can. Xenophilia, in other words, is his vocation. "I will never get to know everybody in the world," he says, "but my purpose is not to become rich, not to become famous—my purpose is to discover what life *is.*"

In doing this work, in talking endlessly to strangers for decades, Zeldin has come to believe that there are no majorities or minorities in the world. There are no strangers or familiars. There are only individuals. Everyone is a minority of one, he believes. Everyone is a stranger. He asks the crowd in Helsinki how many of them feel fully understood. None raise their hands. "No one claimed to be fully understood," Zeldin says, "and that is what you need from other people, to be appreciated, and it's very difficult to appreciate you without knowing you intimately, one by one. It is not by big revolutions that we will change this, but by intimate contact."

Zeldin is also the founder of the Oxford Muse Foundation, which he launched in 2001. This is why I followed him to Helsinki. The Oxford Muse hosts Feasts of Strangers, which are dinners in which strangers are paired up and given a "menu" of intense personal questions—questions that speak to their values, their fears, and their hopes. "The questions are very difficult," Zeldin explains, "because life is very difficult." The conversations that transpire at these feasts—which last two hours and have taken place in fifteen countries—have led to marriages and to deep friendships, even between men who fought on opposite sides of a civil war. More than that, they have taught people not only about others, but about themselves. Attendees "are surprised to find themselves stimulated to say things they had not said before, discovering as much about themselves as about their partner, and having the rare experience of someone genuinely interested in listening to them," Zeldin says.

At the center of the Feast of Strangers is an idea Zeldin arrived at after decades of talking to strangers. That idea is procreation. He feels the old way of belonging—membership in groups—is obsolete. There are simply too many differences among people now, and their individual uniqueness makes a mockery of the idea of a clearly defined group. But he also believes individualism is a dead end. His idea is that the couple—not the group and not the individual—is the most powerful unit in a culture.

"Every relationship between you and me, between you and you, every time you talk to somebody, you discover something about them, and therefore about yourself, and therefore about the world," he says. Zeldin speaks often of muses, but it's not self-expression he's interested in, but procreativity—the result of two minds coming together and producing something entirely new and unexpected that they would not have produced on their own. He tells those gathered to hear him speak on this dreary Friday afternoon, "I hope you will become my muses." And in turn, through conversation, we will become one another's muses.

Zeldin is here to host three such feasts: one for Helsinki's cultural elite, and two more open to the general public. His speech on Friday is the start of things. On his mind is the rise of white nationalism, the political chaos in the West, and Finland's place as a democratic stronghold, as well as its struggles to cope with its newcomers. "Since your population is falling, you've got to realize that other people are coming here, whether you like it or not," he says. "As in every other country migration is inevitable. Because the world is unequal and some places are in such chaos that people have to escape. If I'm not mistaken, the origin of the Finnish people is they came a very long distance to this part of the world. We are all migrants. So we have to know how to deal with strangers. And instead of saying 'Black people are strangers,' we must say we are *all* strangers—I am a stranger to you, and you are a stranger to me, whatever your origins are. I am here to deal with this."

At the end of his remarks, Zeldin tells the audience he wishes to conduct an experiment, "because I want to know who you are. There is no point in me coming to Finland if all I do is walk the streets and eat the food and so on. I've got to understand how each person has got different ideas in their heads." He distributes sheets of paper and asks each person to write a small memoir about their chief achievements, regrets, hopes, challenges, and weaknesses. "In other words," he says, "everything that is important about you."

We all do them, hand them over, and, one by one, quietly, we filter back out into the rain.

Laura Kolbe is a respected Finnish historian and politician. I had reached out to her in the hopes that I could buy her a cup of coffee and pick her brain about the Finns, and she was kind enough to meet me at the University of Helsinki. Kolbe says the stereotype of the silent Finn is just that—a stereotype. There is some truth to it, however, which she says stems from a few factors. She believes it started when German-, Swedish-, and Russian-speaking people arrived two centuries ago. Because they couldn't speak Finnish, they didn't talk to the locals, and the locals didn't talk to them, which was a reticence the newcomers mistook for shyness. Second, Finland is a large landmass with a small population, and it has been agrarian for most of its existence. Rural life is less chatty than urban life. Third, the national mythology, created in the nineteenth century, featured a heroic type: "male, blond, shy, and a little bit stupid, but courageous, honest, loyal, and straightforward," Kolbe says.

She does concede there is indeed a marked difference between Americans and Finns, but she also believes—correctly, as we saw in the last chapter—that American friendliness is in some sense a tool, a means to something else. "When a Finn opens his or her mouth, it happens with honesty; you are not trying to buy anything or sell anything," she says. "Whereas everybody who comes to the States loves the [social] flexibility: The waitress is so social and asks how you are doing, but then immediately when the tip is lacking, the tone changes."

We are joined by Kolbe's daughter, Carolina Forss, a cheerful, bright recent college graduate who studied fashion design. Forss lived abroad in New York City for a summer, which she found open and highly sociable and somewhat liberating. "It was something I really wanted to take back from there," she says. "But it's quite quick: When you come here you become a Finn again."

"What did it mean to become a Finn again?" I ask.

"There's something a little bit inside that shuts down," she says. She loves her country, but her time abroad has made her something of "a stranger," she says: perhaps too extroverted by local standards. "I feel like I'm much more myself when I'm abroad, to be honest," she says. "I'm not a good ambassador for Finland."

A day later, I'm sitting with Theodore Zeldin in the lobby of the Amos Rex museum, and he tells me he's been reading what people wrote after his speech on Friday. "By god, the results are amazing," he says. "About a third of those I read are in a really, really bad way. They feel really left out. They've got no contact with the world." Some of them feel this way because they're foreigners, he says, and some just feel left out. They are lonely; they don't feel as though they belong. We've talked about the loneliness epidemic in this book. Here it is, written across the lives of the denizens of the happiest place on earth. "I felt a bit concerned," Zeldin tells me. "These people need some help, by god."

We talk about his youth. He was born in British Mandatory Palestine in 1933, raised by his father, an engineer, and his mother, a dentist, in a house full of books. A prodigy, Zeldin went to Oxford at sixteen, graduated at seventeen, and obtained his PhD not long after that. He achieved the latter with no doctoral adviser. "Nobody was able to teach me at Oxford," he says. Not the faculty, anyway. But there were other lessons to learn. While there, he met a great many intelligent women. They taught him how to have a deep conversation. "From the point of view of being able to connect with other people, I think I learned it from women. Women can speak more freely about what really matters in life," he says.

The French, he says, were his first strangers. At twenty-one, Zeldin traveled to Paris to dig through the archives of Napoléon III. He had become interested in what makes nations strange to each other, and in confronting the assumptions the French had about themselves. He spent the next thirty years studying them, he says. In the process he evolved a new way of practicing history. He likens his method to that of a biologist. Rather than focusing on sweeping trends and the lives of the most powerful people, Zeldin's interest lay in the molecules and atoms of a society: the people. You don't learn about a country by studying only its leaders and wars and economic systems, he thought. You learn about a country by studying its people, not as a mass, but individually, and by asking how they came to think the way they thought and feel the way they felt.

The first book that resulted from this approach was the mammoth *History of French Passions.* "It's all based on lots of portraits of people as individuals, and showing, as a conclusion, that there are as many minorities in France as there are inhabitants, and therefore all the generalizations which are made about the country collapse," he says. Thus, "the need for understanding each individual becomes the basis of history."

The book angered some, who did not care for having their self-image challenged by a foreigner, but on the whole, it astonished the French. "When the media overwhelmed me with interviews and statements like 'He understands us better than our governments, our spouses, our bosses, and our children,' I was myself extracted from the status of a stranger," he says, "and asked for advice by almost every profession and institution—from the president of the republic and the prime minister to the ultimate rejects of society. Each one bared their troubles to me, and allowed me to penetrate into what is normally hidden from public view. Each expanded my curiosity."

In 2012, France named him a *commandeur de la Ordre National de la Légion d'honneur,* one of the nation's highest honors. At the award ceremony, Bernard Émié, France's ambassador to the United Kingdom, told him, "You are without equal in holding up to us a mirror that accurately reflects both our virtues and our failings. Indeed, you seek meticulously to understand us and to improve not only your compatriots' understanding of the French—and hence our ability to work better together—but also relationships between human beings in general."

The desire to understand the variety of human thought and emotion and experience, to complicate the way we see others and the way we see ourselves, is what drives him today. In his 2015 book *The Hidden Pleasures of Life,* Zeldin writes, "Instead of searching for a niche in which I would be safe, instead of torturing myself with questions about what my true passions or talents are, I shall aim to get a taste, even just a nibble, of what it is possible to experience as a human being. What I cannot experience personally, I wish to imagine by getting to know others who have gone where I have not been. A lost soul is one for whom the thoughts of others are a mystery, and to whom no one listens. [So] instead of 'who am I?' the question I prefer is who are you?" He likens talking to strangers to "a ritual like taking my clothes to the laundry, cleaning my mind of prejudices." He believes if other people do it, it will "change in the way life is lived."

Surely, a change is needed. Today, Zeldin worries that people are walled off from one another, and the problem is deepening with mass migration, inequality, and political discord. He worries countries aren't talking to each other, specialists in different fields aren't talking to each other, coworkers aren't talking to each other, families aren't talking to each other, parents and children, lovers. He's not referring to idle chitchat, but real conversations about things that matter. He's zealous on this point. He believes if you don't understand other people, you don't understand life, and if you don't understand life, you don't know what you can do, or cannot do, and what obstacles might lie in your way. If you don't understand other people, you'll never know how to live among them. Hence his vocation. "I have spent my life discovering the world, one by one," he says.

Zeldin's 2000 book, *Conversation: How Talk Can Change Our Lives,* lays out a vision for what conversation can be. "The kind of conversation I'm interested in is one in which you start with a willingness to emerge a slightly different person," he writes. "It is always an experiment, whose results are never guaranteed. It involves risk. It's an adventure." He cautions against withdrawing from people we don't like. "I would argue that finding something admirable, or touching, in an incomprehensible or obnoxious person, is also profoundly satisfying," he writes. "To find that trace of gold, when it is hidden in apparently stony ground, is one of the most exciting of all challenges."

This is why he wants to talk to everyone. Literally, everyone. "Some people say that what I'm trying to do is too ambitious," he says. "They say, 'Well, how can you speak to seven billion different people?' And my answer is: Think of how many bacteria there are inside one's body; how many cells there are in one's brain. Billions! And you can't tell the scientists, 'Oh, you can't study these things—there are too many of them!' But each person opens up new horizons, unexpected territories to explore. Life becomes a constant surprise rather than a source of anxiety. One is so absorbed and fascinated by one's discoveries, which always lead to something else," he says. "I suppose I should call myself an explorer."

Later that day, Theodore Zeldin stands before a hundred or so people in the museum. In a few moments, we will be paired up and led into a room full of tables for our Feast of Strangers. Zeldin's remarks are both a guide to what to expect and a statement of mission.

He says, "In order to discover what is going on, you'll have to open up your own head and be willing to speak and say what you think. Our civilization is such that politeness prevents us from always saying what we think."

He says, "You'll find that talking with a stranger removes barriers and enables you not only to learn about another person, who is as different from you as you are from every other person, but you learn something also about yourself. You may think you know who you are, but many people disagree and may think you are something else. The misunderstanding that exists between people is the cause of most of our miseries."

He says, "We'd like to expand this to all sectors of society, and indeed to do it between nations. The world is full of danger. We can only save ourselves by learning to talk to people of other civilizations, and seeing the friendship and trust that result from talking to one person. When you talk to a person like this, you will feel like you have some connection with them, and that is the beginning of a relationship."

Zeldin doesn't address the psychology that governs these conversations, but there is a substantial body of research that explains why they can be so profound. We learned earlier about what listening can do. How people who are listened to attentively are less anxious, clearer thinkers, and possess a stronger sense of well-being. We know that when one person expresses something personal, the other person will match them. And we know that it is pleasurable to make personal disclosures, and how, as long as we're not weird about it, that they can make people like and trust us.

But there are also a number of benefits to simply being honest. "Individuals who honestly express their emotions experience lower stress and blood pressure, and develop higher levels of intimacy than individuals who hide their emotions," write psychologists Emma Levine and Taya Cohen in a 2018 study. "On the other hand, individuals who harbor secrets have poorer health than individuals who do not." Levine and Cohen conducted a series of studies that show the effects of honesty. In one, participants were split into three groups. One group was asked to be "absolutely honest" with everyone they dealt with across a three-day period, while the others were instructed to be "kind" or "conscious." The people with the honesty condition expected it would be unpleasant, but found it both was more enjoyable than the other conditions and led to a greater sense of connectedness and well-being, not only in that moment, but for two weeks afterward.

In another experiment, participants were split into two groups—forecasters and experiencers—and given lists of personal questions designed to lead to "difficult conversations." These were very similar to what we would be given at the Feast of Strangers, though they were partly drawn from the work of our old friend Arthur Aron, he of the theory of self-expansion. In 1997 Aron devised a famous list of thirty-six questions that will lead to immediate intimacy among strangers, including "What roles do love and affection play in your life?"; "How do you feel about your relationship with your mother?"; "What is your most embarrassing moment?"; and "If you were to die this evening with no opportunity to communicate with anyone, what would you most regret not having told someone?" The forecasters were asked how they thought these conversations would go but were not asked to have the conversations. The experiencers were paired up and did have them. While forecasters believed the conversations would go badly, the experiencers showed significantly higher levels of enjoyment, connectedness, and meaning, which lasted at least a week. "Moreover, participants indicated that they were grateful for and would want to repeat the experience."

Finally, there's the stranger-on-a-train effect. We have experienced this already, literally on a train. People can be more forthcoming with a stranger than with someone they know well: You know that whatever you say will, in short order, be sunk to the bottom of the sea. There's little chance you'll hear about it again. It won't become part of your home, crouched forever in a corner like an evil-smelling old sofa that for whatever reason cannot be thrown away. "People can sometimes achieve a surprising degree of intimacy with total strangers," wrote the American psychologist Zick Rubin in 1974. "When one is with a passing stranger, a person with whom one has only a present but no past and no future, there is a feeling of unaccountability and invulnerability which can have the effect of increasing openness."*

Rubin did a series of experiments related to how people can match one another's disclosures when they are with such strangers. In one, he had a bunch of students stand at bus stops and start conversations with strangers. They would start by asking neutral questions: When's the bus arriving? Do you have change for a quarter? But then some of them would follow up with a statement about themselves, either a personal one or a neutral one. "I'm really glad this day is over—I've had a really hectic day. How about you?" Or "Well, my day is over. How about you?" Lo and behold, those who received the more re-

---

* In his classic essay on the stranger, the sociologist Georg Simmel noted this, too. The stranger, he wrote, "often receives the most surprising openness—confidences which sometimes have the character of a confessional and which would be carefully withheld from a more closely related person."

vealing statement from the experimenters ended up revealing more about themselves. This, I would argue, is the secret power of the Feast of Strangers.

I participate in two conversations that first day. The questions touch on family, rebellion, priorities, loneliness, friendship, love, fear, and, finally, what you can contribute to the world. In my first session, a young woman tells me if she is rebelling against anything, it's the expectation that she needs to buy a house and marry and get a dog right away, like most of the people she knows. She grew up in a small town but now lives in the city. Her friends' greatest fears are not finding something meaningful to do with their lives, she says, and she herself is at a career crossroads. She says for all the talk of equality in Finland, a male coworker mocks her when she confesses to having ambitions. She hates the rain and the cold, and hopes to end up in a job that might help her live somewhere else. She's close with her family, who always talked to her, encouraged her, and told her she was special and valuable, but she struggles to find friends who can see that, too. She studied abroad and developed a mania for socializing. She realized later that it was because she missed her family so much, that she was trying to fill the absence. When she came home again, she says, she resumed the ability to be alone. She says she used to fear death, but now she knows it's out of her hands—that something above us, maybe destiny, maybe God, is in charge, so there's no real point in worrying until you have to worry.

My second conversation was with someone who, from a very early age, wanted to be a woman of the world, a cultivated, free-flying cosmopolitan. Someone wholly alive. And she was, she says. But then she married a Finn. She came here, and her partner refused to let her learn Finnish, in an effort to maintain control over her. She's been here for many years and has come to hate it. She finds it stultifying, uptight, and passive-aggressive. She says no one looks anyone in the eye. She hates that the locals have never fully accepted her, being a foreigner, but she also wonders if she's resisted being accepted in order to maintain some small glimmer of who she was when she dreamed of a big life. She's leaving, she says, though she hasn't told anyone yet. She's striking out to chase the life she's always wanted. She's very afraid, but she knows it must be done before it's too late.

And as they talked, I talked. For me, what kept coming back was a fear I hadn't even acknowledged to myself. We all talked about growing up—where we come from, what our parents were like. It's unavoidable when you're grappling with big questions. But in both discussions, I kept returning to something that was nagging me: When I was a kid, there were always people around. Family, friends, friends of my siblings, friends of my parents. And I loved that. I loved the churn. And now, I told my partners, I am helping to raise an only child, in a small apartment. And though there were people around, they are also very busy, as we are, and seeing them always involved making plans, often weeks in advance. That freewheeling sociality of my youth—that open door—is much harder to achieve, I tell them, and I worry I am cheating my daughter out of something that to me was formative. I still think about it, constantly. And I'm not sure it would have occurred to me had I not joined these conversations.

I come away with a more sweeping insight as well. Zeldin had said that there is no such thing as a group, that everyone is different, that everyone burns to be understood, and that great conversation makes a mockery of group identity. That when we speak of nations, or religions, or any sort of mass gathering of people who are supposed to be the same, we do violence against the infinite complexity of those around us, and we deny ourselves the opportunity to see the world through their eyes. I came in with an easy, cartoonish, one-dimensional understanding of the Finns. I came out with a much more nuanced one. The happiest place on earth, as it turns out, is not without the sort of fear and desire and humiliation and hope and frustration common to less ostensibly happy nations. I can't help but think Finland's newcomers would like to know this as well, to know that their impeccably clean, impeccably ordered, impeccably well-mannered adoptive homeland is subject to the same roiling human emotions they are subject to, the same confusion and loneliness, even the same crisis of belonging. Maybe, if they get together, disclosure begets disclosure. Maybe that's a good start.

On the flight home the next day, I revisit a dog-eared copied of Zeldin's book *An Intimate History of Humanity,* and find two passages I had missed when I first read them, but which land resoundingly now, given what we've learned. The first is about hospitality:

> A new phase of history begins when . . . ancient and simple hospitality is succeeded by a deeper hospitality. . . . That happens when people become hospitable to strange ideas, to opinions they have never heard before, to traditions that seem totally alien to them, and when encounters with the unknown modify their view of themselves. . . . This is a deeper hospitality because it is not just politeness, but involves admitting new ideas and emotions temporarily into one's mind.

The second talks about our old friend infectious disease, turning it into a good metaphor for what happens when we make an effort to talk to strangers:

> The discovery of how the immune system works has shown that every individual is ceaselessly building up resistance to the unfriendly outside world, and that each has got to do it both independently and in concert with others. . . . It is now clear that everyone needs small doses of foreign bodies, that in order to survive side by side with others, it is necessary to absorb a minute part of them. It is impossible to cut oneself off, or to destroy one's enemies forever. Curiosity about others can no longer be thought of as a luxury or a distraction: it is indispensable to one's existence.

Part III

How to Talk to Strangers

Chapter 15

Okay, So When *Are* We Allowed to Talk to Strangers?

In which we learn that despite the crushing social norms against talking to strangers, and the stifling effects of technology and income inequality, there are times in which it is completely permissible to talk to strangers, including when there is a major disaster, or a mime appears.

I mentioned earlier the phenomenon of this weird stranger mojo—how when you get into the habit of talking to people, people just start talking to you. Ben Mathes from Urban Confessional said once he started free listening, people just started coming up to him and talking. Georgie and Uli told me the same thing. And in time, as I continued my practice, I began to experience it, too. One day, after an intense conversation with a young homeless woman—we'll meet her shortly—I decided to take a walk to process the experience. As is often the case, I got carried away and wound up walking thirty-eight blocks south, ending at my favorite public space in New York: Washington Square Park.

While passing through the park that day, I spotted a young guy sitting at a folding table with a sign reading "Where Are You Going?" I took a seat at his table, and we talked for a while. His name was Judah Berger. He was twenty-three years old and had just started doing this—on a whim, he said, but it was going well. People would sit down and they'd talk—about anything. He'd let them take the lead, and prompt them with open-ended questions as they went, or he'd just ask them for life advice. Afterward, he'd write down anything wise or useful they said in his notebook. It wasn't a social media stunt or anything, he assured me. He had no larger ambitions for it, really. He was just interested in people, and he felt suited to it. "I'm not trying to say I'm special," he told me, "but people always tell me I can talk to a wall. So I figured I'd put it to some use."

Two weeks later I meet Berger for coffee. He's friendly, energetic, engaged, and curious. He tells me he moved to New York a year ago, after graduating from Binghamton University in upstate New York. He worked a couple of tech-recruiting jobs initially, but the business wasn't for him, so he quit to look for something else. He felt a little stuck, frustrated. "We're in New York City, which is the height of Western civilization right now," he told me. (This was before the pandemic.) "It's Rome at the height of the Roman Empire. History will look at this as the place where everything was happening. And I felt like I wasn't meeting enough people."

He had grown up in a small, homogeneous Jewish community in Georgia, and he didn't have many connections in the city. One night, he thought, *What if I just sit and talk to people and see what happens?* He got a table and a couple of chairs and made two signs that he could alternate —one reading "Where Are You Going?" and the other "Where Have You Been?"—and set up shop in Washington Square Park. "I told my parents about it," he says. "They were like, *What?* They were very confused." His mother worried that he was putting himself in danger by encouraging strangers to come talk to him.

Berger says as a kid he was always very curious, and a little intense. He'd go to the library and take thirty books out, and then return them a month later and get thirty more. As he got older, that curiosity started to extend to other people. When Berger went to college, he chose a place where he would be away from his high school friends. There were a lot of Jewish students, but they were from different backgrounds, and there were lots of other kinds of people besides. And as a southerner, he stood out.

"I guess some people were able to tell that I came from a different background," he says, "but over time I just learned to talk to people." He became "the kid from Georgia," and he came to like it. "I kind of took pride in it," he says. His southern friendliness and curiosity helped him meet new and different people. "College really opened me up," he says. After that he moved to the city. "Some people are very happy being in a very small, insulated, supportive community," he says, "which obviously has its pros, but it also has its cons because of, you know—I was always very curious."

When Berger first set up his table and chairs in the park, his biggest concern was that no one would sit down. "I quickly found my fears were unfounded," he said, laughing. Sometimes he'd be trying to jot down his notes from one conversation and someone else would come over and start another one. Sometimes people will start talking to him when he is in the middle of a conversation, and he'll just go with it. "One time, I was talking to this student, and another person came over, and they started talking," he says. "Then they ended up walking off together and continuing the conversation."

He tells me he sits for five or six hours at a time and says he's occupied for 90 percent of it. "It's just a really cool experience, all in all," he says. "You have to learn to interact with a lot of different people, rapid-fire. Every time someone sits down: completely new personality, completely new outlook, completely new background—and you have to find a way to relate to them in a way that they're not gonna be like, *Oh, screw you, you're a dick*. They want to come up with a good experience, so you have to be completely positive."

Sometimes people are suspicious. They'll ask if he's charging money, or they'll accuse him of just trying to find a girlfriend. But the more common question is *Why?* "I always go, 'Why do you think?' And there's always a different answer. That'll get the ball rolling." Some people are easier to talk to than others, he says, but most open up, eventually, and the conversations just go where they go. If there's a lull, he'll ask: "If you can give me one thing to do in life, and I have my entire life to do it, what would you tell me to do?" The genius of that question is that he's asking them for advice, which is flattering, but in order to give it, his partners have to tell him about their own lives. In doing that, they have a chance to talk about their experiences, their values, their pasts, and maybe their hopes for the future.

He had an artist who had hand-painted every article of clothing she wore make him a drawing in his notebook. It was just a little scribble, "but clearly you can see she has talent," he says, showing me. A sixty-year-old woman insisted he go to Burning Man. He talked to a young musical theater director, and a woman who practices "ecstatic dance" who told him if you speak positively to water, it changes its composition. "That can always be debated of course," he says. "But you do meet some very interesting and colorful characters."

Best of all, he's expanding his network. His notebook is becoming "an atlas," he says, a road map to the future. He met the mayor of a small town in England who invited him to visit. He met two students from Italy who gave him a list of places he should travel to and invited him to come to Italy. "I actually have a cool place to go to in Italy because of them," he says. "These are things which I probably never would come to on my own."

"Do you consider yourself an optimist?" I ask.

"Yeah, I think it's hard to do something like this and be a pessimist," he says. "I believe in the goodwill of most people. I don't think this is a risky thing. My mom was like, *Who is going to sit down?* I was like, *Most people are fine.* I'm in a public space. I'm not doing this at three in the morning in some random park. This isn't risky by any means, other than fear of your own rejection. It's always a good experience. And even if you only get to talk with five or six people, that's five or six people you didn't get to talk with previously, and you'll walk away with a new outlook."

We now know about all the things that keep us from talking to strangers, and some of the things that encourage us to. We know that ecology, cultural norms, density, fear, income inequality, technology, and efficiency can keep us apart, and we know the ways cities can conspire against spontaneous connections. But at the same time, we know that cities have exerted a powerful draw over human beings for six thousand years, and we know that people do connect in cities, and they do talk to strangers, just under certain circumstances.

So, as we continue on our journey here, what *are* those circumstances? When are we allowed to talk to strangers?

You remember Erving Goffman. He's the sociologist we met in chapter 11 who came up with the concept of civil inattention—the idea that we often avoid contact because we're overloaded. Goffman also spent a great deal of time in the field studying the circumstances under which it was okay to talk to a random stranger in a public place. He found that a common situation in which the norm is lifted is when you're both looking at the same thing—be it a car wreck, a mime, or a statue. At these times, anyone can talk, "even persons of extremely disparate social positions," Goffman writes. Later, urban planners would describe this as *triangulation,* defined as "the process by which some external stimulus provides a linkage between people and prompts strangers to talk to each other as though they were not."

Triangulation can be pleasant, but it doesn't have to be. People talk to strangers in the event of a disaster, which can temporarily erase racial, ethnic, ideological, and class boundaries. "If the disaster is quite calamitous," Goffman writes, "everyone is likely to be forced . . . into mutual accessibility."* According to Goffman, if an individual is wearing a uniform—a firefighter, or a priest, say—that person was an "open person," and could be spoken to. Old people and very young people can be spoken to at any time, as can anyone "dressed in a costume, or engaged in an unserious sport." (I would place Judah Berger, the young man with the table, in this category.) They "may be accosted almost at will and joked with," Goffman writes. If you and the stranger are visibly members of any minority group in the midst of a majority, you can engage. If someone trips or

---

* Here's a personal example. While traveling back from Kentucky with a friend not too long ago, the plane I was in touched its rear wheels down to the runway, and stayed like that, spanning the runway at a forty-five-degree angle, then shot violently back up into the sky again, with no explanation offered by anyone. As panic consumed the passengers, the young woman next to me, who hadn't said a word the whole time, turned, and said calmly, "So what were you guys doing in Louisville?"

drops something, you can talk to them in order to help. And if you are in need of a free public good—directions, the time—you can talk to anyone. That said, Goffman warned, while you can occasionally ask the date, you shouldn't ask what day it is. Not knowing the date is understandable; not knowing what day it is suggests you are an agent of chaos, and violates what Goffman says is the ideal while attempting to talk to strangers: "To utter something and to not disconfirm that we are sane."

Beyond that, the norms are clear, Goffman found. There are a finite number of situations in which you are allowed to talk to strangers. You can talk to cashiers—but only about things that roughly pertain to the transaction at hand. "You are not entitled to ask a [movie theater] ticket seller flat out, without preamble, whether her hair is natural or not, what she thinks about her mother, and a host of other matters she can call to mind and routinely will when talking to intimates," he writes. "You can tell the ticket seller that you are dying to see the show, and while this might be judged as a little oversociable, it is perhaps forgivably so. But if you chose the moment of contact with a ticket seller to tell her directly about having to take the car in tomorrow to get a new muffler, that would be considered grounds for imputing strangeness." If you're in an elevator, it's best not to talk because "any mutual exchange of glances on the part of the occupants would add almost a touch of lewdness to such already over-cozy sardine formation." That said, if the elevator breaks down, you must talk. The breakdown provides triangulation and a hint of calamity, and to go on as though you were not sharing an unusual and upsetting experience would suggest you are not aware of it, which would also be considered grounds for imputing strangeness.

Sitting close to a stranger for an extended period of time—as on a plane, or a commuter train at a table where pairs face one another—and *not* speaking is also, yes, grounds for imputing strangeness. "During such difficult times, if the individual decides against contact, he may well have to find some activity for himself in which he can become visibly immersed, so as to provide the others present with a face-saving excuse for being unattended to," Goffman writes.

What about specific places? How can we scout out a good location to hone our skills at this? As it happens, the physical characteristics of a place can determine whether people will be comfortable talking to strangers. Cynthia Nikitin has spent nearly three decades studying this in her work at the Project for Public Spaces (PPS), a New York City–based firm that specializes in designing public spaces in cities, before retiring in March 2020. PPS oversaw the transformation of Bryant Park in New York decades ago, which had become so unruly that when PPS staffers began interviewing people who used the park, even the drug dealers complained that it had gotten so bad it was hurting their businesses. Today Bryant Park is a model for what a public space can be. This kind of work is called *placemaking,* and after the chronic neglect and decline of American cities from the 1960s to the 1980s, it has gone global. "It's a new way of governing, planning, and designing our cities," Nikitin says. "Everybody, *everybody* wants this."

In what kinds of spaces are we allowed to talk to strangers? First, Nikitin cites public buildings. Libraries, for instance, are public spaces, which help reduce anxiety over class and racial divisions. "You know that everyone has a right to be there," she says. "It's not like you are there because you can afford a fifteen-dollar craft cocktail."* Nikitin also cites museums and town halls as places where people can talk, because each institution "is there to serve us, which makes public interaction more comfortable and safer—because you're in an environment where it's sanctioned." I would add professional sports arenas to the same category. You are close together for hours, you are watching the same thing, there for the same reason, and in a way you are of the same group: fans, enthusiasts. All these

---

* In my own local library, I see this all the time. Not long ago, I sat next to a Chinese immigrant and her native-born son, and offered a quick hello. Ten minutes later they asked if I could help fill out his financial aid form for college. I said of course, and we worked through it together.

things reduce barriers between us and give us something to bond over.

A good *outdoor* public space, Nikitin says, can encourage interactions among strangers, but by virtue of a much more subtle and complex interplay of factors. Much of what the firm does is inspired by the work of a man named William Whyte, a former journalist who in the late 1970s and '80s set out to understand how public spaces work. He found that the most popular spots had some distinct characteristics: plenty of seats that can ideally be moved around, ample sunlight, trees to sit under, water to drink, food to eat, proximity to a busy corner, a water feature like a fountain or a reflecting pool, and something to look at. They also had multiple uses, Whyte found. The dog park is by the playground, which is by the restrooms, which is by the benches favored by the older people, which is maybe by a small farmers market, and so forth.* All these elements combine to make people comfortable. "And when people feel physically comfortable," Nikitin says, "then they're also more likely to feel open, and safe, and converse with people who don't look like them."

Yale sociologist Elijah Anderson has done a lot of fieldwork on this—the ability of good public spaces to bring strangers together, particularly across racial boundaries. He calls these places *cosmopolitan canopies*. A former Philadelphia resident, Anderson was inspired by spots like the Reading Terminal Market—a bustling food hall—and Rittenhouse Square—a stately park downtown.

Anderson immersed himself in these spaces, and found that they "provide an opportunity for diverse strangers to become better ac-

---

* Farmers markets, it turns out, are especially good for encouraging spontaneous interactions. A 1981 study found that people were far more likely to talk to one another at farmers markets than supermarkets. This is because people tended to come to the farmers market with at least one other person, whereas most supermarket shoppers were alone, and because supermarkets are designed for maximum efficiency, whereas farmers markets are not. In a farmers market, you're forced to wander, to graze. When something catches your eye, you're likely buying direct from a farmer, who is more emotionally and financially invested in their produce and more likely to want to talk about it. When a farmer and a customer are discussing the best way to prepare, say, rutabagas, someone else might overhear it and chime in.

quainted with people they otherwise seldom observe up close." Why? They are public, which is to say egalitarian. Everyone claims a right to be there, and ideally everyone else honors that right by treating them with civility and goodwill. Civil inattention is set aside and people have the chance to look more directly at others as they go about their lives. This can rein in lesser minds and humanize these formerly abstract strangers, fostering empathy and reducing fear. Remember what Gillian Sandstrom found when she did her scavenger hunt study: the participants who were tasked with just looking at strangers felt better and more connected. The same goes for cosmopolitan canopies. People watching is good for us.

Anderson believes that with enough contact, people can overcome intergroup anxiety and become more empathetic and better able to deal with the challenges of an increasingly crowded and diverse world. "Ultimately, lessons learned under the canopy can be carried home to neighborhoods all across the city," he writes. Those lessons aren't that we're all the same, but that we can live together despite our differences by meeting one another not as members of groups, with fixed cultural identities, but as individuals. It provides not just entertainment and edification, Anderson argues. "It provides a life that could not previously be lived."

So those are some of the rules: the instances in which it's considered okay to talk to a stranger in a city. And they're useful to know, because they provide some areas in which we can practice without fear of being looked at funny for violating a social norm. But they're also good to know because our goal here is to move past them, to become adept at breaking that social norm. And to break the rules, you have to know the rules.

We already met sociologist Lyn Lofland. She is a small-town girl from Alaska who took to city life with an immigrant's zeal, placing great value on what she called "the mild but quite pleasant adventures" of talking to strangers. And while she meticulously documented all the ways people avoid doing so, she also observed the two types of people for whom the rules never seemed to apply. Lofland refers to these people as *hicks* and *eccentrics,* and she defines them like this:

> Hicks are persons who don't know how to get along in the city but don't know or don't care that they don't know. The consequences of their ignorance are often rather astounding. They talk to all kinds of people and find that all kinds of people will talk back; they make fast friends in the most unlikely locales and under the most unlikely circumstances; they ask for and receive assistance in situations in which even skilled urbanites would hesitate. They move through the city with confidence, protected from its dangers and pitfalls by the simple shield of ignorance.

"Eccentrics act the same, but may know more than they let on," she writes. Nevertheless, they received the same treatment: "Here are two improbable adventurers . . . illiterate in, or inattentive to, city ways. And what is their reward? Sometimes, at least, friendliness, protection, normalization. The most inept participants in the world of strangers are, on occasion, its most pampered citizens."

Let these be our models, as we set out into the next stage of our quest to master talking to strangers. With them in mind, we return to a classroom in London.

Chapter 16

How to Talk to Strangers

In which we return to London to complete our course in talking to strangers—an experience that involves learning how to listen, ask questions, break norms, build confidence, get free coffee, and stare into one another's eyes for an agonizingly long period of time until the magic happens.

Now we're making some progress. We understand how talking to strangers helps us become happier, more connected, more trusting, and less lonely. And we know that when it goes well—and it usually does—it's because we are wired for it. We know pretty well what keeps us from talking to strangers, but that means we also know what to circumvent, what to guard against. All that is a way of saying, we're ready to learn how to do it.

This brings us back to Georgie Nightingall. We met her at the beginning of this book. She's the founder of the group Trigger Conversations in London, the woman who teaches the class on talking to strangers. I contacted her at the suggestion of the psychologist Gillian Sandstrom. By this point in my quest to become good at talking to strangers, I had participated in a number of group conversations and was having some conversations out in the wild, but I wanted to find someone who could help me get to another level, someone who really understood not just why these conversations can be powerful, but how they actually work, almost down to a molecular level. That was Georgie, and that was how I wound up sitting jet-lagged in a classroom in London, with four other students, learning to talk to strangers.

As the class gets under way, our first lesson is small talk. A lot of people hate small talk, which is understandable, because a lot of small talk is deadly. One student, Justine, says she always assumes that when someone engages her in small talk, it's specifically because they are *not* interested in her. They're just filling time and being nice. I agree with her. I tell the class that when people ask me what I do for a living, I instinctively want to drop to the floor and bellow like a dying animal until they go away. And I love what I do.

Georgie concedes the point. Yes, she says, small talk can be dull. But that's because most people don't understand what it's actually for. It's not the conversation. It's the opener for a better conversation. It's a way to get comfortable with one another and cast around for something that you *want* to talk about. That, she says, is why it's important to be aware that you might be shutting down when someone asks "What do you do?" and that your partner might be, too. You are failing to understand what that question is really asking, which is this: "What should you and I talk about?"

Georgie came to this insight via a couple of sources. She had done improv comedy in the past, and in improv, you have to start a sketch with something familiar to everyone in the audience, something relevant, timely, or present in the room, to bind the group together. Only then can you really take the audience on a ride. That's small talk. But Georgie has also followed the work of social anthropologist Kate Fox, who has studied, for instance, the seemingly inexhaustible English desire to discuss weather. While some critics have pointed to this affinity as evidence of a listless and unimaginative people, Fox argued that weather wasn't the point. Instead, it is a form of social bonding, a greeting ritual. "English weather-speak is a form of code, evolved to help us overcome our natural reserve and actually talk to each other," Fox writes. The content is not the point—familiarity, connection, and reassurance are. Once those are in place, a real conversation can happen.

Once you recognize that small talk is just a door to a better conversation, Georgie says, then it can be useful because it's structured in a way that naturally leads you toward commonality. We have all experienced how these conversations, if given the time, can move in ever tightening circles until you both zero in on something that you have in common and want to talk about.* That small commonality works as a little bond, a signal of mere belonging, as we discussed earlier. It creates a little *us*. With that in place, you can wander, get a little personal, go deeper. But it's probably on you to take it there, Georgie says. "Everyone is interesting, but it's not up to them to show you—it's up to you to discover it."

Now, the best way to discover the interesting stuff, Georgie says, is by breaking the script. Breaking the script means using the techniques of small talk, but resisting the temptation to go on autopilot. For example, you go into a store and say, "How are you doing?" and the clerk says, "Fine, how are you?" and the conversation contains no information and goes nowhere. That's a script. We use them to make interactions more efficient, particularly in busy, dense, fast-moving places like big cities. But in doing so, we deny ourselves the chance at a better experience, and we wall ourselves off from all the benefits that come from talking to strangers.

So how do you break those scripts? With specificity and surprise, Georgie says. For example, when someone says, "How are you?" she doesn't say, "Fine." Instead, she says, "I'd say I'm a seven point five out of ten." She briefly explains why she's a 7.5, asks them how *they're* doing, and then just waits. You recall the idea of mirroring: that people will naturally follow the lead of their conversational

---

* Sometimes these commonalities can be uncanny. I had two friends who, at a party at my apartment, once talked for fifteen minutes, discovering that they were both from the same state, and then the same part of that state, and then the same town, and then the same street, before discovering that one of them had *literally shot the other one's brother with a BB gun*. "I hated that kid," one of them told me. Nevertheless, they hit it off.

partners. If you say something generic, they will say something generic. If you say something specific, they are likely to as well. Thus, because Georgie gave a number, her partner is likely to give a number themselves. If they say they're a six, Georgie will ask, "What'll it take to get you to an eight?" This specificity creates a light atmosphere and makes it harder for the other person to maintain the belief that you're of a lesser mind, because it instantly demonstrates complexity, feeling, and humor: humanity, in other words. "Straightaway, they're like, 'Oh, you're a human,'" Georgie says. "You have that bond, and then naturally things open up."

This technique reminded me of an exchange I'd recently had while buying coffee one day back home. Only this time it was the barista who used it on me.

"Hiyadoin'?" I muttered.

"Me?" he said, "I'm doing amazing. Thank you for asking."

That got my attention. "Are you always amazing?" I asked. "Or is there something about today?"

"I'd say I'm always between great and amazing," he said. "That's how I do. How are you today?"

"I guess great?" I said. "I mean, you set the bar kind of high. After that I can't really say 'Today sucks.'"

He laughed. "See?" he said. "That's how I do."

Georgie moves on to some other techniques for breaking the script, playful ones inspired by her experiences doing improv comedy. They include responding to a shop clerk's question "Can I help you?" with "Can I help *you*?" Or instead of asking people at a party what they do, ask them what they'd like to do more of, or what they *don't* do.* Or instead of asking someone how their day went, ask, "Has it lived up to your expectations?" All these things require a certain measure of confidence to pull off, she says. But they work. And when they do, they will reveal a little nugget of what it's like to be that person. And that is meaningful, because that nugget is indicative of what is beneath the surface. "How you do anything is how you do

* A friend of mine has great success asking people not what they do, but, "Whose job would you want?"

everything," Georgie says. That nugget tells you where to go next in the conversation.

To illustrate this, she asks Nicky—he was the shy one who grew up on a farm and dreamed of traveling the world—what he did last weekend. He says he didn't do much. Then he thinks a moment and says, "I made fudge." Why did he make fudge, Georgie asks. Because he was curious about making fudge, he says, so he made fudge. Georgie asks him if he does that sort of thing a lot. Nicky says yeah, maybe. Now that he thinks of it, he learned how to make pizza from scratch, too, and he's gotten pretty good at it. Georgie says, "Judging from that, you're spontaneous, you try things." Nicky is struck by this. "I never really thought that about myself," he says. And, reader, my heart melts.

Once you've established this little connection, what do you do? The thing I myself would normally do is start asking questions. Which makes sense: I'm showing an interest in the other person, and I demonstrate my interest by indulging my curiosity. But one paradox about talking to a stranger, Georgie explains, is that curiosity is indispensable, but a barrage of questions out of the gate can feel like prying, or an interview, because the other person doesn't quite know where you're coming from yet, they don't know if you have some kind of agenda. Even one personal question posed prematurely can create an uncomfortable dynamic because you're asking something of someone. You're making a demand.

Georgie suggests that statements, not questions, are a better way to open a conversation. A question compels an answer, whereas a statement leaves it up to the other person to decide whether they want to talk. It's not a demand; it's an offer. You notice something about your shared surroundings, you offer an observation and leave it to the other party to respond. If they do, you respond with another statement that builds on what they said. This is a tenet of improv comedy as well—known as "yes, and," in which each performer adds something to what the previous performer said and did. In that sort of environment, if one performer says, "I'm driving a bus," and another replied, "Why are you driving a bus?" it would smother the sketch before it even got started.

Note that these observations should not be moronic—"I've no-ticed that the sun came up today!"—but they can be simple. Like weather talk in England, the point is to indicate a shared experience. Georgie has found that proximity helps, too. If you are at a museum, walking right up to someone looking at a painting and blurting out "What do you think?" is very different from making an observation about a painting after standing next to them for thirty seconds look-ing at it. That's because you have been in their proximity. They have adjusted to your being there, and you—as we saw in greeting rituals—have demonstrated a measure of self-control. Then you can speak. It feels less like an invasion. You're related by the painting. You're a little *us*.

The real genius of Georgie's class, though, is her approach to breaking through social norms against talking to strangers. We learned at the beginning of this book that social norms are one of the biggest hurdles we face in this effort. We don't talk to strangers be-cause *we* don't talk to strangers. But Georgie has developed what she calls a foolproof method that involves not just violating the norm, but openly acknowledging you are violating the norm.

She asks us to imagine riding mass transit—which as we know is the last place anyone ever talks to a stranger. There is someone who strikes us as interesting. We can't turn to that person and say, "Why do I find you so interesting?" because if you said something like that to a stranger on the subway, they're going to assume this is the initia-tion of a chain of events that will ultimately conclude with their be-coming crude homemade taxidermy.

So Georgie suggests something called a *pre-frame*. It's an idea based in the field of NLP, or neuro-linguistic programming, which coaches people to "reframe" negative thoughts, only in this case it's redefin-ing people's expectations for the interaction to come. Ordinarily, we might be wary if a stranger just starts talking to us. We don't know who they are, or what they want, and the fact that they are breaking a social norm makes us wonder if they're all there in the head. What a pre-frame does is reassure them that you are aware of what you're doing.

To do it, you acknowledge out of the gate that this is a violation of a social norm. You say something like, "Look, I know we're not supposed to talk to people on the subway, but . . ." That way, instead of simply breaking the norm against talking to strangers, you show that you're *aware* that you're breaking it. This demonstrates you're in full possession of your faculties. You're probably not erratic, disturbed, or otherwise off in some way. This helps alleviate wariness and open the possibility of a connection. Once that is established, Georgie says, you follow the pre-frame with your statement—*I really like your sunglasses,* for instance. And then you follow that with a justification: *I just lost mine and I've been looking for a new pair.* The justification eases the person's suspicion that you have some kind of agenda, and allows you to talk a little more openly.

That's when questions become more important, Georgie says. Questions serve a multitude of functions. Yes, they help you obtain information. And yes, on a deeper level, they help your conversational partner clarify the point they are trying to make, as we saw with free listening. But they also work on an emotional level, and help us bond with other people. In a series of studies in 2017, psychologist Karen Huang and her colleagues discovered that "people who ask more questions, particularly follow-up questions, are better liked by their conversation partners." They are perceived as higher in responsiveness—which is defined as "listening, understanding, validation, and care." In other words, people like us because we are interested in them.

And yet, the researchers noted, people tend not to ask a lot of questions. Why? Several reasons. "First," Huang writes, "people may not think to ask questions at all . . . because people are egocentric—focused on expressing their own thoughts, feelings, and beliefs with little or no interest in hearing what another person has to say. Or they may be too distracted by other aspects of the conversation that they do not realize that asking a question is an option." Even if a question does pop into someone's head, they may not ask it, because they worry it'll land badly and be "perceived as rude, inappropriate, intrusive, or incompetent. In these cases," people will probably just talk about themselves, which studies show they do twice as often as they talk about other matters, which, ironically, makes people like them less. Good work, everybody.

But what's a good question to ask? Georgie has us complete an exercise in which we are given banal statements—the sort that is commonly offered in small talk—and tasked with coming up with good questions. For instance, one student says she ran along the Thames yesterday. There is almost nothing in this world less interesting to me than running, and usually I'd take this as my cue to begin plotting my escape. But, working from the idea that small talk is the means, not the end, the class brainstorms good questions to ask that might lead to something more personal or interesting: "Do you run every day?" "Is that a passion for you?" "What would you do if you couldn't run every day?" I suggest, "What are you running from?" which is meant as a joke, but the class seems to go for it.*

This should get the conversation going. But what if it doesn't? The prospect of this rejection is, as we've seen, another one of the most common fears people have about talking to strangers. So Georgie moves into a discussion about rejection. Her big insight here is that there is more than one kind of rejection: There are many, and most of them aren't even rejection. Sometimes people are tired. Sometimes people are confused, or they're caught off guard, or they don't hear you. That's not rejection, Georgie says. She advises us that if we are met with confusion to just repeat what we said, more clearly. If people respond with annoyance or hostility, Georgie says, walk away.

"That's them, not you. Leave it," she says. If people seem defensive or scared, however, that means you have misread the situation badly and must apologize and disengage. Only this last response is true rejection, Georgie says. The other responses are about the other person's mood, or they stem from confusion about the breaking of a social norm. In those cases, don't assume they're not talking to you because they don't like you, or because you're bad at this, or because

---

* Later, I deployed this in social occasions and found it worked remarkably well, and took a dull conversation to some very interesting places.

you're bad at everything. "Don't let a rejection reinforce a negative belief about yourself," she says.

When people do start talking, you have to listen, make eye contact, and generally show you're engaged. Two effective techniques to use to signal engagement are paraphrasing what people have just said—"It seems like you're saying . . ."—and something called *echoing,* which is simply repeating things that your partner just said—both of which are commonly used by therapists and hostage negotiators to foster connection and build trust. For instance, if they say, "I guess at that point I was frustrated," you say, "You were frustrated." This seems deeply weird and unnatural, and feels awkward to do, and if you overdo it, your partner is going to think something's wrong with you. But I am here to attest that, done well, it is extremely effective. It's like a magic trick. Researchers have concluded as much. According to the French psychologists Nicolas Guéguen and Angélique Martin, "Research has shown that mimicry . . . leads to greater liking of the mimicker" and helps create rapport during a social interaction.

Throughout the weekend, our class engages in a series of exercises to sharpen our skills, but more important, to understand why we may be uncomfortable talking to strangers, and get past it. One series of exercises involves eye contact. We pair off and look each other in the eye for longer and longer increments of time, to understand why eye contact can feel awkward, but also to get used to it and feel the sense of connection it can inspire. You remember what Gillian Sandstrom said about realizing she was always staring at the sidewalk when she was walking around? Without eye contact, there is little hope for a meaningful interaction.

As it happens, the connectedness we can feel when looking someone in the eye happens on a biochemical level. You remember when we talked about oxytocin, the hormone that is central to social bonding. There's ample evidence that looking into the eyes of another person can stimulate the release of oxytocin, says Larry Young, the behavioral scientist who runs the oxytocin research lab at Emory University. "If you look into the eyes of another person, and give them the sense that they have a connection with you, it can cause oxytocin release in the other person," he says.[*]

The eye contact exercise feels weird, though. At first, it's hard to do without laughing nervously. But as we do it, we get better at it. It starts to feel more natural. Once it does, we're instructed to tell each other things while maintaining eye contact. One person talks, and the other looks, paraphrases, and echoes. We don't ask questions, we don't offer any insights. Georgie asks us to recognize how awkward this can feel for the listener, how it can feel physically uncomfortable, but also how freeing it can be for the speaker to just be allowed to talk to a receptive audience, how it can grant them the space to eventually fumble toward whatever it is they're trying to say, which we saw with free listening. So I sit there and look and paraphrase and echo as Nicky tells me that he wants to get better at talking to strangers so he can be free and travel the world. All I do is nod and listen, and repeat back to him things he tells me. Nothing more. And afterward, he confesses, "It's nice to have someone understand where you're coming from."

As we work through these exercises, Georgie breaks listening down into three levels. There is listening for things you know about. That's the most superficial level. That's when someone says something about baseball and you jump right on it and start talking about baseball. There is listening for information—getting data and asking questions about things that interest you. That's also more about you and your interests. But then there's the deepest level of listening: listening for experiences, feelings, motivations, and values. That kind of listening is more than simply hearing, or self-affirmation. It's paying attention and endeavoring to understand. It is demonstrated with eye contact, echoing, and paraphrasing, and it can be deepened by

---

[*]   This, I cannot stress enough, is different from staring, or glaring, or leering, which triggers not oxytocin release, but flight. An ingenious field study led by the American psychologist and law professor Phoebe Ellsworth had experimenters stand on street corners or sit on scooters at intersections and either stare at drivers or avert their eyes. Experimenters then timed how quickly the drivers pulled away. The ones who were stared at took off significantly faster.

asking clarifying questions—Why? How? Who?—questions that help the person get to the heart of the matter.

In other words, at this level of listening, you are not simply listening for something that you want to talk about, or offering advice, or trying to think of something smart to say in response. It's not about your agenda. It is about helping your partner get to what they really want to talk about, and you going along for the ride. You still want to talk about yourself a little, Georgie says—to give a little, and not leave the person feeling like you've just rummaged around in the bureau of their personal life and made off with a watch without offering anything in return. But you want most of the focus to be on them. It is, again, a form of hospitality. You are hosting someone. You are surrendering a measure of control. You are giving them space. You are taking a risk. That risk opens you to the potential rewards of talking to a stranger.

During lunch and after class I try out some of these techniques around London. Sure enough, I find they work quite well. Granted, I'm an American, which earns me a certain amount of leeway. Every person I talk to replies, "You're an American?" straightaway. It's not the same for me as it is for my classmates. I am forgiven for violating the norm, for I am a Yank. Americans in Europe don't know any better, the thinking goes. We're quite famous for this.

Still, I have some nice little conversations. They're like little conjurings: picking up a completely ordinary hat and somehow pulling out a rabbit. I ask a twentysomething bartender at a pub if the day has met her expectations, and she confesses with very little prompting that yes, it has. She's about to quit her day job. She feels she's been sold a bill of goods about the merits of a straight corporate career, and she's going to empty her savings and travel the world. She hasn't told anyone this yet, she says. But she will soon.

The next morning, I step into a bank to exchange some old pound notes and coins. A young teller at the bank looks at my passport and says, "New York. Better there than here." I ask why he says that—

a clarifying question. He tells me he dreams of going to New York. He was born in London but he hates it. He wants out, but he has a terrible fear of flying, which has trapped him here.

This is my chance to offer something, a statement. I tell him I once developed a pretty good fear of flying after three deeply hair-raising flights in a row. He asks how I got over it. I said I just kept doing it. I told him something a psychologist had told me about overcoming fear through exposure and repetition: "First you stand six feet away from the spider," she had said, "then you look at it through glass, and at the end, hopefully you're holding that spider." That was good to hear, the guy says. He seems bucked up. He's smiling. He changes my bills and coins and hands new ones to me. "Here you are," he says, "in *exactly* the way you gave it to me."

I thank him. "Hey, I hope I see you in New York."

"I hope so, too, sir," he says. "Thank you."

At lunch that day at a Lebanese take-out restaurant, I ask the owner what menu items he's most proud of—because that's what I want. He starts taking bits of this and that and dropping them into my bag. I tell him I grew up in a white neighborhood, and when I was a kid a Lebanese family moved in behind us, and they used to hand us plates over the fence of what was at that time very exotic food. Since then, Lebanese food has always been among my favorites. Curiously, when I eat it, I think about home. That was my statement. The owner tells me that in Lebanon, that kind of hospitality is a big deal; people always make a lot of food for visitors. While he talks, he keeps dropping more food into my bag. When he's done, the bag weighs about five pounds and he charges me for maybe a third of it.

Another day, after class, in yet another instance of uncanny stranger mojo, I happen upon a bunch of college kids outside of the Tate Britain museum. They are approaching strangers and challenging them to throw paper balls into a barrel. Those who do win a prize. Usually when I see this sort of thing, alarms go off. I suspect it's social media play. But I suspend judgment and go over. I try my hand and hit my shot. A kid gives me an origami swan as a trophy. We chat for a couple of minutes, and it turns out they're art students, and their teacher made them do this to get comfortable engaging with strangers, believing that doing so can spark unlikely inspiration and build the social skills that will help the students promote their work. How have they found it, I ask. The kids say it was awkward at first, but the game helps relieve some of the pressure—it gives permission to break a social norm and gives them something to talk about. He says he's met a lot of interesting people.

On the last day in Georgie's class, we pair off and practice all the techniques we've learned. And that's where I arrive at an uncomfortable realization. I've been a journalist for twenty years, so I know how to ask questions. And I know how to find what I'm looking for relatively quickly. If you're in an interview situation, you usually have a finite amount of time to extract something that readers will find novel and interesting. And yes, this requires a somewhat ethically questionable mix of ruthlessness and empathy known well to all reporters.

Which is to say, I'm a little cocky. I'm paired with Paula—the bright young woman who said earlier that she relies so heavily on maintaining a sort of persona in her personal and professional lives that her own friends have told her they don't really know who she is. She tells me that one of her favorite things is making a cup of good coffee for herself on the weekends and just sitting alone. I dig in. In about four moves she is talking about how resentful she is at having to work for other people. I asked if the reason she so looks forward to making and drinking her coffee on the weekends stems from a need to exert complete control over some aspect of her life, and she said, come to think of it, yes, and she'd never thought of it that way.

I'm obviously quite pleased with myself, as I trot back to Georgie with this pheasant in my mouth. But Georgie is less impressed. She delicately explains that while "it's clear you're a person who asks questions for a living," everything about my body language suggested I was looking for something to pounce on. I asked questions too quickly, she said. I was leaning forward. This wasn't a conversation; it was an interview. Georgie suggested asking simpler and more open-ended questions. Instead of saying "Do you think this was because you were a control freak?" just echo, or say, "Why do you think that is?" This is the opposite of what I usually do, but it's what I must learn to do. In a good conversation, you have to relinquish control—your job is to help them arrive at their own conclusion and surprise you, not to ferret out whatever it is, slap a bow on it, and go, *Next!*

Later that day, I ask Georgie a question many people asked me when I told them I was researching this book. How does she do this without feeling unsafe? I am well aware of my own advantage in these matters. I am, after all, a six-foot-tall white guy. The potential physical risk of talking to people I don't know is lower than it might be for a woman, or a member of a minority group in a hostile place. How, I ask Georgie, as a young woman, does she pursue these connections without attracting a glut of unwanted male attention? Especially if she's often being playful, which could be read as flirtatious? Georgie says she usually tells women if the signals are being misread, mention their partner—even a fictitious one—to cool down the interaction. She also says she avoids practicing in places where people hit on each other, like bars. "That's an area where I prefer not to do this so much," she says.

I had asked the same question of Polly Akhurst, the cofounder of Talk to Me—the group that was trying to get people to talk to strangers in London. She told me she got that a lot, too. "Some people were really surprised that [her cofounder] Ann and I, as young, twentysomething women, had founded an initiative encouraging people to talk because of just this," she replied in an email. "For me, there are a few rules: Always talk to people in public spaces, where there are people around, in daylight. If a young guy approaches me on the street as I'm walking and says, 'Hey how are you?' I am not going to respond. But I actually don't think that much about striking up a conversation with a guy," she says. "I don't worry about if he is misinterpreting it. There have been a few conversations where I've realized that the guy I'm talking to thinks I'm flirting with him. But that's really, really few. I try not to be biased about these things, but sometimes it's hard—you do just have to judge the situation and context, and it can be hard as we have preexisting ideas about people."

Georgie tells me later, in fact, that while men and women have been pretty equally represented at her events, she does frequently hear from men that they're worried about striking up conversations with women because they don't want to look like they're flirting or, worse, a threat. Georgie believes there is a sweet spot between not trying hard enough and failing to attract the person's attention, and trying too hard and freaking them out. Her advice is to land in the middle: Be friendly—smile, talk, practice the techniques she has taught—but also give people their space, don't come up from behind them, don't get too close, and be mindful of their reaction at all times. There's no easy way to accomplish this. It's a simple question of honing your social skills, and that takes work.

At the end of the final day of class, Georgie tells us that practice will be everything. Three of us have opted to do an extended class in which Georgie will give us homework and talk with us weekly to discuss our progress. Some encounters will go poorly, she says, and some will be great, but in time, we will get more comfortable with doing this as we internalize the techniques we have learned. We will be able to get a little bolder or more playful. Our confidence, tone, and body language will alleviate people's wariness at the flagrant violation of a social norm of long standing.

Indeed, Georgie is something of a wizard at this. She once started a conversation with a man on the Tube simply by pointing at his hat, smiling, and saying, simply, "hat." She will randomly high-five people in the street, she says. She smiles at people going the opposite direction down an escalator just to see if they'll smile back. She doesn't order an Americano, she orders "the best Americano in the world." And people respond. During a break one day, I walked into the campus Starbucks to get more coffee. Georgie was already in there, talking animatedly with a barista she'd never met before. When she and I walked out she told me he gave her the coffee on the house.

Chapter 17

Talking to Strangers in the Field

In which I look people in the eye, say hello, and attempt to start conversations despite what the rules of engagement tell us.

For the next three weeks, Georgie Nightingall sends us homework assignments via WhatsApp. These assignments, which vary in degree of difficulty, will give us a chance to try out our new skills in a real-world setting. "You have to make time for this, and go out, and be bold," she tells us. In the first week, she gives us three assignments. For the first, we are to make eye contact with strangers and smile. Just smile. For me, this proves to be the hardest of all the assignments. I had been led to believe that locking eyes with a stranger and smiling— and *only* smiling—is generally interpreted as a prelude to dismemberment, and I imagine people will give me a wide berth when I start doing it. But I do it for science. And at first, it doesn't seem to be working. People either look away, or they don't notice at all.

I message Georgie. "So say we're approaching someone, it's just you and them, on a quiet street," I write. "When do you make eye contact? Just occurred to me as I held eye contact with a guy for like 50 feet, which began to feel somewhat menacing."

"It depends," she replies. "I prefer starting eye contact when they are a little away so you have time to connect as they get closer. But not that far away. That is a standoff. Key thing is to follow up with the smile after any eye contact to show you're not a threat. Maybe shorten to less than 50 feet!"

Fair enough. I also go home and try to replicate the smile I was making out on the street. I realize that it is the smile—rather, "the smile"—I usually affect when I'm impatient, in a hurry, annoyed, or all three. My wife refers to this as "the tense smile." My friend Julia once described it as malicious. So clearly, I had to figure out a way to perform a normal human smile —also known as the *Duchenne smile,* in which your cheeks and eyes get involved—and not merely a grimace. I practice this in the mirror, trying to get my mouth and eyes to work in concert to convey some facsimile of human warmth. It feels unnatural to be smiling like this, unprovoked, and I think it makes me look insane—so much so that even doing it in the privacy of my own bathroom makes me feel self-conscious. Like I am worried there might be a neighbor in the bathtub watching this charade.

Nevertheless, I hit the streets and start smiling at people. Making eye contact is hard, holding eye contact is hard, and smiling is especially hard. I feel completely exposed. I feel like I should explain, *This is a stunt! I'm trying something for a class!* But, as far as I can see, my discomfort at behaving like this on a city street proves invisible to my fellow citizens. On my second day of doing this, sure, some people look a little confused or surprised, but most smile back. It happens enough times that my fear of doing it dissolves. Instead of expecting the worst, my expectations are brought into line—they reflect reality.

And the thing is, people were pretty receptive. I did it most often while walking my daughter to school and then walking back home afterward, and I will say it felt surprisingly good. The world felt smaller, more manageable. I felt more connected to my neighborhood, and I felt better about my neighbors. I still say hello every morning to some of the people I smiled at then.

There have been a number of studies that substantiate my experience. Researchers have found that we like people who make eye contact more than those who look away. We believe that people who look us in the eye are interested in us and, if we speak, in what we're saying. Eye contact has been found to signal inclusion and positive regard, and indicate "the degree to which others regard their relationship with the individual as valuable, important, or close."

A lack of eye contact, on the other hand, has the opposite effect. In one study by psychologist James Wirth, participants who were placed in a situation in which someone refused to make eye contact with them reported feeling ostracized and aggressive toward that person, and they experienced diminished self-esteem. In a 2012 study, psychologist Eric Wesselmann had experimenters cross paths with students on a college campus and either make eye contact, make eye contact and smile, or not make any eye contact at all. Only 45.4 percent of the students who were looked at noticed, but those who did reported feeling less disconnected than the students who were ignored. On the whole, by making eye contact—again, positive eye contact, not leering or glaring—you're telling someone that you consider them valuable and fully human, and that you believe you're both in this together. And when they look back, they are indicating the same thing to you. It's another function of a species that, when it feels safe, naturally seeks connection.

After a few days of smiling, I take it further. I start wishing people a good morning or, if I feel especially brazen, say something like, "Give 'em hell out there today." The latter, I find, works exceptionally well. People laugh, or they wish me the same. I really get into it. One day, I say it to Bill de Blasio, the mayor of New York City. He and I get coffee in the same coffee shop in the mornings, but I had never actually talked to him before. Time to end that, I think. I say, "Good morning, Mayor." He says hello back, and I say, "Give 'em hell out there today." He smiles and replies, "Always." This turns into a series of interactions. In one, we talk about an interview he had done the night before on Fox News; in another he sees my Red Sox hat and starts talking about the game. I have nothing to add and am in fact frozen with fear. At the end, standing at the door of the café, he exclaims, "We'll get 'em next year!"

"You know it!" I said, having been previously unaware the season had just ended.

One day I walk in, and my friend Craig is sitting two tables from the mayor.

"Hey, Craig," I say.

"Hey, Joe," he says.

"Hey, Mayor," I say.

"Hey, man," the mayor answers.

This is going well, I think.

Georgie gives us a couple more "light" assignments like this, which I find initially embarrassing but ultimately useful. One is based on the Buddhist idea of *loving-kindness*. People practice this as a form of meditation, and it works as a series of concentric circles. They start by wishing good things to themselves and those closest to them, and gradually wish good things for friends, acquaintances, strangers, and, finally, all of humanity. To many, this may seem like a strange idea, but several studies have shown the benefits for the meditator. One led by psychologist Bert Uchino at the University of Utah in 2016 found that six sessions of loving-kindness meditation reduced depression and negativity in participants; increased well-being, life satisfaction, and the perception of social support and social connectedness; and improved existing relationships. A 2008 study led by psychologist Cendri Hutcherson found that even a few minutes of loving-kindness meditation fostered a stronger sense of social connection with, and positivity toward, strangers, suggesting that "this easily implemented technique may help to increase positive social emotions and decrease social isolation."

The Georgie version of this practice involves looking at a stranger and silently wishing them a great day. The idea here is that you notice another person, you recognize your shared humanity, you ponder their life, and you think something positive about them. It's a sort of training to counteract our tendency to dehumanize strangers. Georgie says when she does this—she actually wishes them "the best day ever"—she feels more grounded, and more comfortable about approaching people, because this moment of human recognition is like a relationship in embryonic form. I struggle with this part, though, because I keep getting hung up on what their best day ever is. Is it a promotion? Is it winning the lottery? Is it a bank heist? Patricide? I feel I don't have enough information to make that judgment. So I try something different. I just imagine them smiling. Each stone-faced person who walks by, I imagine them breaking into a smile. While this exercise at first feels silly to me, it does something. I, too, feel calmer, more grounded, and more positive about my fellow humans from doing it.

More assignments arrive from Georgie. We're told to follow our curiosity, and comment on something we've noticed about another person. We're told to commit "random acts of authenticity." When someone asks how we are, we're told to answer honestly. To deviate from the script. We're told to start a conversation with a stranger using a statement, and practice listening more deeply with people. "When someone shares something, be curious about what certain words mean to them. Put to the side your interpretation of their events and their meaning and ask them to say more," or just echo their words. I do all these things in the weeks that follow. I leave my headphones at home; I keep my phone in my pocket. I notice things. I talk to people. And indeed, it works far more often than it doesn't.

Inspired by Gillian Sandstrom's experiment at the Tate, I go to the Metropolitan Museum in New York. I see a guy staring at Ellsworth Kelly's painting *Blue Panel II*. A deep-blue geometric shape. Following Georgie's advice about proximity, I walk over and stand next to him for a few moments. He takes a photo of the painting and of the plaque with the artist's information. I use a pre-frame. "Can I ask you a question?" I say. "What do you like about it?"

Slightly embarrassed, he says, "The color . . . and it's from 1977, when I was born." He's a tourist from Spain, he says, and anywhere he goes he visits museums and takes pictures of anything from 1977. I tell him I was born in 1977, too, and he lights up—the power of the minimal similarity in action. He shows me dozens of photos of artwork from 1977 on his phone.

In another gallery, I follow my curiosity. I ask a security guard something I've long wondered. I use a pre-frame. "Can I ask you a weird question?" He's wary, but says sure. "Do people ever touch the paintings?" His reply is deadpan. "All the time. So many times. Every day," he says, in a slight accent. He says sometimes people seem to lose themselves and touch the paintings, and sometimes they just don't seem to know you're not supposed to. "That's why we're here." He seems tired. I remember something the tech entrepreneur Paul Ford once argued is the best conversational opener ever: When someone tells you what they do for a living, always respond, "That sounds really hard," and watch what happens. So I give it a shot.

"Wow, that seems like a hard job," I say. "You're standing here all day, but you're also supposed to be on alert the whole time."

"Exactly," he says. "We have to always be looking. Always."

"Or else they'll touch all the paintings."

At this he finally cracks. He laughs. "Yes. Exactly."

I put the same question to another security guard. Do people ever touch the paintings? "All the time," he says, annoyed. I ask why they do it, and he says, "Frankly, I don't care. It damages the paintings. Touching a sculpture I can understand, even though that damages the sculpture, too. You can see it in the brown spots." I ask if he likes this job. He shrugs, but says he shouldn't complain. He's surrounded by masterpieces, every day. I ask if he ever becomes numb to the beauty, and he opens up. "Oh no," he says. "No, no, no, no, no." He says it helps that they rotate him and the work, so he doesn't have to stare at the same pieces every day. "It's a living thing," he says of the museum.

"So it doesn't gather dust," I say.

"It *does*," he corrects me. "But do you know what the dust is? It's human skin. Sloughed-off human skin. The maintenance guys told me that."

"So I guess people are touching the paintings whether you like it or not."

He laughs. "I guess they are."

Outside, I buy a dirty-water hot dog from a cart.

"Heyhiyadoin'?" says the vendor, a Middle Eastern guy. And this is where we usually go to the script: I'd say fine, order my hot dog, and go. But this time I try an honest disclosure.

"I'm a little ragged today, to be honest," I said. "My daughter kept me up like half the night last night."

"How old?"

"Three."

"Three is a good age," he says. "Is she a good kid?"

"She's charming but volatile."

"Aren't we all," he says.

A Black teenage cashier at a bodega asks me the same question, and I answer it the same way. She tells me she has a little sister and reassures me. "It gets better," she says, kindly. She is the greatest.

As I do this work, I also realize that you can tweak the standard greeting to break the script, as Georgie put it, and get people talking. "How are you doing?" seldom if ever gets a real response. But something more specific like "How's the day been?" does a little better. And my new go-to—"People behaving themselves?"—works great. It always gets a conspiratorial smile, and sometimes a story. One morning, at the market by my apartment, I put that question to a young cashier.

"People behaving themselves today?"

"Most of them," she sighs.

"Not all of them?" I say.

Her coworker happily jumps in. "She got yelled at today."

"You got yelled at?" I say. "It's like eight-thirty in the morning."

They start telling me about this outwardly normal-seeming woman who yells at them over something every single day. This morning was unusually bad, the first woman says. She yelled at the cashier first. "Then she went out and yelled at one of the delivery guys." We chatted a little more, while they recounted more stories about this woman, shaking their heads at the lunacy of it. Afterward, when I grab my bag to go, one of them says, "Thank you for being nice."

That thank-you inspires another idea. I start thanking people sincerely. Looking them in the eye and thanking them. Bus drivers, people who hold a door open, people who give me some space as I push a stroller down a narrow sidewalk. Never just "thanks," which would be to follow a script, always something more, like "Hey, thanks for doing that. I really appreciate it." People seem taken aback, but pleasantly so. I discover later that there is research on this as well. A 2020 study by psychologist Guy Gunaydin featuring hundreds of commuters in Turkey found that expressing gratitude to strangers led to higher levels of happiness and greater feelings of well-being. And the more people did it, the better they felt.

Another day, I see a trumpet player busking in the park. He's quite good, and he looks like a theater actor: trim, and well dressed in black. I always give money to street musicians, but this time I stop and chat with him after he finishes up. He says he's been playing trumpet for twenty years, since he was a kid, and he's been playing for six years in Central Park. Starting out playing in public was a humbling experience for him. "If something's off," he says, "New Yorkers will let you know." That occasionally brutal feedback—which could range from artistic criticism to outright verbal abuse—has actually helped him grow as an artist and as a person.

"Because if you lose your composure, you're done," he says. "If you get mad and it goes a certain way, you might get arrested." So he learned to read audiences, to play to them, to treat everyone as an equal. He says if you give off positivity, you'll get back positivity. He has an accent, so I ask where he's from. He says he's from Ghana. His parents came in the visa lottery. He says he thinks about this a lot, what his life would be like if he wasn't here in America. He says he was a dishwasher for years, and now he plays. "I wake up every day and I play my trumpet," he says. He's immensely proud, immensely grateful. "To do *that*?" he says. *"In New York?"*

At a restaurant downtown one night, a friend of mine unwittingly tries Georgie's hat gambit. You remember—when she pointed to a guy wearing a hat on the subway and said "hat," and they had a conversation. We're sitting at the corner of the bar, and a young man sidles up and orders an espresso martini. "Espresso martini," my friend deadpans. This, let's just say, is not offered in a spirit of genuine curiosity. Yet within seconds the young man is telling us why he is drinking an espresso martini: He is fortifying himself for a meeting uptown in which he will quit his finance job. He hates finance, he says, he's sick of New York. He has purchased a little bit of land in the South and wants to open a brewery. He tells us all about his plans. He finishes his espresso martini, thanks us for the chat, and steps out into the rest of his life.

But these are, in the grand scheme of things, pretty low-hanging fruit. Yes, it's challenging to start conversations with any stranger out in the world. But these interactions were still somewhat structured—a shop clerk and a customer; a musician and an audience member. They were fun and surprising, and felt good, but our roles in them were pretty clearly defined. I want to try something a little more challenging. Something completely unstructured. And I start with the ultimate taboo of talking to people on mass transit.

On a city bus, I sit down next to an older white guy wearing a blue bandana. A young mother gets on at the next stop and props her baby up so she can see out the window. The guy looks at me and smiles, and then he turns to the mother. "That's a beautiful baby," he says. I agree. That's triangulation, like we talked about. We're looking at the same thing, and it fosters a little connection. The mother is absorbed with the child, so I ask the guy if he has any kids. He has one he says; he's forty-seven. I ask if he's proud of him. "Of course I am, man," he says. "But I'm proud of everybody. I love the human race. Unless the aliens are in charge—then I'll love them, too. Unless they're cannibals!" This is not what I expected that man to say.

I have a few small chats on the subway—I go on a bit of a welcoming-foreign-tourists jag, inspired by my readings on hospitality. If someone seems lost, or is studying a map, I offer to help them. If people are taking a selfie, I offer to take it for them. I end up walking some Belgian tourists to their destination. I welcome all these people and tell them I'm happy they're here, which is a departure from my customary attitude toward tourists. But that feels good, too, and they seem to really like it. That leads to some nice chats, and it helps me see my town through fresh eyes, which I realize is a rare and wonderful and sometimes challenging thing.

As Ben Mathes—the founder of Urban Confessional—put it, I am now flexing my openness and advertising my accessibility, and as a result, people just start talking to me more often. Uli Beutter Cohen from Subway Book Review experienced the same strange phenomenon, and so did Georgie. When I told her it had been happening to me, she said, "I'm glad that it's now being reconfirmed by somebody else, because I was talking to a friend about this. I said, 'Suddenly I'm now the person that everybody speaks to anywhere I go. They'll stop me on the street, even when I have headphones in, to have a conversation.'" That didn't happen before, she says. To me, either. Until now.

One day on the subway, a big guy, Latino, maybe late thirties, clad in sweatpants and a hoodie, comes barreling onto the 6 train and drops hard into a seat, and I can just sense it: the stranger mojo. I can feel his attention being steered to me. It's uncanny. I sit next to him and he looks over and gives me a quick "Hiyadoin'?"

I'm not going to just say, "Hiyadoin'" back, because that's a script. I try something a little more specific. "I'm doing all right," I say. "You doing all right?"

He says yeah, he is. And I just wait. A brunette woman stands to exit the car, and the guy leans over to me. He quietly tells me that's the "shape" he likes. At this point I am slowly filling with dread, assuming that what is coming next is going to be unpleasant. But I've also been training for this. I've done free listening; I've taken the class. I know that giving someone the space to talk can take you down some interesting roads. So I choke down my discomfort and I echo him.

"That's the shape you like," I say, quiet enough that no one else on the train can hear me saying this.

"Yeah," he says. He elaborates on his preference. He says the reason this is the shape he likes is because he distrusts anyone who looks "perfect." I gamely nod and hold eye contact. He says he prefers stretch marks and cellulite because, as he says, "That is meaning. That is the sign that you've lived your life."

"That you've lived your life," I echo.

"That's right," he says. He says he learned that from his late mother.

And we're off.

When she died, he says, tons of friends came for the funeral, and they all told him that she taught them how to live. She abided no taboos, for one, he says. One woman said his mother had pushed her to get together with a Black man she was interested in decades ago but worried about what people would say. My seatmate's mother said the hell with other people. Go for it. The woman heeded her advice. "They're still married," my seatmate says proudly.

When I do talk, I ask clarifying questions and hang back. I let him say what he wants to say, and he says it. As the stops streak past, he tells me his mother lived in Puerto Rico, and she smoked just like her mother. He begged her to stop or else she'd die, just like her mother did, but she wouldn't listen. She developed emphysema, and the disease aged her. She started getting plastic surgery to try to regain her youthful looks, and the result disturbed him. He could barely recognize her anymore. It really upset him. Then Hurricane Maria hit Puerto Rico in 2017 and killed her.

We get to my stop and I say I have to go, but "thank you for telling me this, and I'm really sorry about your mother." He tells me his name, and offers a hand. I take it, and he slaps his other hand over mine and gives me a firm two-handed shake without saying anything. I step out onto the platform at Fifty-ninth Street, and the train lurches away and he's gone.

Then there is L.* I meet her on a sunny summer day. She was camped out on Forty-second Street, doing a crossword with a plastic cup full of change in front of her and some watercolor paintings for sale. People who are homeless are often invisible to those who are not. We know that. I'm far from immune to that particular form of blindness, myself. But L caught my eye because of a sign she had hung up, which pushed back against the lesser minds problem. It read, "I lost everything but my smile and my hope." So I walked over and asked her

---

* She has asked me not to use her name, because she does not want this part of her life immortalized.

how she stays hopeful. "Because I know it's not forever," she says. I ask her if I can buy her a coffee. She says yes. I go get it, come back over, and ask her about herself.

"I'm not the average person you meet on the street," she tells me. "I'm educated. I'm not addicted to anything. So when people actually speak to me, they realize there's no difference between me and them." Usually you would think this is a good thing. They see themselves in her. The problem is *they see themselves in her.* Meaning, she is an unwelcome reminder, perhaps, of the precariousness of their own lives—standing proof that no one is immune to catastrophic reversals and that the world is far more complex than we may be comfortable with. "That can turn into fear so quickly, and that fear turns into hate so quickly," L says. "Because I represent the idea that anyone can become homeless. I had a bright future up until a couple of years ago, and one chance meeting turned into this."

Raised in New Jersey, she was a dancer when she was younger, but she got injured, and as she recovered a great-uncle bought her a sketch pad and a couple of pens to help her pass the time. She drew everything she could. She signed up for every class available. She went to college for fine art in Los Angeles and was accepted to graduate school.

Then the spiral commenced. She came back to the East when her father became sick with cancer. He was young and healthy before, but he died quickly. She had no siblings, no other living parent, no living grandparents, no other family. After the funeral, she was preparing to return to California when she was mugged. The mugger stole her identity, or at least sold her wallet to someone who did. That person drained her bank account and wrecked her credit. L was stranded, and she's been on the street ever since. "I'd never be out here in a million years if my father was still alive," she says.

I ask her what it's been like, and she says it's horrible. "I hate it. I hate it." She was raped by a man who lured her to a movie theater, offering her a hundred dollars to accompany him. She was relentlessly targeted for harassment by a police officer who started writing her tickets for an illegal display—her sign—dumping out her change, and chasing her off her spot where she sold her paintings. She lost months of income. Another time a man grabbed her by the foot and tried to drag her into the park—on a Sunday morning. Passersby just walked around them as she screamed for help.

L asks if I've ever heard of a Native American story about the wounded dog. I say I hadn't. "I don't know the exact legend," she says, "but the idea is that the best and the worst of us are attracted to an injured dog, because the best can feel its pain and want to help, and the worst are attracted *because* of the pain, because it's vulnerable and they want to hurt it more. That's kind of like what it's like being out here," she says. "It's like the best and the worst people are attracted to you, because the best want to help and the worst want to take advantage. And everyone else kind of gets lost in an ocean."

She tells me, with a laugh, about an old and seemingly affluent woman who comes by almost every day, hits her with her cane, and tells her to get a job. "And she's a little old lady, so if I say anything or do anything, people yell at me for yelling at the old lady." I ask what she would say to her if she got the chance. "I would probably tell her, 'Try to see me as one of your grandkids. If they were in my position, would you want someone treating them this way?' I mean, I don't see any of the anger that people give out toward me as directed at me, like it's my fault. I'm like an emotional garbage can for people. I'm like a quick way to get rid of some anger or angst in their life."

And yet, she still has her hope, and her smile, as the sign indicates. Strangers represent darkness and fear for her, but they also serve as causes for hope. "I have people who come out of their way to see me," she says. "I have people that have given me their cellphone numbers, and that check up on me on a daily basis. They make sure I'm okay. I've made friends for a lifetime." When the man tried to drag her into the park, a night manager at a hotel nearby who brings her breakfast every Sunday ran out, tackled the assailant, and sat on him until the police arrived. Another friend who had political ties heard about the police harassment and went to the mayor's office to lodge a complaint. The cop was fired, she says, shortly after.

She's cautiously optimistic. She has some leads on part-time teaching gigs. A lawyer has taken her case pro bono to try to untangle her credit mess. She still wants to go to grad school. I ask her what her first big art project would be, coming out of this. She says she wants to write a graphic novel about her experience out here. She wants to make it "serious enough to get the point across," but she also wants it to be funny. And she is a very funny person.

"Funny beats everything," she says. "If you want to reach people, you've got to make them laugh." I tell her I once saw a letter to the Irish comic writer Flann O'Brien lamenting the fact that people think it's easier to be funny than it is to be sad. "That sums it up so well," she says. "It's so much harder to laugh about everything than it is to just mope. It's so easy to be sad. And no one wants to be sad. That's the kicker. Nobody wants to see someone crying, and self-loathing, and beating themselves up. People love a redemption story. People love to laugh, and to know that you're trying."

The research tells us that when we talk to strangers, it helps us feel rooted in our worlds, it helps us feel better about the people around us, and it helps them feel better about ourselves. These are great reasons to talk to strangers, and I can attest that I felt them, too, when I sought out these interactions. I felt calmer and more reassured; I laughed more. I smiled more. Some of my friendliness was nerves; some was no doubt tied to a human tendency for what psychologists call *positive self-presentation*. When we put our best face forward, researchers have found, people tend to respond in kind, causing a loop. What starts as a bit of a pose triggers a real emotional response in our partners, and when they're friendly back to us, we feel genuinely good. That clears the way for a meaningful interaction.

But there is a deeper benefit, a more important one, though it can be unpleasant to cope with. When you talk to a stranger whose life is so radically different from your own, it forces you to confront some uncomfortable things. You realize that though you inhabit the same space, their world is very different from your world. A street that to you is familiar, even delightful, is full of fear and peril for them. Earlier, we talked about Bryant Park being a perfect public space. I have spent a lot of time there. I have nothing but positive memories from the place. For L, however, it was a place a stranger tried to drag her into in order to rape her.

My point is this: You cannot hope to be a good citizen, you cannot hope to be a moral person, if you do not make an effort to see that the world is a very different place for the person sitting next to you. That their strangers are not necessarily your strangers. And the way to understand this, across social boundaries, or racial boundaries, or ideological boundaries, or any other boundary that has been thrown up to keep us apart, is to talk to them. And this, as we'll see, is a major challenge.

Chapter 18

Talking to *Them*

In which we learn about why it can feel so daunting to talk to someone from another group, what can make it even harder, and what we can do to overcome it.

Thomas Knox can't explain why he decided one day to get a table and two chairs and head down to the subway to set up shop on the platform and try to get people to talk to him. He just did it. "I don't even know, man," he tells me. "It's a question I get so much and I still don't know how to answer it. I'm just good with people. I've always been, since I was a kid. I just like people. I'm fascinated by them. Why do they wear the things they wear? Why do they say the things they say?" he says. "I think if we did a better job of communicating what we're comfortable with, and what we're uncomfortable with, we'd be in a better place as a society."

It goes without saying, then, that Knox didn't really have a plan for how it was going to work. "The first day I did it, I just took a bunch of flowers with me," he says. "I said, 'I'm gonna give flowers to everybody—I don't care if it's a guy, girl, kid. Everybody gets flowers.' And I sat there and people kept talking to me." In time, Thomas added a new feature: the game Connect 4. So now people could sit and talk while they waited for their train, or they could play a game, or do whatever they wanted. Knox was just offering himself as company. Once the conversation started, he was all in. He'd follow it wherever it went. That's his gift. "It's always been a breeze," he says. "I guess it's just the way I am. . . . I'm just built this way."

"How do things usually play out?" I ask.

"Everybody is unique. Some people are super rude. 'How desperate can you be?' they say. People think it's about me, or about love or romance. But I'm not doing it for love. Once I break that down, we're the best of friends. They start, and they have their purse clenched to their chests," he laughs, "and like fifteen minutes later it's on the floor."

Knox and I got coffee together in early 2019, and I found him energetic, game, charismatic, and pretty irrepressible. It's not hard to see him disarming people on the subway. Which is no mean achievement, given what we know about the rules of decorum on the subway. "We all initially have our guards up," he says, "because growing up, we were taught to not talk to strangers and watch your back, especially in New York. But I'm always in discovery mode. Every coffee shop I go to, I talk to the barista. Everybody wants to tell a story. Everybody. They just have to feel comfortable enough to tell it to you. And I can break that shit down. Give me ten minutes with a person! Maybe I should have been a psychiatrist. That's what Tracy Morgan told me: 'You're like a free psychiatrist!'"

As a kid growing up in New York, Knox was forever getting in trouble for just leaving: walking out of class, out of school, going to the park. "I was just living my life, man," he says, but it drove his parents crazy. They used to call the cops to go find him, he says, but eventually they gave up. Nothing could contain him, and besides, he'd always come home eventually. His parents lived apart—his father in Brooklyn and his mother in Staten Island—and he toggled between boroughs. "I'd get in trouble in one and they'd just send me to the other," he says. He laughs. "I was like Dora the Explorer. *Thomas is off doing his Dora the Explorer.* I love it, man. I can go to any city by myself. I only go to the places no one wants to go to. That's just my style. As long as I've got a hundred bucks in my pocket, I can make it work," he says. "I feel like I can handle any situation."

His first time down in the subway turned into what he called "Date While You Wait," his subway salon that in 2015 attracted ample press coverage. Knox was working for Apple at the time and had to take a week off just to deal with the thousands of messages he got in response to the coverage. They're still coming in, even today. He pulls out his phone and shows me his Facebook messages. People thanking him for doing this, asking for help. The messages scroll forever. He's since been doing public speaking engagements, advising teachers, reporters, and athletes about communication, and giving talks to schoolkids about the importance of human connection.

"Some people—they don't want to talk to strangers," he says. "And when you're uncomfortable with something you automatically make it negative. But if I can break that down, the sky's the limit about what you can find out about somebody."

What does he want to find out?

"I'm just excited about the person," he says. "Like, where are you from? What have you done in your life? Why do you love what you love, why do you hate what you hate? I'm the type of guy, I'll sit down with someone who hates Black people. A real racist. And we will leave best friends. I'll be like, 'Why do you hate us, man? Tell me why you hate us.' He'll say, 'I don't know, man, a Black guy killed my mom.' And I'm like, 'I can totally understand that. I totally sympathize with you. I'm sorry you had to go through that. I respect that you feel that way.' And we leave mutually respecting each other's feelings. When there's a mutual respect there it's more than enough. You don't have to be best friends."

I tell him he seems pretty confident. "I'm not afraid," he says. "There's nobody better than me, but I'm not better than anyone." Which is the most quintessentially American thing I have ever heard another person say, which makes Thomas Knox one of the most American people I have ever met.

———

One of the messages Knox got in the initial Date While You Wait deluge came from a young woman who was worried about her friend. He was painfully shy, an artist, she said, and she thought Knox could help him. Knox said, "Sure, why not?" and got in touch with him. After some back-and-forth, Knox designed a pilot program for the young man. "I trained him," he said, laughing. "I said, 'Train your mind to become comfortable with rejection.' If you can become comfortable with rejection, you're good. Nobody can stop you."

The first lesson was simple. "I said, 'Every morning, say hello to everyone. Everyone. I don't care who it is. Guy, girl, everyone. Make eye contact, and say good morning.'" The young man agreed, and disappeared. A week later, he was dodging Knox. He admitted he didn't finish the lesson. Knox gave him an ultimatum: Do the work, or I'm out. A week later, they talked again. The first assignment was complete. "He went around, he said good morning to everyone," Knox recalls. "I said, 'How'd it go?' He said, 'Well, some people thought I was crazy; they paid me no mind. Some people would nod, and some people would say good morning back.' I said, 'Cool. You did that for a week. This next week, the people who say good morning back, say "How are you?"' The next week he called me, like, 'Bro, I can't believe this thing is working. I've had like three conversations with random people!'"

I meet Knox and this young man, Francis Hernandez, for coffee a few months later and they talk about how Knox helped him. Hernandez is in his midtwenties, an artist, and he was at a low point when the two met a few years ago. "During that period I wasn't working on my artwork; I wasn't getting creative or anything like that. I was stuck, essentially," he says. "That was it. It was clear I was stuck. And I was like, *Shit, I'm hopeless.* Once you start feeling hopeless, you know how that goes." Hernandez was a withdrawn kid, born in Puerto Rico and raised in the Bronx. "Very closed up in my room, stuck in my room kind of shit," he says. He never liked art class, but he nevertheless started creating pieces. "Back then I was just so angry. Just *fuck you to everyone* kind of stuff. I put that on a canvas and someone actually bought it. They thought it was art."

"My biggest issue is I don't want to fall under the myth of the introverted artist," he says. "I had some depression and things growing up. I don't want to be the artist who cut off his ear, you know what I'm saying? I don't want to be viewed as that hidden-genius artist that no one knows about until he's dead. Who wants that?"

"Nobody!" exclaims Knox.

Hernandez admits he was resistant to Knox's plan at first. "I felt stupid," he says. "I say hello, and nobody says anything back, and then I think I'm the problem—you know what I'm saying?" He says he knew how to have a conversation, but he'd freeze up on the spot when trying to start one. He'd get stuck in his own head. Then he'd force himself to do it, and he'd come on too strong and it would go sideways. But he stuck with it, and it started to get better. "Everything started to click," Hernandez says. "When you told me to do things, and I knew they were right things to do."

"They may not have been the right things to do!" says Knox.

"But they seemed very basic and simple and humane," says Hernandez. "They were very simple things, easy to do, and to that I was resistant. Everything is clicking now. Now I'm decent. I'm not a crappy human being anymore."

"I don't think you were crappy!" Knox says. He turns to me. "I will say, looking at him now, he's just so much more confident. Like, that kid I met, he had shaggy hair, he just seemed like, *Whatever, I'm trying to get through*. Now he seems way more powerful, way more vibrant."

I ask Francis if he feels that way.

"Yeah," he says. "Because I'm exposing way more of myself. Especially artistically." He says as he's gotten better at connecting with people, he notices more people are offering to help him. His bosses at his day job at a gym have become mentors. His mother always told him never to ask anyone for help, and so he never did. But now he does. "Asking for things is my next thing to work out." A friend—the same one who introduced him to Knox—has stepped up and helped him organize his first art show. The support he's gotten has ratcheted up his confidence, and that has filtered into his artwork.

"It's all connected," he says, "because the reason I wasn't in touch with people is because in general I closed myself. I asked people to keep away, and it affected everything else."

"It's clicking now," he says. "It's starting to click."

"You're blooming, man," Knox says. "Take your time. There's no rush."

"It's a bit overwhelming because now, like, I have so many people helping me out and not asking anything in return," says Hernandez.

"The best thing you can do for me is continue to develop and keep finding ways to free your mind," says Knox. "I think you hold a lot in. Free your mind, man. Life is simple." A glass shatters on the other side of the coffee shop, and Knox looks over. "If I drop that glass, they're gonna sweep it up," he says. "It's not the end of the world. That's how I kinda look at things. That's what I would challenge you to do. Be open-minded. Things will be okay."

Hernandez nods. "I'm throwing everything out there," he says.

When we first met, Knox was dividing his time between New York and Philadelphia. We got to talking about New York. Inspired by his optimism and enthusiasm for strangers, I told him I find New York to be far friendlier than people give it credit for. Certainly friendlier than my hometown. I told him that when I went back to Boston for Christmas after moving to New York, I went to a high school friend's Christmas party and got a lot of guff for moving. "How's fancy New York, Mister Fancy New Yorker," he bellowed at me. I told him it's a place where people actually help when they see someone struggling to get something heavy up the stairs in the subway. I told him I feel like if anyone in Boston stopped because someone was carrying a stroller up a flight of stairs, it'd be in the hopes that they'd fall. My friend considered this and replied, "You know what? You're right. And you know what else? If you don't like it, *get the fuck out!*" And he high-fived another friend.

I got a little carried away talking to Knox about New York. I told him that people are brusque, and they're in a hurry, and they'll hiss at you if you're in the way, but they pay attention to one another, and they'll help you out. I told him I felt like the only reason an agglomeration of ten million people doesn't spiral into chaos is the small amount of effort expended by every person on a daily basis. I told him about the frequent sight of people helping people carry baby carriages or suitcases. I said almost every time I drop something, someone picks it up and gives it back to me. Same for my daughter. I said I'd wiped out on the sidewalk in Midtown on no fewer than four times on icy days, and each time a couple of strangers had me back on my feet in half a second. There were no pleasantries attached, no effusive thanks, but they'd have you back up and on your way.

Now, Knox's expression at this point could be described as *polite*. So I stopped, and I asked him, "Doesn't that happen to you?"

"No," he said.

It was winter, and we decided to go for a walk. As we gathered our things, he realized he'd dropped something. He turned around and saw that his scarf had fallen on the floor, and had been inadvertently kicked away. He picked it up and showed it to me. *See?* he seemed to say.

Thomas Knox is a master of talking to strangers—something I hope to become as well. But I'm a white guy, and he's a Black man, and this is America, and his strangers don't always act like my strangers.

There is another great irony concerning life in a city that really applies to any place that has seen an influx of immigrants, or rising levels of diversity. Ideally, life among different types of people affords us a chance to grow, learn, expand, and gain access to new ideas and social networks. Researchers have established a connection between diversity and creativity in companies, for instance, for one. More important, though, as our friend Uli Beutter Cohen discovered while running Subway Book Review, contact with members of other groups also helps us understand one another's lives, that our realities are not necessarily their realities, which is a requirement for a healthy democracy in a diverse nation, and the stuff of wisdom. As John Stuart Mill wrote in 1848, "It is hardly possible to overstate the value . . . of placing human beings in contact with persons dissimilar to themselves. Such communication has always been, and is peculiarly in the present age, one of the primary sources of progress."

And yet, psychology and culture can conspire against these sorts of connections—especially when the boundaries between us are hardened due to conflict, segregation, or entrenched prejudice. Examples of this are not difficult to come by. But let's just look at race in America, for one example.

A 2017 study led by John Paul Wilson of Montclair State University, for instance, asked non-Black American participants to compare photos of same-size young white men and young Black men. Again and again, the participants perceived the Black men as being larger, more muscular, and more threatening than the white men. As a result, they believed that police would be more justified in using force against the Black men than the white men. That study followed years of research that have yielded a raft of related findings. Non-Black study participants were more likely to misremember a Black man holding a weapon. They were more likely to confuse a mundane object for a weapon in the hands of a Black man. White people were also more sensitive to signs of anger in Black faces than in white faces. And they're less able to tell Black faces apart—unless those faces are angry, in which case, they remember.

This helps explain, for instance, why Black Americans are shot by police at a significantly higher rate than white Americans. It is why I can unhesitatingly tell my young daughter to run to a cop if she's in trouble while knowing full well that if my child were Black, and especially a boy, I would not do so with such unexamined confidence. It's also, perhaps, why no one in the coffee shop picked up Thomas Knox's scarf.

It comes as no surprise that this effect is heightened in people who show higher levels of prejudice. But even those who don't believe they are prejudiced are capable of dehumanizing strangers from other groups, of perceiving them to be of lesser minds. The Black American writer Hanif Abdurraqib beautifully captures what it's like to be on the receiving end of this: "What I am told most often now is that I am kind," he writes. "I am told this more by white people than by anyone else. . . . People who don't know me particularly well talk about how they can see a kindness in my eyes, or feel a kindness that I have deep within. I generally laugh, shrug uncomfortably, and give a small thanks. I know, particularly when it is by people who aren't familiar with me, that what they are actually complimenting is an absence of that which they perceived, perhaps expected."

Dehumanization goes beyond race, though. The history of sexism is a millennia-long exercise in dehumanization, neatly captured in the 1997 romantic comedy *As Good As It Gets,* when someone asks a famous romance novelist, played by Jack Nicholson, how he writes such good female characters, and he replies "I think of a man, and I take away reason and accountability." That's dehumanization.

We also frequently see it between urban and rural people, going both ways. A Jewish acquaintance of mine from the Northeast went to college in Oklahoma, and was, no joke, asked by an otherwise friendly classmate where her horns were.* Meanwhile, any American southerner who went to college in the North can tell you how surprised northern students were to discover that, yes, they were intelligent. "I sound a lot less southern, almost undetectably so, than I did when I was a kid," writes Whet Moser, a native southerner, living in Chicago. "Once you get into higher education, you learn to go with a generic Union accent fast."

New immigrants are constantly subjected to a similar kind of fear, condescension, and dehumanization—likened to animals or viruses, believed to be cognitively inferior and incapable of controlling brute urges. In his landmark history of nativism in America, the historian John Higham compiled a veritable catalogue of horrible things people said about immigrants: calling them "an invasion of venomous reptiles," "long-haired, wild-eyed, bad-smelling, atheistic, reckless foreign wretches, who never did an honest hour's work in their

---

* In one of the greatest rejoinders I've ever heard of, she smiled and told them, "They only come out when I'm angry."

lives," "rag-tag and bob-tail cutthroats of Beelzebub from the Rhine, the Danube, the Vistula, and the Elbe," and "Europe's human and inhuman rubbish."

Back then, people were freaked out about Germans. Today we see the same line of attack in many nations that have experienced an influx of immigrants and refugees from non-European lands. I often think of the San Diego man who turned up to protest the arrival of a busload of refugee children in California a few years ago, worrying aloud to a reporter: *"What kind of criminality will happen?"**

So, yes, we have a tendency to dehumanize people of different groups, especially when cultures reinforce the belief that they are somehow deficient. Given that, it only makes sense that the prospect of interacting with them—especially if we've had little-to-no positive interaction in the past—can make us anxious. There is a term for this: *intergroup anxiety,* and according to the psychologist Walter Stephan, who has studied the phenomenon for years, "[it is] why such interactions are often more complicated and difficult than interactions with in-group members."

Pretty much everybody is subject to intergroup anxiety to some degree, but it is especially pronounced among people who are prejudiced, people who identify very strongly with their own groups, people who previously have had little contact, or, worse, negative contact with the other group, and in situations where there is competition, or an imbalance in terms of numbers or status. This anxiety not only manifests on a psychological and emotional level, but on a

---

* There are real threats in the world that activate this anti-immigrant response, but the fear, as it happens, doesn't actually need to be moored to reality. In fact, it's stronger if it isn't. The historian and political scientist Ariane Chebel d'Appollonia has shown that anti-immigrant sentiment isn't tied to the state of a nation's economy, like you'd think, but is far more likely to be a response to a *symbolic* threat—a belief that *they* represent a threat to our way of life, say. This is driven in part by a chronic overestimation of the scale of immigration. In 2006, for instance, 12 percent of the U.S. population was born outside of the country. And yet 25 percent of Americans surveyed believed that number was closer to 25 percent, and 28 percent of Americans surveyed said it was higher. These "perceived ethnic threats," she writes, "are largely indifferent to realities."

physical level as well—these interactions have been found to result in elevated blood pressure and levels of the stress hormone cortisol.

At this point, we know a good deal about what can keep us from talking to strangers—ranging from social norms to walking speeds. Stephan adds four more fears to the pile: We worry they will hurt us, harass us, lie to us, or contaminate us with a disease; we worry about "being embarrassed, misunderstood, fearful, confused, irritated, frustrated, or feeling incompetent"; we worry they will dislike, mock, or reject us; and we worry that our own side will disapprove of our associating with them. Additional studies over the years have shown that people are reluctant to talk to members of other groups because they believe their differences will be unbridgeable, or because all they have to go on are negative stereotypes, or, as we saw in chapter 2, they think the other person simply isn't interested in talking to them. These beliefs can occur regardless of whether the person is a member of a majority group or a minority group. Straight people can be anxious about talking to gay people and vice versa; studies have found the same with white people and Black people, and Americans and non-Americans.

It's obvious that more prejudiced people would avoid talking to strangers from groups they don't care for, or are at odds with. But because the prospect of talking across these boundaries induces anxiety even in less overtly prejudiced individuals, intergroup anxiety can prompt people to simply avoid one another altogether and stick with their own kind. We see this in politics, for sure. The journalist Bill Bishop has argued persuasively that the growing self-segregation in America, which he calls *the big sort,* is a primary driver behind political polarization. When we avoid other groups, we never develop a more complex—which is to say accurate—perception of one another. We never come to understand one another's lives. This allows stereotypes to remain unchecked and prejudice to fester, and it creates a significant obstacle to what psychologists call *intergroup contact,* which is the most effective way we know of to alleviate tensions between different groups. (We will return to that shortly.)

What's even weirder, and more insidious, however, is that while historic levels of immigration make societies friendlier and more emotionally expressive, an influx of strangers from different groups can actually keep people from engaging *with members of their own groups* as well. At least in the short term. This was the unhappy discovery by the great political scientist Robert Putnam, who found in 2007 that when places become more diverse, people show a tendency to withdraw—not just away from the other groups, but away from their own kind, too. After noting that immigration and diversity in the long run "are likely to have important cultural, economic, fiscal, and developmental benefits," Putnam showed that diversity can cause people to "hunker down," leading to declines in trust, altruism, community involvement, and number of friends.

"Diversity, at least in the short run, seems to bring out the turtle in all of us," he wrote, continuing:

> Diversity does *not* produce "bad race relations" or ethnically-defined group hostility, our findings suggest. Rather, inhabitants of diverse communities tend to withdraw from collective life, to distrust their neighbors, regardless of the color of their skin, to withdraw even from close friends, to expect the worst from their community and its leaders, to volunteer less, give less to charity and work on community projects less often, to register to vote less, to agitate for social reform *more,* but have less faith that they can actually make a difference, and to huddle unhappily in front of the television. . . . Diversity seems to affect men and women equally, though with minor variation across different indicators of sociability. The impact of diversity on sociability seems somewhat greater among conservatives, but it is significant among liberals, too. The impact of diversity is definitely greater among whites, but is visible as well among non-whites.

No one group holds a monopoly on this tendency. It seems to affect men and women equally, and while conservatives are more likely to withdraw amid greater levels of diversity, liberals do it as well.

The political scientist Eric Uslaner has taken issue with Putnam's conclusion, though. It isn't diversity per se that leads to distrust and alienation, Uslaner has found. It's segregation. "When people live apart from one another, [the meaningful contacts] essential to build trust and tolerance are unlikely to develop," he writes. This lack of contact can drive down social trust not just among groups, but across societies. Cities, and increasingly towns, can be diverse, but if the residents are kept separate—either by their own choosing, or if they're compelled to segregate—they will be able to go through much of their lives without meaningful encounters with members of other groups. That means they will remain anxious at the prospect of talking to them, so they won't, and their stereotypical views of them will remain intact, and those stereotypes will be used to reinforce the separation. They will remain permanent strangers to one another and they will suffer, and so will their societies.

This seems grim, because, well, it is. It's an exceptionally complicated problem. But the (cautiously) good news is that, should we make the effort to interact with these out-group strangers—positively, as opposed to "interacting" in the context of a shouting match or civil war—it will likely go better than we expect. We saw in chapter 2 how people tend to be extraordinarily pessimistic about the prospect of talking to strangers. They're afraid to do it because they believe it will go badly, and they're shocked and delighted when it doesn't. People are even more pessimistic about talking to a stranger of a different group.

The psychologist Robyn Mallett led a series of experiments in 2008 to see if these fears are based in reality. First, the researchers asked white study participants to imagine sitting in a plane next to a Black person or a white person, and asked them to predict "how likely it was that they would feel annoyed, resentful, nervous, angry, afraid, enthusiastic, relaxed, happy, excited, and cheerful when interacting with the person." The participants expressed significantly more anxiety about interacting with the Black seatmate. In the next study, participants—mostly white, but with Asian, Black, and Latino students as well—were divided into two groups. People in one group, the *forecasters,* were asked to imagine how they expected an interaction with a member of a different group—gender, race, sexual orientation, class, etc.—would go in a few different contexts. The other half, *experiencers,* were asked to actually talk to them and report on how the exchange ultimately went. It went well. "As predicted, forecasters anticipated that they would feel more negative emotions during intergroup interactions than experiencers reported feeling," wrote the authors. This happened regardless of the person's gender or race.

The next study focused on perceived differences, and found that both Black and white participants—forecasters and experiencers alike—expected to have little in common with members of the other group. Once the experiencers actually spoke with someone from the other group, however, they reported they did in fact have things in common, and enjoyed the conversation more than they expected to. What's more, participants reported that they felt as much in common with the person of the other group as they did with a conversational partner of the same group. "In many cases, people who find themselves on an airplane, seated next to a stranger who is from a different social group, will anticipate a long and uncomfortable journey," the authors concluded. "Our data suggest that if they strike up a conversation with the stranger, the interaction would be more pleasant than they anticipated."

Robert Putnam, author of the hugely influential book *Bowling Alone,* argues that in order to alleviate racial and ethnic strife in America, "Tolerance for difference is but a first step," he writes. "To strengthen shared identities, we need more opportunities for meaningful interaction across ethnic lines where Americans (new and old) work, learn, recreate, and live." In other words, we need to learn to talk to these strangers, before avoidance and isolation curdles into hatred and violence.

In America, a small but devoted cadre of people are trying to correct this, to build bridges between groups. One of them is a brilliant thinker by the name of Danielle Allen.

Danielle Allen is an introvert, but she talks to strangers. She got this from her parents. "I was, in meaningful ways, raised by people who see the good in other human beings, and are always open to seeing what other human beings have to offer," she says. And she got it from where she grew up in Southern California. "In the town I grew up in, you had to say hello to people that you were passing on the street, regardless of whether you knew them or not," she says. "And then I went to college on the East Coast, at Princeton, and it was a massive shock to my system. I remember in my first year I would go around campus, like, waving at everybody, saying hi to everybody, and nobody would return my greeting," she says. "And I just could not figure it out. What was this place I've landed in—where people didn't even acknowledge each other's presence? It started there."

Allen is Black, and when she was at Princeton, there were a host of controversies surrounding race. The lack of sociality and the racial stress got her thinking about how trust works—what makes people trust others in their communities, and what engenders distrust? She came to believe that the reason the East Coast was less friendly than the West Coast was related to age: The East Coast was more rigid historically in terms of race and class than California was, more hierarchical. She came to call these "fossilized boundaries of difference." Those kept people divided from one another, estranged. How did Allen deal with this social chilliness? "It's fair to say I withdrew."

A few things changed that. First, she studied in England. Despite what Londoners believe about themselves, she found everyone easy to talk to. "Britain is a talking culture; it's a much more verbal culture—more playful, more joking. It was powerful to see a place that has a long-lasting culture for what talk amongst strangers can do," she says. And then she landed at the University of Chicago and began to study the lines of division between the community within the school and the community around it: namely, the South Side of Chicago. "I was literally being told by people, *don't walk here, don't drive there.* And I could feel some of my essential capacities shutting down," she says. "I could feel the atrophy of my social knowledge and my ability to navigate the universe around me. So I started thinking about the way in which the fear [my colleagues] had about the larger world of Chicago was actually diminishing their intellectual capacities." Contact with strangers, as we know, can expand us. They were missing out on that.

Allen then began to think about "how to get people out of that trap where fear of strangers was actually eroding a lot of their intellectual and also social capacities. . . . It really brought my attention to the value of those bridging social connections. The value is intellectual, the value is human, and the value is emotional. That doesn't mean that there's no stranger danger, but the point is, you can actually learn how to prepare, manage, mitigate, and reduce it." These insights led to a widely celebrated study of the South Side of Chicago, and then on to a formidable body of work that has earned her a professorship at Harvard University, a MacArthur "genius grant," and international renown as one of America's top thinkers.

In her 2004 book *Talking to Strangers: Anxieties of Citizenship Since Brown v. Board of Education,* Allen offered a path to reducing racial distrust in America, which was rooted in American history and Greek philosophy and set in a framework of learning to talk to strangers. "Engage a stranger in conversation across a racial, ethnic, or class divide and one gets not only an extra pair of eyes but also an ability to see and understand parts of the world that are to oneself invisible," she writes. "Real knowledge of what's outside one's garden cures fear, but only by talking to strangers can we come by such knowledge." She continues:

> Most of us take positive pleasure from living among strangers. They are, more often than not, a source of wonder to us, and wonder is (as Aristotle put it) the beginning of philosophy. Strangers help feed the human desire to learn. Wisdom about the world we currently inhabit generally can't be gotten from books, because they can't be written, or read, fast enough. Strangers are the best source. Take Socrates as an example. He gave living form to the injunction "know thyself" by talking freely with everyone, Athenian or foreigner, he came upon. A direct ap-

proach to curing one's fear of strangers would be to try especially hard to engage in conversation those strangers who come from worlds and places one fears.

She has made a practice of talking to strangers, too, and it has made her feel safer in her day-to-day life. "I am no stranger to frightening personal attacks, but strangers are now for me a remarkable source of pleasure, and not fear. Beyond that, they are a source of empowering knowledge that enables me to move through the world freely and to roam widely. This personal self-confidence is one of the great rewards of claiming one's political majority by talking to strangers."

I ask Allen what she's learned by having these interactions, what her approach is, and how to increase the chance that a conversation—especially one across racial boundaries, which as we know can be fraught—is fruitful. "I think one of the things I learned is that talking to strangers is about gift giving," she says. "And I think giving a gift means sharing something about yourself that the person wouldn't otherwise know."

When she was a kid, trying to work herself out of introversion, she thought the way to start a conversation was about asking questions. "I literally would give myself a list of questions that I could try to use to talk to people," she says. "Of course, what that does is just make people feel like they're being interviewed." She laughs. "I came to understand that the whole point is about reciprocity. Yes, you ask people how they are, and hear them when they answer, but you also need to give them something, you need to share a piece of your own life or a piece of your own perspective, or something like that. And the more comfortable you are sharing in that regard, the more comfortable other people are sharing back. There's a kind of relationship between that gift-giving practice, and an acceptance of some degree of mutual vulnerability. That's the starting point for an interaction."

Talking to strangers comes more easily to her now, Allen says, though as an introvert she still needs some time alone after a lot of it. But more important, it's helped her feel better about the world, which is no mean feat for someone who has spent her career studying social, racial, and political division. "I like humanity as a whole more

because I talk to strangers," she says. "I learn things, and I'm surprised by things I get from people because of my openness to them.
The positives vastly outweigh the negatives." So much so, that she's
hoping to scale it up.

In 2018, Allen signed on as co-chair of the Commission on the
Practice of Democratic Citizenship, a bipartisan group convened by
the American Academy of Arts and Sciences consisting of some of
the best minds in academia, business, law, the nonprofit sector, tech,
and politics. Its goal is to address, and hopefully help reverse, the
rapid disintegration of American civic life. In 2020, the commission
released an ambitious report called "Our Common Purpose," which
contained a thirty-one-point action plan for reforming our system
of government, reinvigorating civic participation, and binding together Americans who, at the moment, would prefer to live on different planets (or at least prefer that the other side live on a different
planet). The commission held some fifty listening events across the
country, and found again and again that, even "in this era of profound
polarization, Americans are hungry for opportunities to assemble,
deliberate, and converse with one another."

It's hard not to hear echoes of what we've encountered throughout our little quest in this statement. People want to talk, but they
don't know how. They don't know where to go to do it, perhaps.
Maybe they don't think the other people are as interested in talking
to them as they are in talking to the other people. Maybe they're
afraid, or worried they'll say the wrong thing, or that they'll be rejected, or scorned by their own side by fraternizing with the enemy.
Whatever it is, the commission proposed creating a National Trust
for Civic Infrastructure, which would support efforts to get people
of different backgrounds and persuasions together, via public spaces,
programs, and events. In essence, they are proposing a national effort
to help learn anew to talk to strangers.

Now, just say, hypothetically, that they do manage to put these people in a confined space together. What would they do then? What
sorts of skills would they teach them that would allow them to actu-

ally interact, instead of remaining on opposite sides of, say, a Plexiglas door screaming at one another? How would they get these hardened partisans to feel comfortable enough with the mere sight of one another that when the door is opened, they don't charge through and tear one another to ribbons, but instead touch fingers and pant-hoot happily before sharing a banana? Okay, I may be torturing this metaphor. But how can we get strangers who hate each other to talk? For this, I'm going to ask you to join me on one last trip, to St. Louis, Missouri, where hundreds of political partisans are waiting for us.

Chapter 19

How to Talk to Enemy Strangers

In which we learn how to straitjacket our inner chimps, summon our inner bonobos, and start chatting with our foes, in an effort to heal our nations before everything really goes to hell.

Holly is a private home-school teacher. That's not her real name. I've agreed not to identify her because if I did, she believes it could cost her her livelihood. She's a Republican in a small, predominantly Democratic city in the South. Yet her experience is more unusual than the typical fish-out-of-ideological-water case, because half of her students are from Republican families, and half are from Democratic families. "Of course, I maintain complete neutrality, which is only appropriate for any teacher," she says. "My political or philosophical or religious structures are inappropriate to a classroom." Still, if the Democratic families found out she is a Republican, she believes she would lose half her business. Some of the Republican Baptist families already eye her warily, possibly due to her refusal to disclose her party affiliation. A few have politely inquired as to whether she might dabble in witchcraft, for example. (She does not.)

All of this means Holly has to walk a very fine line, day after day, week after week, month after month, and year after year. Her neutrality helps her maintain the trust of both sides, which is no small feat, because over the past five or six years, she's watched in dismay as relations among the students have begun to break down across party lines. "I have noticed a distinct coalescing into two different tribes," she tells me. During school hours, the students are able to be cordial, to cooperate, and to share space together without incident, she says. But outside of school, there is no longer much contact. These are students who have been friends since they were little kids, she says, and they are on their way to becoming strangers to one another.

The reduction in social contact has allowed stereotypes to take hold. The Republican students think the Democratic students are agents of moral decay, and the Democratic kids think the Republicans are morons and Jesus freaks. Holly tells me about a "brilliant young man" from a Democratic family. She was holding a class in a church she had rented one day, and the kid wouldn't set foot in it. "He was lingering outside, looking awkward," she says. "And I shooed him in and said, 'What are you doing? You're late.' And he said, 'I don't feel comfortable going into a Baptist church'—as though they're going to spontaneously seize upon him, lay hands on him, and speak in tongues. He was terrified."

Holly sees this estrangement as the start of what could become a terminal slide. She worries "that once they ossify, and once they solidify into their political self-definition, there will be no crossover. And there will be *judgment*." They have known one another for years, but they are coming apart. She believes the parents are responsible. "They're wonderful people on both sides, but they don't mingle. It's very rare to see a crossover friendship and a family alliance. And I want that for these kids," she says. "I mourn the fact that these kids are not looking at a lifetime of alliance."

"And so," she says, "I came to Braver Angels in a search for this."

It's at this point glaringly obvious that political polarization makes strangers out of fellow citizens—both in the sense that they do not speak, and each lack an accurate picture of the other. A 2018 poll published in the *Journal of Politics* found that Republicans vastly overestimated how many Democrats are gay, Black, and atheist, and Democrats likewise overestimated how many Republicans were old, rich, evangelical, and southern. Ideological warfare obliterates our understanding of human complexity, especially at our current moment, in which the divide is so wide and the grievances so bitter that each side not only abhors the other, but has turned a refusal to engage with the other side into a moral virtue, even an imperative. With that, polarization begins to morph into something much more dangerous—sectarianism. Civility is perceived as docility, and a willingness to so much as talk to the other side is viewed as a betrayal to one's own. It's parasite stress writ large. To hazard contact with an out-group member is to risk infection and spread it to your own kind.

Braver Angels is an organization that aims to teach Republicans and Democrats to literally sit in the same room and speak to one another. It's a depressing reminder of how far gone we are that this most basic of human capabilities—speaking to another human—should suddenly seem so prohibitively difficult that an organization would be required to teach it to grown-ups. But that's where we are. And by now we know why. Humans are often ambivalent toward strangers. But when placed under threat, or even made to feel a sense of threat, we can violently close ranks, swear off contact, and dehumanize the other side. That's oxytocin at work. But you recall that while oxytocin helps us throw up walls, it also helps us build bridges. When we feel reasonably comfortable, we can expand the *us*. We devise ways to connect with strangers and we gain the power to cooperate, innovate, and share ideas—which is, again, the basis of human civilization.

That's the mission for Braver Angels. They attempt to teach a completely rudimentary social skill to as many adults as possible, in the hopes that once those adults become more comfortable in the company of political strangers, they will develop a more nuanced understanding of the other side, which may help them discover things they have in common, which may lead to some small cooperative projects, which may, in time, god willing, set this gibbering basket case of a country to rights. It's a goal that is at once laughably small and impossibly ambitious. But it's not the first time we've seen people attempt something like this. Whether it's with greeting rituals, hospitality, or the rise of culture or religion, humans have long sought ways to reconcile the fear of strangers with the opportunity they represent, and when they were successful, they eliminated strangeness and cleared the way for cooperation and belonging on a much greater scale.

Braver Angels is the brainchild of three men: two veteran political operatives, David Blankenhorn and David Lapp, and an eminent family therapist by the name of Bill Doherty. Shortly after the 2016 election, Blankenhorn called Lapp to see if they could gather a group of ten Hillary Clinton supporters and ten Donald Trump supporters in a room in Ohio, and see if they could get them talking to each other. Blankenhorn called his old friend Doherty and told him what they had in mind. He said they wanted him to figure out a way to structure the gathering to maximize the chance that something productive might come out of it, and minimize the possibility of people yelling past one another, as is the current fashion. Doherty agreed, thinking the idea had a whiff of bravery to it, and the men put out feelers to find a group of partisans who may be interested in such a thing.

The first group was convened in South Lebanon, Ohio, in December 2016, for two days of workshops. The goal was not to change anyone's political views—only to see if it was possible to get them to have a productive conversation. The program Doherty had created for the gathering consisted of a few parts. First, the attendees took turns saying why they came. "Most of them said, 'We have a community to run here—we have hospitals to run, and roads to build, and schools to operate. And we have to figure out a way to do that despite our differences,'" Doherty recalls. They were under strain and needed to find a way to cooperate, in other words.

Once they'd established that, they had to get over the first big hurdle: negative stereotypes. We know now that stereotypes can aggravate intergroup anxiety and keep people from talking to one another. So Doherty separated what he called the "reds" and the "blues" into two rooms and had them come up with a list of what they believed were the top four stereotypes the other side had of their group. Republicans pointed to the accusation that they're all racist, for example, and Democrats picked the criticism that they want big government to solve all problems. Then a facilitator asked the participants two questions: One, *What's true instead?* And two, *Is there a kernel of truth to the stereotype?*

The aim of this exercise was to confront negative stereotypes immediately, but to do it in a way that wouldn't kill the conversation before it started. If each side was asked to name the top four stereotypes about the *other* side, then it would feel like an attack and the walls would go up. But by naming the stereotypes of their own side, and both pushing back against them and acknowledging there may be some truth there, the attendees were able to show self-awareness, restraint, humility, intelligence, and good faith. The exercise functioned like a greeting ritual. Both sides were initially wary, but once it was performed, there was reassurance in a common humanity, and a pathway opened. This step was critical. "If people land the kernels of truth: bang, the workshop takes off," Doherty says.

Next was the fishbowl. For this, one group sat in the middle, and the other sat in a circle around them. The inner group was asked two questions: *Why are your sides' values and policies good for the country?* and *What are your reservations or concerns about your own side?* They discussed the questions among themselves, as the outer group listened, and then they switched positions. Both sides were prohibited from talking about the other side or characterizing the other side's beliefs. "You don't say, 'Unlike the other side, we believe in responsible government,' because a lot of the breakdown that occurs in communication across difference is when people characterize the other group's position," Doherty says. As these discussions happened, each side was able to watch the other display intelligence, introspection, self-scrutiny, doubt, sincerity, and so forth: many of the complex human characteristics we can be loath to attribute to groups we don't like. After the session, people were paired up and asked what they learned about the other side and whether they had anything in common with them.

Next, each side was given a chance to ask the other side questions. We know how important questions can be when talking to strangers. Asking good questions can show other people we're engaged, and it can make them like us more, and it can help the other person think more clearly. But here both sides turned out to be terrible at it. They had gone so long without being curious about the other side that they had forgotten how to be—*curiosity* being the first body thrown off the back of the truck during polarized times.

"It was not good," says Doherty. "People don't know how to ask those questions." He says they were more accustomed to "making declarations." They'd say, "Obamacare is a disaster." Or they'd say, "Marriage is between a man and a woman," which doesn't invite discussion. Or a red would be making an argument about policy and the blue would call them sexist or xenophobic. "It just shut down the conversation," Doherty says.

So Doherty separated the groups again and had each work with a facilitator to come up with four good questions that would actually gain them insight into the other side's way of thinking. In essence, this forced them to be curious about one another. Once they came up with better questions and asked them, the participants were permitted to ask only follow-ups that further clarified their understanding of the other side's stance.

The question exercise had a couple of unintended effects, Doherty says. Respondents, having been asked good questions about why they believe what they believe, sometimes realized they didn't have as firm a grip on the issue as they had thought they did. They had spent a lot of time talking to people they agreed with, and an intellectual laziness had set in. For them, arguments weren't for changing minds or clarifying points. Arguments were for signaling membership in the group. Other participants simply realized how bad they had become at giving even the slightest thought to their opponents' positions. But they all practiced listening, and thinking, and they got better at it.

Doherty was worried that the first session would come flying off the rails. But as he watched, real conversations occurred, and friendships budded across partisan lines. One of those friendships involved a man named Kouhyar Mostashfi, a software engineer who came to the United States from Iran in 1994 and lives in the Dayton, Ohio, area. Mostashfi had become involved in Democratic politics during the George W. Bush administration, but he had boiled over with the election of Donald Trump. "It caused me to lose faith in Republicans," he says. "I flat-out saw them as the enemies of the state. That was my line of thinking: I hate them. I hate all of them! I hate every Republican in my neighborhood, in my work. I don't want any association with them." Nevertheless, when a Democratic chairperson circulated a flyer advertising that first Braver Angels (initially called Better Angels) meeting, he was intrigued. He didn't think there was anything they could do to change his mind, and he didn't expect that anything they said would make the least bit of sense to him. But still, he was curious. "I really wanted to meet these people," he tells me. "It's like when you're watching these science-fiction movies, and you see the alien, and you're interested to see how they behaved. That was really my motivation."

That initial meeting delivered a few surprises for Mostashfi. Partisans on the other side were more complex than he'd given them credit for. One red was an evangelical Christian who believed homosexuality was a sin, but also took care of his terminally ill gay brother. The man told the group he wasn't going to allow his religious beliefs to ruin their relationship, he said. Another conceded that Republicans were wrong to give Barack Obama such hell when he was president. Another still was Greg Smith, a former law enforcement officer and devout Christian who voted enthusiastically for Trump. During the session, Smith—a bearish, gregarious, and emotional man—approached Mostashfi and asked him about ISIS, a line of questioning Mostashfi was by then pretty tired of answering. He told Smith that Islam has its extremists, like other religions. But they talked more and got friendly. In a brief documentary made of the first gathering, Smith beams after the session, calling him, "My Muslim buddy."

Because of the setting—the rules, the structure, the moderator, all of which kept hostility and defensiveness in check—each group was allowed to be curious about the other side without fear of it blowing up on them. It was like a free pass, a temporary cessation of hostilities, and the effect it had on its participants was transformational. "You know, we tend to put these people in the same bucket, and that is really not the case," says Mostashfi. "That exercise really helped me try to see them as human beings as opposed to just members of a cult." He and Smith met up for lunch after the gathering and talked for three hours about religion. That turned into a friendship that endures today. Together, they formed Braver Angels of Southwest Ohio, a local alliance. Smith became a chair of Braver Angels for a year. (When I met him at the Braver Angels annual convention in St. Louis in 2019, Smith later told me he believed that God brought him to that first meeting. He also told me, "I'm the funny one and Kouhyar is the smart one.")

Doherty says that first gathering "was successful beyond our expectations, and we decided we had to keep working on it," Doherty says. As of December 2020, Braver Angels had thirteen thousand members and chapters in all fifty states. It's a modest number, but it nearly doubled between 2019 and 2020, providing for its members a source of hope in a time in which we think very little of one another. "It is just so noble," says Mostashfi. "Not every day is easy. I have my bad days. I have the days that I'm just so sick of the news that I come home and I vent to my wife, 'What is someone like Greg thinking? How could they love this guy?' But I still go to these meetings. I still want to have a conversation. Because, you know, the alternative is chaos."

We can certainly debate the long-term merits of the Braver Angels approach. I'm confident many hardcore partisans will think it is either goofy or some kind of secret indoctrination effort. Admittedly, when I first made contact with them, I was skeptical that such a thing could work on a scale large enough to make a difference. I worried that the worst offenders, the most divisive people, would never come anywhere near something like this. Doherty conceded that point. "The real haters are beyond our reach," he said.

And to be honest, I wasn't without hate myself. Like many, I had become deeply contemptuous of the other side—to the point where there are days when I'm convinced the republic is through, and I'm not sure I even care, as long as I don't have to share a house with those people anymore. But I'd also become frustrated and disappointed by liberals on my own side, which I guess makes me a lousy partisan. So maybe there was hope. Certainly, the project appealed to me on one level, because while I certainly struggle with a deep and abiding cynicism, I have found that it is often held in check by an abundance of personal experience that tells me that people, if engaged in the right spirit, will almost always surprise you. And I wondered if a lot of the refusal to talk to each other comes from the fact that we have simply forgotten how—something we've seen repeatedly in this book. Doherty said something similar. "I think some people, if you asked them, would say they would like to be able to communicate," he said. "But they don't have the skills for it."

Despite the group's high-minded aspirations, my main interest in Braver Angels was in the techniques they used. I wanted to see how they defused hostility and distrust among warring groups, how they were able to coax people over a barrier that had come to feel insurmountable. Conversations with strangers can be difficult, as we know. They can be intimidating, even in ideal cases. I wanted to find the most difficult version of those conversations, and see if there were ways to get better at them. And I wanted to see if the established benefits of talking to strangers—happiness, belonging, trust—would translate into the inhospitable hellscape that is American politics, or if such an effort was doomed to fail, like peonies planted in a bucket of salt. So I flew to St. Louis to attend Braver Angels' annual convention, whereupon I promptly found myself in a large college hall surrounded by hundreds of Republicans and Democrats from all fifty states wearing red or blue lanyards, singing the national anthem in a display that felt both subterranean and subversive, readying themselves to spend a few days talking to the people they hated.

All of which is to say, the start of the 2019 convention was awkward, even by the standards of conventions, which are always sort of awkward. There were three hundred delegates milling around—150 blues and 150 reds—and they were anxious, maybe a little shy, and certainly guarded. Every delegate was made to wear a lanyard announcing their side, which some said made them feel exposed and vulnerable, like they had a target painted on their chests. Newcomers were skeptical that anything could come out of this. Some of them told me that their friends thought it was a bad idea to fraternize with the other side. A TV news crew was there, and some of the delegates ducked any time a camera came out. If you could power the lights with intergroup anxiety, it would have blinded us all.

The challenge for Braver Angels was to get past this anxiety and distrust, to engineer ways to make these attendees feel safe enough and comfortable enough to start talking to one another, and, more important, to start listening. The apparatus they have constructed in order to do this is a howdy door for politics: gradually getting strangers used to the sight of one another, curious about one another, reducing the instinct to attack, and slowly, carefully, and under close expert supervision, putting them together to see if a working alliance can be formed. This is what the convention needed to accomplish, and Braver Angels would attempt to do it through workshops, parliamentary debates, speeches, parties, and mixers.

The debates are new, an effort to attract conservatives, who, composing about 30 percent of the overall membership, have been less enthusiastic about this venture. The liberals tend to like the personal conversations, and the conservatives tend to like the debates, which lines up with political science research. Generally speaking, liberals tend to have what is called an approach motivation, meaning they like to build bridges and connect, while conservatives have an avoidance motivation, meaning they value structure, view other groups with wariness, and are focused on protecting their own. In other words, one likes to connect, one likes to defend. Which is to say it should come as little surprise that some conservatives might suspect that the kumbaya element of Better Angels is a trap set by a coven of socialist witches.*

For our purposes, the most relevant aspect of the convention is the

---

* It's also worth noting that the political scientists Ronnie Janoff-Bulman and Nate Carnes have found that the most smoothly running societies are the ones that land squarely between the conservative and liberal orientations. In such societies, a conservative mentality "may minimize risks associated with free riding and social loafing," they write, while a liberal one may maximize the social benefits of connecting and cooperating across group boundaries.

one-on-one conversations. These will give us a template that we can use to have difficult conversations with strangers from groups with which we are at loggerheads. They work like this: A red and a blue are seated across from each other. They take turns talking about their lives and their beliefs. Each tries to understand where the other is coming from, and in doing so, they try to find any areas of agreement. Because we are essentially back in the chimp research facility, there are myriad rules in place to minimize the potential for conversational breakdown, or worse.

Participants are told that they are here as individuals, not representatives of a party, and not to assume that the other person holds any particular views—unless they explicitly say they do. They are to describe only their own views and not characterize the views of the other person. They are told to stick to the spirit of the activities designed for each stage of the conversation—so if the question is *What have we each learned from listening to the other?* that's all they may discuss, even if it means resisting the urge to correct the other person. And throughout, they are to take turns, be respectful, share time evenly, and not interrupt. The fact that participants require so many rules and so much supervision in order to have a very basic human interaction is indeed depressing. But the rules are indispensable. They are like training wheels, or maybe crutches. They help participants build the needed muscles and hone coordination without hazarding a head injury.

The conversation itself is divided into several parts. Delegates are told to first explain why they decided to participate in this conversation. This shows they are earnest, they want to fix this mess, they feel there is common cause. Next, they're asked to share something personal about themselves—their family, where they live and for how long, and any hobbies or interests they may have. This is the sort of personal disclosure that invites other personal disclosures, and enhances liking and trust, as we've seen. It's also what Danielle Allen talked about in the previous chapter: a gift. You give it, and you get a gift in return. After that gift is accepted, and a connection is made—and *only* after that—delegates are to describe their political values, but in a personal way, describing what life experiences brought them around to those views, and explaining why they think they are good for the country. Finally, they are to express any reservations they have about their own side.

The genius of this approach is that it forces the participants to invert the way we tend to address one another in a political argument. Usually, we lead with the hottest of hot-button issues. If the argument is happening online, often we take a person's views and then reverse engineer a conveniently simplistic idea of who that person is based entirely on that view. Then we thrash that straw man into dust, to the delight of our allies. This creates a loop. The more we trash, ridicule, or dismiss them, the more we become convinced that they are one-dimensional subhuman enemies. The more we become convinced that they are one-dimensional subhuman enemies, the less inclined we are to try to understand them or talk to them. *What's the point?* we think. It's like trying to talk sense to a mosquito. Better to squash it, or avoid it. And they think the same of us. Northwestern University's Nour Kteily found in 2016 that the single biggest driver behind dehumanization is the belief that the other side is dehumanizing us.

At Braver Angels, however, because the conversations start with biography, participants are immediately confronted with the full complexity and humanity of the stranger sitting across from them. As they talk, inevitably they'll find something in common, because that's how humans talk—at least when they're comfortable. Maybe they both have a dog. Maybe they'd both been on a cruise. Whatever. It doesn't have to be much. Just a little bridge, an incidental similarity, something to establish a rapport, a mutual sense of liking between two individuals, which can then serve to keep the conversation on the rails when it gets into more contentious territory. Without that connection, the conversation is doomed. You can't put a strange liberal and a strange conservative in an enclosed space and shout, "Abortion: Go!" because one would say, "You're a murderer," and the other would say, "You hate women," and that would be the ball game.

But once there is a little bond in place, you can open the howdy door a crack. When the participants get to know each other as people—

with lives outside of partisan politics, beliefs rooted in real experience, a sense of self-awareness, and a capacity for self-scrutiny—the conversation can then move on to thornier issues. At this stage, one person is asked to talk about their view of an issue that is important to them. And then the other person does the same, ideally addressing any areas of potential agreement. Then the order is reversed and they go again. If they have time, they can get into two bonus questions: "What are your hopes and aspirations for the country?" and "What did you hear the other person say about their hopes and aspirations, and do you see anything in common?" The point of this, we're told, is not to win an argument or change the other person's thinking. As Doherty put it, the goal is to be able to sum up the other person's argument in a way that would make them say, "Yeah, that's right."

I watched as the reds and the blues went through this process. At first, people were a little uneasy, and rigidly polite. But as they moved through the steps and followed the rules, you could see them relax. They got more animated. Not irate, but engaged. You heard some laughter. After ten minutes, the place sounded like a bar. When the moderator asked them to talk to the group about their conversations afterward, everyone professed enjoying it. They all said they really liked their partners.

There is a substantial body of research that underscores what is happening in these conversations, based on an idea called *contact*. In 1954, a psychologist by the name of Gordon Allport formulated what is known as his contact hypothesis. It was inspired by findings that members of integrated military units and residents of integrated housing projects often displayed lower levels of prejudice than people who did not routinely mingle with other groups. Allport hypothesized that when people from different groups meet under certain conditions, it can reduce prejudice and cultivate "the perception of common interests and common humanity." You remember how Theodore Zeldin likened talking to strangers to "taking my clothes to the laundry, cleaning my mind of prejudices." Here it is again: Contact immunizes us against prejudice. Allport's conditions were very specific, though. Ideally, the people had to have equal status, common goals, a shared task, and the support of some sanctioning power—like a group, a law, or a social norm governing conduct—in order for contact to work. Braver Angels, you'll note, meets all those conditions.

Other researchers, however, have found that contact even under less optimal conditions can still make an impact. Thomas Pettigrew and Linda Tropp, two leading experts in the contact hypothesis, conducted a sweeping analysis of hundreds of studies. Ninety-four percent of the samples in their study showed that contact reduces prejudice. They found that it's ideal to have all of Allport's conditions in place in order to make progress. But they also found that contact of any duration can increase liking, and "generalize" beyond the individuals who we meet. That means the white American, say, can come away from a positive contact with an Iranian immigrant not only with warmer feelings toward that individual, but toward Iranian immigrants as a group, for instance. And if they become actual friends, that's the most effective way we know of to alleviate prejudice—not just between the friends, but among the friends of friends as well. In other words, say my good friend's friend is an evangelical Christian. That won't make me agree with evangelical Christians, and it won't make me accept them unconditionally as a group, but it will soften and complicate my view of them. It will help me see them as individuals, which will help reduce prejudice. And I will be reassured that contact with their group is possible by watching my friend. He will model for me how it's done.

Now, once contact is established at Braver Angels, these strangers' views are presented verbally and in person. That, too, is key. Juliana Schroeder and Nicholas Epley, the psychologists who conducted that subway experiment in Chicago, did a series of experiments with psychologist Michael Kardas in which they presented participants with a series of views on divisive topics. Some of these views were presented as a transcript, some were conveyed via a voice recording, and some were presented in a video. The researchers then asked the recipients of these messages a series of questions about how they perceived the people offering these views. Did they think they were refined? Open-minded? Responsive? Warm? Or were they superficial, cold, robotic, or "more like an object than a human"? In other words, how human did they believe these people were?

Schroeder and her colleagues found that across the board, people rated those with opposing views as less human—which is depressing. But they also found that when these views were conveyed verbally or visually—via the recording or the video—participants perceived those who held them as more human than they did in the transcript condition—even if they disagreed with the opinion. The authors believed that the presence of paralinguistic cues—tone of voice, pitch, articulation—was the reason why. When we see a stranger speak, it's harder to convince ourselves they aren't fully human. It's a check against lesser minds.

Juliana Schroeder repeated this experiment later, first with voters expressing their preferences for primary candidates in the 2016 presidential race, and then with the nominees. She found the same effect, only it was more extreme this time. Participants *reading* the views of someone who supported a candidate they opposed declined to attribute any humanity to the speaker at all. But when they saw and heard the views being expressed, they responded much more warmly to the person holding them.

Again, this is a world apart from political discourse online, where it is much easier to dehumanize the person on the other side, because you don't see them. You don't see their face, you don't hear their voice, you don't know their story. For you, they are a political view incarnate, nothing more. But in person, one-on-one, it's very different.

I spoke to one of the participants in this workshop, a Georgia Republican with a great languid drawl named Pat Thomas. His partner in the exercise was transgender, he said, whereas he always believed you're either male or female and that's it. "She's a very nice woman; we had a lovely conversation," he told me. "It made me think that people have these experiences that I can't relate to, but I should be open-minded about it." Likewise, he thinks he may have informed her opinion on his big issue, "the proper role of government."

These workshops are all about relearning to have a conversation—

to develop discipline and attentiveness, to learn to listen to understand and speak to be understood. Once people get comfortable, they can potentially take the training wheels off and attempt to have conversations outside of the safety of the structured workshop. When they are ready to take that leap, and start pursuing these sorts of conversations out in the wild, Braver Angels held another workshop showing them how.

The trick, attendees were told, is to set the tone of the conversation out of the gate so as not to trigger defensiveness or hostility. To do so, we have to express honest curiosity about the other person; we have to mention our partisan affiliation at the outset so it doesn't feel like a potential ambush; and when we ask questions, we should first ask permission—"Can I ask you something about this?"—so we demonstrate self-control and self-awareness and it doesn't feel like an interrogation. It's a pre-frame, like we learned from Georgie Nightingall. It establishes the nature of the exchange that is about to occur. After that, as we saw with free listening, we are to ask clarifying questions. Something like "Why do you feel that way?" opens doors, where "How can you say that?" does not.

And when our partners answer our questions, we're told to listen attentively, nod, make eye contact, mirror, and paraphrase what they say, so they can see we're trying to understand—just like Georgie taught us, right? Listening is critical to the Braver Angels approach, and a growing body of psychology research shows how powerful it can be in the context of partisan politics—for the person listening, and the person being listened to—when done well.

The Israeli business professor and psychologist Guy Itzchakov, whose work we encountered earlier, has found that when people feel they are being listened to, they relax, and they are more likely to share their true thoughts and feelings. Itzchakov calls this a "safe state" and argues that it "enables speakers to delve deeper into their consciousness and discover new insights about themselves—even those that may challenge previously held beliefs and perceptions." In other words, when you don't feel you're under attack, you're more likely to think, as opposed to simply parrying or repelling the other side. We've all experienced this, those moments when you're talking to a good listener and you have a sudden epiphany about what you believe. That's what Itzchakov is talking about. By listening well, we help each other think.

Even more promisingly, attentive listening can also reduce a speaker's more extreme beliefs. Itzchakov found that when speakers were anxious, they were more likely to experience what psychologists call *defensive processing*. This is when we essentially block out any information that contradicts our existing beliefs. We all do this—when we're stressed-out, or overloaded, say—but if you do it enough, it can block out all new information and keep amplifying the beliefs we have. Being listened to attentively, however, reduces anxiety, and thus reduces defensive processing. And when defensive processing is reduced, a curious thing happens. The speakers become aware of inconsistencies in their own positions and develop a more nuanced understanding of both sides of the argument, something called *attitude complexity*.

In a 2018 paper, Itzchakov and his colleagues "found that speakers who conversed with a good listener reported attitudes that were more complex and less extreme." In other words, *simply being listened to,* as opposed to being argued against or presented with more accurate data, clarifies your beliefs, enhances your understanding of the nuances of a particular issue, and reduces extremity. In 2020, Itzchakov published the results of another study into high-quality listening, this time to see if it could alleviate prejudice. He had hundreds of Israeli participants discuss a personal prejudice. Some were treated to high-quality listening—with support, empathy, and understanding; others were treated to low-quality listening. Itzchakov found that the ones who were listened to well experienced a drop in the intensity of their prejudice; those who were not listened to well stayed the same. He believed this was because the people who were really listened to felt less defensive, and that allowed them to explore their beliefs more fully and be less reactive than those who were not really listened to.

Back at Braver Angels, we're told that when it's our turn to speak in a conversation—after we have expressed curiosity, asked good questions, and listened to the answers—we should try to personalize our response. We can do this by using "I statements" instead of more sweeping assertions. "I worry we're approaching a tipping point on global warming," we can say, as opposed to "We're approaching a tipping point on global warming." We can offer something critical about our own side to demonstrate that we are not partisan automatons. We should point out any commonalities, but when we do disagree, say some version of "I hear you" first, to show you actually do. And we can earn their attention by telling stories, because stories make people listen in a way that facts do not.

Guy Itzchakov studied this, too. He ran another experiment in which speakers told listeners either meaningful stories or strictly informational ones about buildings. The ones who told meaningful stories were listened to more closely. "We concluded that when speakers share meaningful stories they make their partner listen well and consequently experience higher psychological safety and lower feelings of social anxiety."

Insecurity and social anxiety, as we know, are fuel for polarization. Only if you can find a way to reduce them can you even hope to have an actual conversation or debate. That's what many of Braver Angels' techniques are aimed at. When successful, they can lower suspicion, stereotyping, and hostility, seed a kernel of good faith, and set us on a path toward understanding something that is both head-smackingly obvious and utterly elusive, but which comes up often when we discuss talking to strangers: That they are not just mindless drones or witless suckers. That they are, in fact, complex. They defy pigeonholing. They have something to offer us—insights, ideas, surprises—and us them. Convincing ourselves that this is true is remarkably difficult because every iota of our politics, as well as our informational ecosystems, are aligned against it. But as we've seen throughout this book, the best way to do so is to take the risk, muster the faith, and talk to these strangers.

And I'll admit it. They got to me. I spent four days talking to people—reds and blues from all over the country. A young, shy liberal who told me he feels like he learned to have a conversation this weekend. In one exchange, he said he was "shocked" at the depth of the other person. "It felt like exercising a new muscle," he said. A Republican psychiatrist from D.C. told me that she never publicly discloses her party affiliation, because it would kill her business, but also that living with a secret that could affect her livelihood made her a far more empathetic therapist for her transgender clients.

I watched Bill Doherty tell a room full of people, "Neither side is going to vanquish the other; we need to find a way to get along," and I found myself nodding. I heard his cofounder David Blankenhorn take objection to the idea that fostering these discussions is an admission of weakness or a lack of resolve. "What if that's the weak way to think?" he said. After all, "is there anything more demanding, or rigorous, or serious than love your neighbor?" I listened to John Wood, Jr., a Black Republican from South Central Los Angeles, call for "patriotic empathy," which is the idea that we have an obligation to our country to choke down our loathing and empathize with our political opponents. That we have to become curious about their lives and invested in their fate. I thought of that corny American virtue I spoke of earlier that turns up in so many obituaries: *never met a stranger,* and for the first time felt like, with enough work, it could be made applicable across lines that now feel uncrossable.

Late in the convention, I asked Pat Thomas, the Georgia Republican, what his experience had been like. He took a drag of a cigarette and said he's never been one to shy away from conflict—"I'm Irish"—so it wasn't like he needed a sense of safety to express himself. But still, the convention had surprised him. "I thought there'd be more acrimony from the sides, but everyone here is reasonable," he said. "We're all Americans, we're all *reasonable* Americans. We can self-govern. We can talk to each other. We've all experienced that this weekend."

I told him watching this as an outsider had been interesting for me, because I saw everyone start out a little anxious, but then once they got comfortable, it turned almost giddy. It was like summer camp. Lunchtime in the school cafeteria was practically deafening, and blues were seeking out people in red lanyards to talk to, and vice versa. I told him my idea about relief, about how when I have a good interaction with a stranger, it always feels like a relief. I wondered if that was part of the giddiness. "Everyone here feels that relief, including me," he said. "It's really refreshing. . . . We're all relieved that we can actually talk to each other. And we can actually convince the other side to look at something a different way on some subjects."

He leaned back and took another drag of his cigarette. "This is a phenomenon that can spread like wildfire," he said. "I think it could be a big thing, this Braver Angels movement."

And I felt a change on a personal level as well. As a city dweller in the Northeast, I probably have more in common with people in Tokyo than I do with people who live a hundred miles north of me. The greatest strangers to me—strange almost to the point of being incomprehensible—are rural Republicans. My exposure to them is almost always filtered through media and social media, and it's never flattering. Yes, the internet carries the promise of connecting me with a diverse array of intelligent views, but the algorithms governing Twitter ensure I just keep getting more of what I already agree with, and Facebook, before I quit it, seemed to be largely an engine that manufactured bizarrely irate confrontations with a childhood friend's angry coworker who somehow saw my post. None of this left me with a complex perception of who the other side was.

I got to spend time with these people in St. Louis. And though we disagreed, vehemently, on many things, the fact that we could sit and talk, make each other laugh and think, and tell stories and enjoy one another's company was a revelation and a relief. Now, in the heat of partisan battle, whenever the urge strikes to dismiss them en masse, I think of those conversations and of those individuals. They act as a natural buffer against the prejudice I've long held against folks like them. It's the contact hypothesis at work: When you meet members of a group as individuals, in person, as equals, and you imagine yourselves part of a common project, it's harder to write them all off as interchangeable parts of a monolith. You have included them in the self; you have expanded. And at the very worst of a very bad 2020, I found myself thinking of them often. People would characterize an entire region in a negative way, and I'd think, "Yeah, but I met this guy in St. Louis who told me something interesting. . . ."

I'm certainly not saying that the Braver Angels approach can, or will, solve everything. The organizers would certainly never make that claim. Many of the things that to me need to be addressed in order to help America fulfill its founding promise for all its citizens are questions of law and policy. They are complicated, and they will be hard to repair and reform into something that benefits everyone. It might take a decade, or two decades, or more, before we can get to a point where the country is fully functional. But just because it's hard doesn't mean we shouldn't try. Heraclitus wrote that harmony comes from the strain of binding opposites, after all, and learning to talk to your fellow citizens—people who have become strangers because of shifts in culture and politics and circumstance—is just a start. But in a time devoid of hope, a start feels momentous. It feels like everything. It feels like the only thing.

A few days after the convention, I called Holly, the teacher we met at the beginning of this chapter, to see what her takeaways were. "I am still on a complete dopamine high from that experience—which was really one of the top experiences of my life," she says. "Having that confluence of people, and intent, was transforming. I'm a zealot now. I just wish I'd had this all my life." She had already started reaching out to local organizations about organizing Braver Angels debates, and so far people had been receptive. She wants to teach the skills she learned to her students, and hold classroom debates based on the Braver Angels model. She envies young people who might be exposed to this model. "They need to develop those intellectual muscles early, and have the guts and stamina to know that this is a powerful way of being," she says.

Going into it, she says, her husband was skeptical. "He definitely belongs to the tribe of reds who are concerned about being shouted down, insulted by, treated poorly by the far left," she says. "And condemned as stupid. It's a humiliating and infuriating situation to be in." When she told him she wanted to go, he thought it would be a nice social occasion, but in the end wouldn't do any good. But she had spent several days having deep conversations with strangers about philosophy, religion, and politics without fear of it devolving into name-calling, contempt, and dismissal. She had seen how the workshops and debates helped shape people's behavior, and led to better discussions and clearer thinking. She says she learned that there was a lot more nuance not just on the blue side, but the red side, too.

"I know I sound like some crazy convert," she says, "but it's joyous—it is a joyous thing to invite someone into. With seven thousand people perhaps it isn't hugely powerful, but what's the alternative? To give up in despair?" She's not afraid of the long odds. "The early Christians, there were only a handful of them, too." She laughs. "They seem to have made a rather large impact."

A year and a half later, in December, after the 2020 election, I talked to a spokesman from Braver Angels. He said they had to cancel the convention, but they had been doing more conversations over digital platforms. He says turnout has been strong, and he was excited about the way that technology could so easily bridge the physical distances between reds and blues. He said that in November, thirteen hundred new dues-paying members signed up—which was a record. That was 10 percent of their entire membership—what was then thirteen thousand—in a single month. And he said that they have been aggressively reaching out to more people of color, more working-class folks, and of course more conservatives—who they'd begun to reach via partnerships with civic organizations and churches. It was hard, he said, but it was progress.

I also emailed Holly to see how she was doing. Using the language of Braver Angels—Republicans are reds, moderates are purples—she reported the following: "I am no longer participating in Braver Angels. None of my red friends are, and the self-proclaimed 'purples' in our local group have all Red Pilled [that is, have turned hard to the right]. I've had it, and alternate between denial, despair, and fury. We Americans are all strangers now."

Which is to say, we have our work cut out for us.

Chapter 20

Upon Encountering a Stranger

In which we imagine the first day of the rest of your life as a xenophile.

You step out of your house in the morning and into a world of strangers. Where do you go? Do you walk somewhere to catch a train, or a bus? If so, look at the world around you. Take it in. Notice. Keep your phone in your pocket. Remove your earbuds.

Are there other people around? Look at them, and remind yourself that they are not instruments, they are not obstacles, they are not of lesser mind. Wonder about them. What are they doing? Where are they going? Don't be a creep. Just be curious. When they get maybe fifteen feet away, make eye contact. Pay attention. Do they look back? Yes? Good, then smile. Wish them a good morning. Some might not even notice you did it, but a surprising number will, and they'll smile back and return the greeting. Note how that feels to you, and keep walking.

What's next? Coffee? Of course, it's coffee. What kind of question is that? Remember that in situations like these, social norms and our desire for efficiency conspire against making connections. Remember that friction can make us social. You get to the front of the line and the guy asks how you are. Remember that he's following a script.

Break the script. Be clever and authentic. Shrug and say, "Eh, I'd say about a 6.5 out of 10." Ask him how he is. Notice that he follows you. He says he's maybe a 7.5. Build on what he says. Say, "Man, I'd like to hit 7.5 today. You got any advice for me?" How he answers this question will give you a glimpse of who he is, and what it's like to be him. And you've asked him for advice. That's a compliment. It demonstrates that you think he is more than a coffee-delivery mechanism. If there are other people in line, thank him, grab your coffee, and go. If there aren't, keep talking if you want. If you're worried about the right way to end the conversation, just be honest. "I gotta run—it was nice talking to you" never fails.

How do you get to work? If you commute by car: Sorry, your options are going to be limited. But if you take a bus or a train, you're in luck—even though the prospect of talking to someone scares the hell out of you. You're worried they'll reject you, or that you won't be good at it, or you won't have something to talk about. You're worried about violating a social norm. Those fears are completely natural and completely understandable. Take them and drown them in a bucket.

You get on the bus or the train. Now look around. Is there a seat? Are you going to be standing? Whatever it is, try to talk to people at your level. Talking to someone who is sitting while you're standing could make them feel like you're looming over them, or trapping them. It can be done, but you have to be mindful of the awkward dynamic that can create. Ideally, talk to the person sitting next to you, or standing next to you. So who is next to you? Here's where you follow your curiosity. Is there anything interesting going on? Do they have a coat you like? Are they reading a book you've heard about? There's your opener. Be mindful of pluralistic ignorance: Just because they may look like they don't want to talk doesn't mean they won't want to talk. But at the same time, read the signs. If they have noise-canceling headphones on and their eyes are closed, leave them alone.

But if you get the sense they may be open—and you will develop very keen radar for this after you practice a few times—start with your pre-frame. This is your greeting ritual, your way to show that you are a self-possessed human of sound mind and not an agent of chaos. "Sorry," you say, "I know we're not supposed to talk to people on the train, but I really like your coat." They might not be expecting this, so you may have to say it again. If they're responsive, follow that with your statement. "I've been looking for a new coat. Can I ask, where'd you find it?" or some such. And maybe you talk about coats. That's great. You've made a little connection. How does it feel? Do you feel reassured? Relaxed? Happier? Connected? Did it go better than you expected?

Maybe you talk more. Remember that small talk is a door, a way to get comfortable with someone and figure out how you fit together, as you search for some kind of commonality, some sign of mere belonging. Maybe they're into something you're into. Maybe, in talking about the coat, they give you a glint of who they are. If that's the case, engage with it. Smile, nod, paraphrase what they say or echo it, and maybe ask them a general question: *Why is that? When did you realize that?* Remember that the way people do small things is the way they do big things. You can get a lot from a little detail. Maybe you learn something, or gain an insight you might not have arrived at on your own. Maybe there's something that stays with you, an image, or a statement or perspective that you can carry with you. Something that expands you a little, that makes the world feel a little more comprehensible, a little more manageable, a little less dauntingly large.

Or maybe they just didn't want to talk. That's fine, too. They might be tired, distracted, or prejudiced, or just private. It's okay. Move on.

Maybe later, during lunch, you go to a little park with good seating and shade and perhaps a fountain: a public place where a mix of different types of people go to relax. Not a river, like a city street. More like a tide pool where people collect. Here you don't really have to use the pre-frame, because the norm against talking to strangers is relaxed in places like these. You're all participating in the same space, and you all have equal right to it. You end up next to a person who's from a different group: maybe they're a different color, or they're older, or they're disabled. Whatever it is, you feel a little anxious. You're worried that it might go badly, that you might say the wrong thing, or they'll reject you in some way. Those fears are completely natural, too. Nevertheless, drown them in the bucket and proceed.

Remember the idea of triangulation. If you're both looking at the same thing, or experiencing the same thing, it forms a little *us,* a little bond. Maybe kids are playing basketball, and you turn to the person and say, "I used to love playing basketball." That can lead to a conversation about your childhoods, or exercise, or whatever. Or, just comment on the weather, in the English fashion. Just be specific, and offer a statement. Don't say, "Nice day." Say, "Nice day. Thank god it's fall." This is not a scientific claim, but when you mention a preference for weather to a stranger you will very soon be discussing where you both came from. That can take the conversation somewhere interesting.

Remember that when you offer something a little more personal, they will probably tell you something personal in response, and that doing so—as long as you're pacing one another and not saying anything gross or weird—will make you like and trust each other a little more. Listen closely. Don't interrupt or fidget. Make eye contact. Pay attention to the nonverbal signs. Watch your partner's body language for indications of approval or enjoyment. Know that you're both likely underestimating how well you're doing, and how much the other person is enjoying the conversation. Think of the tradition of hospitality. Once you both get comfortable, that's when it gets good. Let the conversation go where it goes. Let it surprise you. If you seem to have an especially good rapport, maybe ask for advice on something. That will give you another glimpse of who this person is, and it might actually solve whatever problem it is you're having. In any case, by asking for advice, you've made yourself a little vulnerable. You've taken a risk. That's key to this enterprise, because people tend to respond to it.

Afterward—"Well, I gotta run, it was really nice talking to you"— think about how you expected the interaction to go, and compare that to how it went. This will help you recalibrate your ordinarily dismal expectations for how these encounters can go. Who knows, maybe you'll feel less anxious around other members of this group in the future, with this interaction under your belt. Maybe the effect generalizes, and leaves you with a more positive perception of that group—or at the very least shows that you are capable of talking to one another—as individuals and as members of your groups, and that is a victory for you and for society. You have both learned a little about what life is like for another, and your own lives are richer for it.

How do you feel? Are you tired? Relieved? Reassured? All three? Perfectly valid. Take a break. Recharge. These conversations are demanding; if you're tapped out, they won't go as well. If you need some alone time, take it. This is hard to do when you're tired.

I'll give you an option for this next step. You go to a bar, a town hall meeting, or a cocktail party at a friend's house. Whatever you're more comfortable with. While you're there, some stranger makes a remark, and you bristle. You could ignore them, or you could go after them. But you take a breath. You know that going on the offensive will likely result in the usually pointless and exhaustingly common spectacle of two people angrily talking past each other, leaving both just angrier and more convinced that they are right and the other side sucks. And that's fun sometimes, but in the end, you can't escape the sensation that you just ate a whole bag of potato chips.

So you decide to take a real risk this time. You choke back the urge to lash out. Which is hard, because lashing out is what we do. You take a breath, and you start in. You say out of the gate what side you're on, but maybe you temper it with an acknowledgment of a stereotype the other side has of your side: "Look, I'm but a low-level functionary of the Communist Party here, so take this with a grain of salt. . . ." You don't attack the other person's argument. You don't call into question their motivations, and you don't assume. Instead, you state your own belief. You don't frame it as a matter of unquestioned fact, handed down by god or nature or whoever is keeping the lights on up there. You frame it as an I-statement: "I've found that . . ." And then you work in a little bit more of your story: how you arrived at that belief. Remember that while peppering people with facts tends to repel, stories attract—they flesh you out and make it harder for the other person to maintain the belief that you are not all there. Show the other person that you don't have all the answers, you're trying to understand, and this is your best effort. Show that you have a couple reservations about your side, too. In doing this, you have set the terms of the exchange.

Hand the mic back to the other person. How did they arrive at this belief? Who are they, as individuals? Know that what they say is going to set off alarm bells. You are going to want to pounce. Do not pounce. Hold fast. Be curious. Ask open-ended questions. Don't grill. Don't say, "How can a person who thinks like this be trusted to ride a tricycle, much less cast a vote?" Say, "Why is that so important to you?" Say, "What were your parents like, politically?" Your goal in this is to understand the person better, and to be able to articulate their position in a way that rings true to them. In this way, you are extending hospitality. Give them space, let them talk. Where have they been? What's the news from distant lands?

As the conversation wends along, notice how much calmer you feel than when this started. Notice how you think differently when you're comfortable. Are you revising your position, even a little? Is he giving any ground? You don't have to change each other's minds. That's an unreasonable expectation for a short encounter. What you want is to understand each other, to bring seemingly irreconcilable factions a half an inch closer. To maybe find something you can agree on, even if it's tiny and beside the point. But if not that, fine, too. At least you've seen firsthand that with practice and some discipline, reasoned conversation can be had. By now, after all, you have confidence. You have gazed upon the enormity of other lives, and though it's daunting, you have not flinched. You are an explorer, a traveler without a destination, and you are making contact. That's enough for now.

Chapter 21

A New Social Renaissance

As you've probably gathered by this point, I have a fondness for the old stories. So let's you and I end our time together with one of those.

In the beginning, there was a man and his god in a pretty place. In this pretty place was a forbidden tree of knowledge, and the man, Adam, was curious about it. This is understandable. He was a human being, after all, and humans are helpless in the face of curiosity. It's strange that God would design man to be curious and then make satisfying his curiosity a sin, but we'll leave that one aside for the moment.

For a time, Adam was able to keep his hands off the forbidden tree, and all was well. But then he got lonely. It's also strange that God would put man in paradise and then make him susceptible to loneliness, but then this is the same God who created a whole race of hyper-cooperative apes, and then punished them for being *too* cooperative in building the Tower of Babel. We'll leave that one aside for the moment, too.

God fashioned Adam a companion: Eve—the first woman, which means she was also the first woman to be blamed for everything (see also: Pandora). Eve was curious about the tree, too, only she was persuaded to act on her curiosity by a trickster snake that God had put in the garden for reasons both unclear and unlikely to stand up in court.

Eve pressed Adam to eat the apple. Adam yielded. Maybe it was because to pick a fight this early in the relationship would likely result in an immediate curtailment of newly discovered erotic possibilities. Maybe Eve just made the better argument.

Whatever it was, that was that. Out went the lights. Adam and Eve became strangers to themselves—ashamed of their own bodies—and strangers to this world, evicted from the only home they had ever known. If you're a believer, their decision to satisfy their curiosity was the original sin, and its taint pooled ever outward, staining our souls and the souls of our children. You believe that it's the reason we've all been sentenced to live in this vale of strangers; that it's why we seem to be programmed to need all these intangible things that the world does not readily provide, like belonging and meaning and attention and security; that it's the reason, to quote the great philosopher Immanuel Kant, that we're all crooked timber, out of which nothing truly straight can be built; that it's the reason, to quote another great philosopher, why we ain't got no home in this world anymore.

We are living in strange times. The world has changed, and the world is changing, and the world will continue to change. It was ever thus. We know that we are built to move, and we're built to mix, and we are extraordinarily capable of adapting. And we know that change can be good. It can help us improve our lot, and it can, and has, helped us to survive. But it also makes us crazy. Many people have watched as social, cultural, economic, and technological forces have combined to turn the world they know on its head, to render strange what was once familiar, leaving them feeling afraid and alone amid a cascade of social emergencies.

In America (but not only America), political polarization has become so entrenched that it's almost impossible for fellow citizens to imagine a future together. We may share a country, but we have become strangers to one another. Inequality has become so severe that the ruling classes' perception of the lives of the people below them is informed almost entirely by bias, conjecture, or nonsense, but seldom by personal experience. They are strangers to one another, but only one of them holds the keys. Millions who have been historically marginalized are now demanding to be recognized and included and afforded the rights that their fellow citizens have long taken for granted. They have been strangers, and they wish to be known. War, poverty, and climate instability are causing immense migrations of immigrants and refugees to strange lands. They are strangers, too. Strangers and sojourners in exile, a long way from home.

Amid all these changes, it's easy to feel disoriented. Humans have long identified themselves in the contexts of where they lived and which group they belonged to. But as those places change, and those groups hybridize or dissolve and new groups appear, offering novel innovations and ways of being, we can feel unmoored, unnerved. If who I am is based on the world around me, what happens to me when that world changes? Who am I then?

That's a big question. James Baldwin wrote in 1976, "An identity is questioned only when it is menaced, as when the mighty begin to fall, or when the wretched begin to rise, or when the stranger enters the gates, never, thereafter, to be a stranger: the stranger's presence making *you* the stranger, less to the stranger than to yourself." When you root yourself in the world, and the world changes, you can become a stranger among strangers.

When we struggle to understand how we relate to one another, and how we fit in, that uncertainty can tip into anxiety, and anxiety into feelings of threat or abandonment. These can lead us to withdraw from society or lash out against these new strangers and these new changes in the hopes of restoring a lost order, and with it, our old feelings of comfort and belonging. But that's a fool's game. You can't restore society to the way it was any more than you can return to your own childhood. When you think you can, you're guaranteed a crushing disappointment. When societies think they can, they are almost guaranteed war.

But I get it. I understand what it feels like to be a stranger in a strange land, to some small degree. In the past, belonging and identity were fairly simple things for me. I was a white, male, Irish Catholic writer from Boston, Massachusetts. I knew what a man is and does, I knew what a Catholic is and does, I knew what a writer is and does, and I never thought much about what it was to be white, to be honest. I had deep roots in a specific place with a specific character that resonated with me. I was surrounded by siblings, two fairly traditional parents who grew up close to where they raised us, and a rotating cast of familiar people around. While I chafed against this occasionally, it was also a source of great comfort and stability, and the root of how I came to see myself. It still is.

So what happened over the past twenty years? Boston changed into something I hardly recognize. Catholicism imploded in a cloud of lurid scandal. The internet destroyed much of print media and redefined the writer's place in society. Traditional gender roles were shuffled, revised, and discarded. I became a father who is expected to devote far more time and energy to parenting than any previous generation of men have, while working full-time. And I moved to New York City: America's Capital of Strangers. So who am I in this welter of revolutions? What do I belong to?

And for that matter, who are you? And what do you belong to? It's a big question. Perhaps the biggest. But it's not unanswerable.

The world is strange, and it's making us lonely. The COVID-19 epidemic drove our isolation to new extremes, but we were already suffering from an epidemic of loneliness before the coronavirus arrived. Since the 1970s, Americans, as well as people across the West, have retreated from public life and from one another. Robert Putnam calls this cocooning. Activities that were once done with others out in the world—dancing, clubs and civic organizations, churchgoing—have been replaced with activities conducted at home, either alone or with a small number of people. "Our society appears to be in a state of social decline," writes psychologist Oscar Ybarra, "not one in which the environment is chaotic and people fear for their lives, but one in which people have fewer interactions and relations with others."

This trend overlaps with a steep decline in social trust, and a rise in loneliness and depression. This can form a loop. Psychologists have found that on some occasions, lonely people can withdraw even further from society as a result of the pain of their loneliness. Maybe the prospect of interacting becomes intolerably stressful after a long time alone. Maybe their social skills erode so significantly they simply forget how to be social. Maybe they forget that they even need to be social. We know that healthy relationships are critical to our physical and mental well-being, but we are not getting what we need, and we are flailing, and that flailing is causing havoc.

We are alone, but that's not to say we're independent. We know that our hunter-gatherer ancestors became social because they recognized they were dependent on one another to survive, and bands and tribes met regularly in order to maintain sustaining relations with one another. Socializing was survival, and survival was socializing. This is how we evolved, and how we came to flourish as an ultra-cooperative species. The irony for us is that, though we have withdrawn socially, we're far more dependent on others than our distant ancestors were.*

Take me, for example. I am hopelessly dependent on others. I can't sew. I can't hunt. I can't fish. The one time I grew tomatoes, they came out looking like an offense to nature. I'm not even sure I can change a tire. I am functionally useless in almost every imaginable way. But most of the strangers I rely on in order to manage being alive in the world are invisible to me. I tap my phone and food appears by my door. I tap my phone and a plane ticket arrives in my in-box. I don't have to look at anyone or talk to anyone. I am not an outlier in this. We have all of the dependence and virtually none of the social contact, and now we are stressed-out by the prospect of calling another human to order a pizza. This is quite an arc for a hyper-social species.

Meanwhile, rendered invisible by technology, the legions of strangers who serve our needs become little more than instruments for use, condemned to a permanent strangerhood. Michael Tomasello, the developmental psychologist whose work on the evolution of morality we looked at in chapter 4, makes a connection between interdependence and morality. "There can be no fairness or justice

---

* It's worth quoting George Bernard Shaw on this one: "Independence? That's middle-class blasphemy. We are all dependent on one another, every soul of us on earth."

among individuals who are totally self sufficient in procuring everything they need on their own," he writes, paraphrasing the Scottish
philosopher David Hume. "To be concerned with fairness and justice, individuals must have some sense of their dependence on one
another." We are as dependent as ever, but many of us have also figured out a way to eliminate the unpleasantness of ever having to see
the faces or learn the names of the many strangers who keep us alive.
This is a recipe for social and moral disaster.

It will also cost us, personally. There is an idea in economics that
interacting in market economies teaches people how to behave
around strangers—that it hones our social skills and trains us to trust
them. The anthropologist Joe Henrich, who we heard from earlier,
found that people who live in cultures with strong market economies
are more likely to trust strangers—even strangers of different ethnicities or races. It comes from interacting face-to-face with them
and having your trust repaid enough times that you simply internalize it. When all transactions are conducted virtually, however, we
might gain efficiency, but what do we lose? We lose contact. That
carries a steep price. The rarer these interactions become, the more
our social skills erode. The more our social skills erode, the more
anxious we become about talking to strangers; the more anxious we
become, the less likely we are to talk to strangers; the less likely we
are to talk to strangers, the harder it is for us to comprehend that they
are human, same as us.

These are strange times. I started this project as my own country
seemed to be on the verge of collapse. I am finishing it in the midst of
a plague. The former has accelerated our political estrangement. The
latter has accelerated our retreat from the physical world—at least for
those of us with the perverse luxury of quarantine. For many people
during the COVID-19 crisis, almost all interactions were conducted
digitally; most purchases were made over the internet and resulted in
"contactless delivery" at one's front door; school was conducted via
online communication platforms. What had been a gradual progres-
sion toward digital life became a jarring replacement of all in-person
contact with remote contact.

Quarantine was traumatic to many people. People were shut off from most human contact, living under stress. Depression rates tripled, according to one study, and psychologists began to worry that the experience would permanently alter children who lived through it, giving rise to what they called "Generation Agoraphobia."

But the experience was also illuminating, in that it gave us a taste of a future that until then many of us were just passively defaulting into. It gave us a chance to pause, and think, and ask ourselves: Do we like this? Do we like living almost entirely online? Do we want to keep doing it? Because that, to me, is where this road leads: to a nation of people alone in rooms in front of screens, rarely if ever in the physical company of others, all their material needs delivered silently and frictionlessly by increasingly vulnerable people who may as well be ghosts. And it's foolish to think that accelerating everything that was making us lonely is somehow going to make us happy.

But that is only *a* future. Not *the* future.

Here's another story. An old one, though not as old as the Garden of Eden.

The Tuareg people are pastoral nomads who live mostly in Mali. For Tuareg men, most of life is conducted in the vast emptiness of the western Sahara desert, which they call *Ténéré*. This is how they earn their living, and it requires them to frequently be away from the people they know and love. Life in the desert, in all its enormity, infinity, and eternity, causes a feeling they call *asuf*: a word that can translate to "homesickness," but, as Malian scholar Ibrahim ag Youssouf and colleagues note, a more precise definition is "a desperate effort to put up with the absence of men, to ignore one's human insignificance and frailty in the huge, hostile Land of the Djinn," or desert people.

The desert is dangerous, and so, too, can be its inhabitants. The desert tribes have a history of warfare and feuding. So when one encounters another, they must proceed with extreme caution. When one sees the other from a great distance, they have to acknowledge one another. To be seen and then to disappear is to be suspected of mounting an ambush, and invites violence. If they are across a gorge, or walking in opposite directions, sometimes a shout will do. But if they're moving toward each other, there is no question that they must meet.

When they do, it is with profound ambivalence, because they are experiencing *asuf,* but they are also keenly aware "that interaction is not always harmonious, and the knowledge that most of the harm done to men is done by other men." A greeting ritual must be followed. For this, one man greets the other—*Salaam*—and after that, they are required by custom to shake hands. This is an extremely delicate matter, much more so than the way we might shake hands, precisely because of that sense of ambivalence. On one hand, men suffering from *asuf* are desperate for human bodily contact. But on the other, this kind of bodily contact could result in their being pulled from their camels, and left to die in Ténéré.

So they have to be careful when they shake hands. Shaking too firmly might be interpreted as an expression of distrust, of a prelude to an attack. Or a lonely Tuareg might resent being suspected of ill intentions when all he wanted was to feel the hand of another human being. They must both be careful not to appear too suspicious, or arrogant. They must be curious, but not too curious.

And all the while, they must be polite, because as in cultures of honor, to give insult is a grave matter. And they must do this while sitting on camels. But once they complete the handshake, the rest of the greeting ritual can follow. They can exchange news, they can point each other to water, or food, or a camp. They are lonely people, living in a dangerous place, struggling with thoughts of insignificance amid a great and disorienting expanse. And by engineering a way to make contact with a stranger, life is made easier and less lonely. We've talked a lot about how the success of the species is based on our ability to reconcile our fear of strangers with the opportunities they present, and how that is the beginning of social innovation. Here it is in microcosm. In our way, we are in Ténéré, we are suffering from *asuf,* and we must, too, learn the art of the Tuareg handshake.

These are strange times, but they are not unprecedented. As we have seen, again and again, human beings have responded to existential threats and societal collapse by creating new ways to cooperate with strangers and new modes of belonging within a changing world. The capacities of the hyper-cooperative ape have been scaled exponentially, from the rise of sociality among hunter-gatherers to the dawn of cities and major religions, and further: to the invention of democracy, the dawn of the Enlightenment, and civil rights, and human rights. We have seen a vast expansion in our capacity to attribute humanity to strangers.

Without question, these movements were and are all deeply imperfect. Many left out women, or rejected equal citizenship for all. Some replaced many small conflicts with a few very large ones. I am aware that I am speaking from a privileged perch, having not been tormented or killed for being an alien, a heathen, or some Other—that I have never been marshaled into formation and used as cannon fodder in a clash between kingdoms or civilizations. I am aware of the horrors humans can visit upon one another. I brood on them. Humanity for me can inspire as much terror as hope. But I am hopeful.

And I think you can be, too.

"The stranger is no longer the exception, but the rule," wrote the sociologist Lesley Harman. "Where once he was relegated to the margins, he has taken over the page." But how do we live in this new world? The first step is to recognize, paradoxically, that the more we drift apart from one another, the more we actually do have in common. We saw how the early adherents of Western religions were strangers and sojourners in a fallen world. Far from dooming them to permanent estrangement, it became a source of strength and solidarity. The world had become strange, the thinking goes, and they responded by creating a new conception of belonging and identity that was rooted in the experience of having been a stranger. In ideal cases, this gave them heightened empathetic powers. They knew what it was like to be strange, therefore they could imagine what it was like for others to feel the same way. When everyone is a stranger, the saying goes, no one is a stranger. What had been the source of our division can also be a source of solidarity.

For thousands of years, the powerless, the enslaved, and the oppressed have been strangers. They've always been subject to forces that scatter them, trample their humanity, and impose cruel fates upon them, while also training the rest of the culture to believe that these strangers are subhuman, that they can't be talked to or understood, that they can never really be incorporated into the dominant culture.

Now, however, a far less severe but still traumatic version of that estrangement is affecting the people who previously represented the majority, the monoculture. I'm one of those people. We can attempt to reverse the social and cultural changes that made us feel this way. But it won't work. It never does. Instead, if we acknowledge that we feel disoriented, confused, maybe afraid, we can imagine that others do, too. If we feel lonely, we can begin to awaken ourselves to the loneliness of others. That's the beginning of moral clarity, and I think it's the beginning of the answer to our present difficulties. "To encounter oneself is to encounter the other," wrote James Baldwin. "If I know that my soul trembles, I know that yours does, too: and if I can respect this, both of us can live."

How will we live? Who will we be? That's the question. As I was researching this book, I frequently came upon the idea of cosmopolitanism. I've long been skeptical of the strain of cosmopolitanism that calls for the elimination of borders and nations and group identities, advocating for a unification of all of humanity as one big mega-tribe. Beyond my practical reservations about governing such a mass— whom will I call to get this pothole fixed?—I'm not sure a newer, bigger group is what we actually need. At least not in the way we ordinarily think of groups. During my time at the Braver Angels convention, a Republican who was raised by Colombian immigrants was talking about *e pluribus unum—out of the many, one*. She got the *pluribus* part, she said, but what was the *unum*? If we were all going to be one, who gets to decide what the one is?

The political scientist Danielle Allen, whom we met earlier, has argued that we need to move away from the concept of being *one* to the concept of being *whole,* which, she writes, "might allow for the development of forms of citizenship that focus on integration, not assimilation, and on the mutual exchanges and appropriations that have already occurred among different groups and that will always keep occurring." I think she's right. I think forming larger and larger groups got us to where we are, but I'm not convinced they will get us to where we need to go. To put it in technological terms, I suspect that what we need is something less like network TV and more like blockchain. We don't need fewer bigger things, in other words. We need more smaller things that can work in concert, based on a simple assertion that we're not all one, but we are all here.

That's where cosmopolitanism starts to jibe with our project here. Not as a group identity—there's a smugness to the word that we'll need to irradiate—but as a mind-set, a way of behaving as an individual among individuals. The UCLA historian Margaret Jacob has a definition of cosmopolitanism that captures this nicely. She calls it "the ability to experience people of different nations, creeds, and colors with pleasure, curiosity, and interest, and not with suspicion, disdain, or simply a disinterest that could occasionally turn into loathing." This kind of cosmopolitanism represents the idea that the way to live in a diverse world is to train yourself to be curious about others—not morbidly curious, but curious in a way that is based on a belief in your shared humanity, a belief that whatever your respective statuses, you are equals. It doesn't mean you can't be proud of your heritage, your nationality, your creed. It just means that you recognize that there are other ways to be, and to be curious about them and the people who represent them.

This is challenging. In some ways, it's against our nature—at least that part of our nature that can be so easily roused by the mere presence of cultural strangers. In deep history, this kind of wariness was likely an advantage. "One outcome of the tribal psychology mind-set is that people may be inclined to perceive threats where none exist," argues Walter Stephan, the psychologist who studies intergroup anxiety. "Perceiving threats when none exist may be a less costly error than not perceiving threats when in fact they do exist. Thus, by default people may be predisposed to perceive threats from outgroups."

In a hyper-diverse world, however, seeing out-group threats where there are none is no longer the less costly error. It is a profoundly costly error. It is, potentially, a fatal error. And it is one that can be avoided by mustering curiosity about the lives of others.

As we saw, curiosity can be a defense against prejudice and division because to be curious about a stranger is to reject the tendency toward lesser minds, to believe that there is more to them than what you may initially see, or what culture has told you to see, and to believe that your curiosity will, in the end, be rewarded. That's why zealots abhor curiosity. Viennese psychologist Alfred Adler wrote, "It is the individual who is not interested in his fellow man who has the greatest difficulties in life and provides the greatest injury to others."

The sort of cosmopolitanism I imagine is the antidote to that. It's a kind of renewed civic faith. One that is practiced daily by talking to strangers, and rooted in the ideals of hospitality, of listening, greeting, inquiring—all the things we have seen over the course of this book. The more you practice it, the more you interact with strangers, the more comfortable and skillful you become at crossing boundaries that keep people apart.

This sort of faith is challenging; it requires a leap. But as we've seen with mass religions, we have it in us to scale faith in strangers. Plus, talking to strangers isn't as hard as we think it is. When you practice it—in person, but also online, if you do it in the right spirit—it serves as a balm for many of the problems of the age. It makes you feel better, happier, more connected, less lonely. It helps you think more clearly. It reassures you about the people with whom you share a world at a time of declining trust, and they you. It reminds you of that world's infinite complexity, and in so doing, it instructs you on how to live in that world. It doesn't tell you that we're all the same, because we're not, and life would be boring if we were. But it does reassure you that despite all evidence to the contrary, we have the capacity to communicate and cooperate despite our differences.

The wellspring of this faith, however, isn't a mysterious presence in the ether. It's not bound up with ritual, or sacred objects, or dogma. It is drawn entirely from the people around you, and that makes it endlessly renewable, as long as you're willing to do the work. When you do the work, you become happier and healthier. When enough people do the work, the world changes for the better. It doesn't solve all of our problems. As I said earlier, many systems need to be reformed as well in order to fulfill the promise of the species. Levels of stress driven by real and perceived threats and struggle and privation need to be reduced, because that's what can fuel the fear of strangers. And I am under no delusion about how difficult that sort of reform is. But I also believe that we will get precisely nowhere if we remain strangers to one another. I believe that rebuilding ourselves as social creatures, by learning to talk to strangers—those like us and those unlike us, one by one and day by day—is where it begins. I believe that this act of engagement—this turning toward one another—can be our next social renaissance.

I don't think we're unfit for this challenge. I don't think we've somehow blundered into a world we're not capable of flourishing in. On the contrary, I think everything that has come before has trained us for it. Immanuel Kant defined cosmopolitanism as the "ultimate purpose" of nature, the culmination. And I'm inclined to agree with him. There has been a process at work for thousands of years. All of the social innovations we've seen have been engines for manufacturing trust in strangers on a larger and larger scale. If we can keep it up, and somehow avoid exterminating ourselves through ecological disaster or nuclear misadventure, we stand a chance of continuing with this project.

Its success will fall to us as individuals. The old social innovations involved external controls to keep us in line, like ritual or tradition or monoculture, or the belief in a god who will punish us if we misbehave, or law, but many of those controls are now fading. In one sense, that makes it seem like the world is falling irretrievably into chaos. But in another sense, we can see many of these old ways for what they might really be: training wheels for what comes next. And we can see that we have agency, as individuals. After all, the story of human evolution isn't just about nature or nurture. It's about both, working in tandem. For the entirety of our time here, humans developed a way of doing things. If it helped us flourish, we enshrined it as practice or tradition, and in time it became encoded in our genes. It became our nature.

That nature is, as ever, a work in progress. What it will ultimately be will be up to us. We are the only species with this much control over its own fate, as careless as we've been with the world and one another. But I'm hopeful that we can meet the challenges of the moment and flourish in an uncertain time. In 1751, the French philosopher Denis Diderot defined cosmopolitans as "strangers nowhere in the world." Let that be an ideal for what we might become, and what others might say about us, and let us graft onto it that old cliché, which works like a beatitude and points the way forward: *Never met a stranger.*

But we were talking about the Garden of Eden. I can see the appeal of it—this image of a warm, safe, unworried place populated by a small group of familiar individuals. I'm drawn to it myself sometimes, when things are hard. But I'm also easily bored. I like new people and places, new ideas and jokes, new stories and foods and drinks and songs, and I like when they mix with one another and make newer and more unexpected things. I've personally felt Theodore Zeldin's idea of the procreative act of talking to strangers—how it created conversations and insights from nothing, but also how it changed me, how I've grown from exposure to their lives and their stories. My assumptions about the world have been challenged, and yet I'm reassured, even as the world around me rattles and groans.

So I have a different take on the Eden story. I don't think it's a fall. I don't think it's a sin. I think we should build monuments to Eve, and maybe the snake, too. I think incuriosity is the real sin, and curiosity is a cure for loneliness and strife. I think that without Adam's expulsion from the garden, he would have stayed what he was: an unlettered man in a pretty place with an empty head instead of what he became, which is to say, a stranger. If it were me, I'd eat the apple, too. I'll take the world. I'll cast my lot with the strangers.

ACKNOWLEDGMENTS

Books, I have discovered, are difficult to write. I've been reading them for years, and I had long ago fallen into the trap of believing that they must be as easy to write as they are to read. Okay, I'm joking, but developing, and pitching, and reporting, and writing, and editing this book, while juggling parenting duties, and attempting to survive a yearlong toddler sleep disorder, a plague, and the near collapse of my country, made what was already a challenging endeavor that much more so. The first person I need to thank, with all my might and all my heart, is my wife, Jean, for putting up with my craziness through this process, and for all her love and support over the years. I am immensely fortunate to have met this stranger twenty years ago in Cambridge, Massachusetts, and that she took a chance on what was then a noisy, opinionated, and unemployed man who just happened to be hanging around in the right place at the right time one day.

I offer a slightly qualified thank-you to our daughter, June, who tried to kill me with her sleep issues, but she has since learned that I cannot be killed quite that easily. Kid: You are an inexhaustible source of hilarity, joy, weirdness, and inspiration. Though you forbid compliments, I am proud of you, and I love you. You are my sweetpea, whether you like it or not.

And I owe a massive debt of gratitude to my parents, Joan and Ed Keohane. Watching the two of you live your lives the way you do—always moving, always talking, always making new friends—is an example that I consider a model for a successful life, and I intend to follow it to the end. Thank you. This book is, in no small part, for you. The same goes for my siblings: Kris, John, and Den: You three are smart and endlessly entertaining, and you are a big reason why I am who I am, for whatever that's worth.

This book lurched into motion one morning at Eisenberg's Sandwich Shop in Manhattan, over breakfast with my former boss at *Esquire,* David Granger, formerly known as the greatest magazine editor in history. I was telling him about the cabdriver I'd met in Nantucket, who leads this book off, and we started to wonder if there was a book in it. I wrote a short proposal and he loved it. And then I revised that proposal and he disappeared and started ducking my calls because it was so bad. Fortunately, he reemerged and we beat the proposal into shape, thanks to his peerless editing abilities, and, more important, his enthusiasm and support. In no way would this book have happened without his involvement, and I owe him a great deal for it. He's a great editor, a great guy, and a promising upstart in the lit agent game.

I met Mark Warren several years ago, also when I worked at *Esquire,* and I knew from the moment he got mad at me for cutting one of his pieces to make room for one of my own, that we were destined to work on a big project together. His wise counsel, good company, and sharp edits helped this book immeasurably. He's a great editor and a legitimate literary man, with the perfect mix of good humor and moral seriousness. Plus, he holds the title for the greatest edit note I've ever received from an editor. To wit: "Something happened at the end of this chapter—we were humming along, building a point, and then we lost focus, and started talking broadly and amorphously about strangers, lurching around in time and meaning. . . . Please have another go . . . robustly, and with focus. Thanks." Deadly. All writers should be this fortunate. Thanks, Mark. Go get some sleep.

Also at Random House, thank you to Andy Ward, Tom Perry, Chayenne Skeete, and Dennis Ambrose for the great care you have taken with these pages, and for your patience in the bargain.

Throughout this process, Kevin Alexander was a font of ideas, diversions, insights, weird text messages, and book industry insights, helping to explain the inexplicable to me, and keeping me sane at my most crazed—even as wildfires rained ash on his house. His notes on the manuscript were, as ever, spot on—smart, funny, merciless, and energetic. He is one of my favorite writers, and my favorite collaborator, and I am now in his debt, which I hate. Drinks on me at Raoul's when this is all over.

Nate Hopper—friend, colleague, and occasional partner in crime—also gave me exceptionally smart and helpful feedback on the manuscript. He's an inordinately gifted editor, a real natural, with a genuine hatred for bad writing, cliché, and shoddy arguments, and this book wouldn't be what it is without his insights. Nate: thanks for all your help, and for your company over the years. I'm sorry Nizza and I were so mean to you back in your rookie season but that's just the business.

To the late Dr. Robert Wilkinson from Villanova University. You were the best teacher I've ever had, bar none, and I would not be doing this for a living if it weren't for your encouragement, enthusiasm, indulgence, and wise counsel. I hope wherever you are, here's good company, good music, good books, and a great bottle of scotch. Thank you.

It goes without saying that this book would not have worked if not for the brilliant and very busy people who generously and perhaps irrationally took the time to hang out and answer all my stupid questions. Most notably: Gillian Sandstrom, Georgie Nightingall, Nic, Juliana Schroeder, Polly Akhurst, Ron Gross, Joyce Cohen, Michael Tomasello, Douglas Fry, Joe Henrich, Polly Wiessner, Gabriel Kahane, Andrew Shyrock, Ben Mathes, Sarah Tracy, Nikki Truscelli, Cris Tietsort, Larry Young, Hunter Franks, Cliff Adler, Joaquín Simó, Judah Berger, Cynthia Nitkin, Jae Quinn, "L," Ronald Inglehart, Nairán Ramírez-Esparza, Ceyda Berk-Soderblom, Theodore Zeldin, Laura Kolbe, Aleksi Neuvonen, Cal Walsh, Muhammad Karkoutli, Uli Beutter Cohen, Thomas Knox, Danielle Allen, "Holly," Bill Doherty, Ciaran O'Connor, Earle Ikeda, Imam Khalid Latif, Rabbi Ethan Tucker, Father Thomas Reese, Mat McDermott, Steven Angle, Yale University for letting me use the HRAF, as well as the dozens of others who responded to my emails, and generally pointed me toward the good stuff and away from the bad. And thank you to Linda Rost and Nick Thomas for letting me crash at your lovely place in London.

This book began in a taxi in the middle of the night in Nantucket. I was there thanks to a fellowship from Screenwriters Colony, and without that, I never would have had the idea that sprouted this book. So, to Lydia Cavallo Zasa and Eric Gilliland: I'm sorry I have thus far failed to sell a show or a screenplay, or secure any meaningful work in Hollywood, but I hope this book will come as some small consolation for having wasted so much money on me. And to the other three writers from the program that year: Meg Favreau, Kaitlin Fontana, and Jai Jamison—you three comprise the most intense text message relationship in my life. You are all dead funny, garishly talented, unreasonably supportive, and great people besides. (F-Tom.)

Thank you to Jenn Johnson—the most capable human I have ever met—and Emma Whitford—ace reporter—for helping me out of a couple of research binds. And thank you to erstwhile strangers Stevie at the Brooklyn Central Library and Jen at Café Martin for being friendly faces and dispensers of much needed coffee while I worked on this book.

Finally—this book was edited and revised and finished during the COVID-19 crisis in New York City. I saw this big, bad city of strangers come together in a way that I will never forget (while also remaining a safe distance from one another). America handled this crisis about as poorly as anyone could, but New York was an inspiration. I will never forget all the New Yorkers hanging out the windows at the very worst of it, banging pots and pans together, and singing "New York, New York." I'll never forget the effort people made to say hello to strangers in the street, and ask them if they were okay. They were gritty, and tender, and tough, and warm. They were marvelous. So, to the great City of New York, and everyone who lives in it, and everyone who died in it during that terrible time: Thank you. I love you. This book is dedicated to you.

A NOTE ON SOURCES

The Power of Strangers is the product of a great deal of reading and research. That includes dozens upon dozens of books, and a library's worth of studies. To save paper, and to spare readers from having to carry around more of it than they need to while enjoying this book in transit, I have opted not to include endnotes here. I encourage anyone so inclined to find them at joekeohane.net/strangersnotes. I have also included an extended bibliography there. It includes every work cited in this book, as well as a number of great things I was unable to include, in the interest of keeping this book under eight thousand pages. For anyone interested in digging more deeply into the topics addressed in this book, there is plenty there to help get you started.

Now, please: Go talk to a stranger.

INDEX

ABOUT THE AUTHOR

JOE KEOHANE is a veteran journalist who has held high-level editing positions at *Medium, Esquire, Entrepreneur,* and *Hemispheres.* His writing—on everything from politics to travel to social science, business, and technology—has appeared in *New York* magazine, *The Boston Globe, The New Yorker, Wired, Boston* magazine, *The New Republic,* and several textbooks. An avid parallel parker and occasional working musician, he also won a prestigious Screenwriter's Colony fellowship in 2017 for a comedy television pilot that remains, sadly, unproduced.

ABOUT THE TYPE

This book was set in Bembo, a typeface based on an old-style Roman face that was used for Cardinal Pietro Bembo's tract *De Aetna* in 1495. Bembo was cut by Francesco Griffo (1450–1518) in the early sixteenth century for Italian Renaissance printer and publisher Aldus Manutius (1449–1515). The Lanston Monotype Company of Philadelphia brought the well-proportioned letterforms of Bembo to the United States in the 1930s.